Informational
Diagram Collection

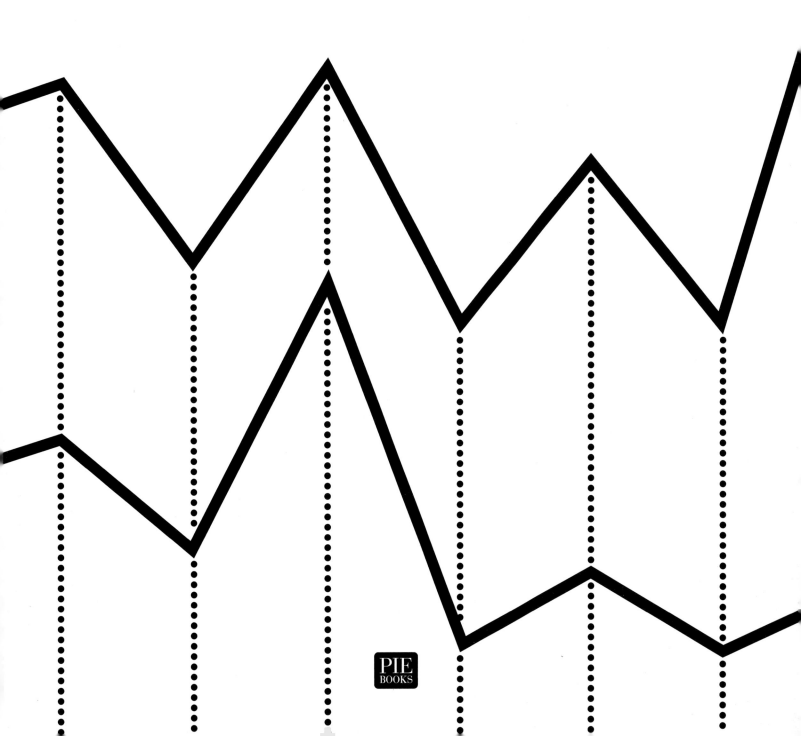

PIE
BOOKS

Informational Diagram Collection

PIE BOOKS

2-32-4, Minami-Otsuka, Toshima-ku, Tokyo 170-0005 Japan
Phone: +81-3-5395-4811 Fax: +81-3-5395-4812

editor@piebooks.com
sales@piebooks.com
www.piebooks.com

ISBN978-4-89444-810-0 C3070
Printed in Japan

CONTENTS

"Now and Future Diagrams"

By Katha Dalton
Project Manager; Hornall Anderson Design Works, Inc.

Today we share a world where visual information is simultaneous and omnipresent in staggering amounts. Growth of online, electronic and interactive media ensures that in the future still more of it will come alive, not only in two and three dimensions, but in a potent fourth: motion. This is good news, not only for the public, but also for designers whose palette for expressing visual information is enriched. Why? Because the old cliché is, and will remain, true: "A picture is worth 1,000 words."

How does this work? It is in part because through design, visually presented facts and statistics are able to simultaneously communicate data and trigger emotional responses to that information based on its appearance.

In the past, designers typically used diagrams for a more aesthetic purpose—as visual filler on the page—than to relay information. However, in today's world, we are continuously barraged with an onslaught of information, and diagrams are more important than ever. They are a critical form of communication that helps us assimilate complex information and respond to it in appropriate ways.

One such example of using diagrams in this manner can be found in the 2002 annual report for an aircraft-operating lessor client. In an effort to illustrate fiscal results in a more reader-friendly manner, the client distills a complex global business into digestible bits using simple, illustrative diagrammatic metaphors, such as "don't put all your eggs in one basket," the Wall Street bulls and bears, and the team success of bees in a hive.

With the ongoing challenge of filtering the myriad details we receive on a daily basis, informational diagrams will continue to play a key role in softening, simplifying and supporting clients' messages now and in years ahead.

Profile

At Hornall Anderson Design Works, we have always had two main goals: first, to give our clients design solutions in tune with their marketing objectives; and second, to do the best work in the business, striving to elevate every job above the ordinary. The plan has succeeded. Started in 1982, Hornall Anderson has become one of the largest, most respected design firms on the West Coast.

ダイアグラムの現在と未来

キャサ・ダルトン
ホーナル・アンダーソン・デザイン・ワークス　プロジェクト・マネージャー

現在、世界には驚くほど多くの視覚情報が同時に遍在している。インターネットや電子媒体、そしてインタラクティブなメディアは、平面や立体だけではなくモーションという面でも今後さらに発達していくに違いない。これは一般人だけでなく、視覚情報を表現する手法が豊かなデザイナーにとっても朗報だ。なぜなら、昔から良く言われている「一枚の絵は千の言葉に値する」という言葉が、今も、そしてこれから先もまさに真実だからだ。

これらは実際にはどう作用しているのだろうか。ひとつとして、事実と統計をデザインによって視覚的に提示することで、データを理解したり、見たままの情報に対して感情的な反応を引き起こしたりが同時に行えるという点が挙げられる。

昔、デザイナーは情報を伝えるというよりもページを視覚的に埋めるといった、デザインを美しく見せる目的でダイアグラムを使うのが一般的だった。しかし、現在の私たちは絶え間なく情報の集中砲火を浴びており、ダイアグラムはかつてないほど重要性を帯びている。複雑な情報を理解し、適切な方法で情報に反応する手助けをしてくれるダイアグラムは、コミュニケーションに欠かせないひとつの形態だ。

こうした意味でダイアグラムを使ったひとつの例に、航空機リース業者であるクライアントのために作成した2002年度アニュアル・レポートがある。決算報告を読者に分かりやすく表現するため、クライアントの複雑なグローバル・ビジネスを、「ひとつのカゴからすべての卵を取り出してはいけない」、「ウォールストリートの雄牛と熊」、「蜂の巣の蜜蜂チームの成功」といった、シンプルで一目瞭然なダイアグラムのメタファーを使用した具体例へと落とし込んだ。

日々受け取る大量の情報を常に選別していくという挑戦のために、インフォメーショナル・ダイアグラムは、現在も、そしてこれから先も、クライアントのメッセージを分かりやすく明快にし、支援するのに中心的な役割を果し続けるだろう。

プロフィール
ホーナル・アンダーソン・デザイン・ワークスでは、常にふたつのゴールを目指している。ひとつは、クライアントのマーケティング目標に合ったデザイン・ソリューションを提供することで、もうひとつは、すべての仕事で水準以上の結果を目指し、ベストを尽くすことだ。このプランは非常に成功している。1982年の設立以来、ホーナル・アンダーソンはアメリカ西海岸で最も大きく評判の高いデザイン会社の地位を保っている。

"No change"

By Gilmar Wendt, Creative Director; SAS

My favourite diagram is the London Underground Map, perhaps not a surprising choice. But living in London makes things slightly different. When I mention it to my English friends they either say 'you are such a tourist', or start to moan about the dirt and the delays they experience every day. Londoners love to hate the tube. To them, the diagram is just part of it, a commodity, helping you find the quickest way from A to B.

I don't mind that. After all, helping you understand something better is what diagrams are about. The tube map has simply become so much part of my friends' daily routine that they're unable to see what it really is. Which is, a perfect piece of information design. Designed by an engineer, Harry Beck, in 1931, with the single aim to make it as easy to understand as possible, it has revolutionised the way we design tube maps around the world. And even though it has been altered over the years, to me it has lost none of its graphic qualities. I love the colour coding, the clarity, simplicity, and, of course, the beautiful Johnston typeface.

These are interesting times for designers. New media has brought new dimensions to information design-and new challenges too. I'm fascinated as to how animation and interactivity can be used to explain a complex structure, or make a process clear. But as we expand our tool box and explore ever-changing fashion styles, there's one thing that remains. Information design is for the user. Helping him understand how to get from A to B is what its all about.

Profile

Gilmar Wendt is the creative director of SAS, the London based corporate design company. SAS has been running for 15 years, helping their various blue-chip clients communicate more effectively with their investors, business customers and employees.
www.sasdesign.co.uk

ノー・チェンジ：今も昔も変わりなく。

ギルマー・ベント
SAS クリエイティブ・ディレクター

私の大好きなダイアグラムはロンドンの地下鉄マップだ。おそらく、この答えはあまり意外ではないだろう。しかし、ロンドンに住んでいると多少事情が異なってくる。私がこのことをイギリス人の友人に話すと、「君は旅行者みたいだな」と言われるか、日々経験している地下鉄の遅れやら汚さに不満を言い始めるかのどちらかだ。ロンドンっ子は地下鉄の悪口を言うのが好きなのだ。彼らにとって、そのダイアグラムは愛すべき嫌われものの一部でしかなく、A地点からB地点へ最も早く行ける方法を探すための必需品なのだ。

私にしてみればそんな事はどうでもいい。結局、ある物事を良く理解するための助けになることがダイアグラムの目的だ。地下鉄マップは単に、私の友人たちの日常にあまりにも深く関わっているため、彼らには本当はそれが何なのか、ということが見えなくなってしまったのだ。つまり、本当は地下鉄マップは完璧なるインフォメーション・デザインのひとつなのだ。1931年、できる限り分かりやすいものを作るというたったひとつの目標のもと、エンジニアであるハリー・ベックがデザインした地下鉄マップは、世界中の地下鉄マップのデザイン方法に革命を起した。さらに何年もの時を経て部分的な修正はされてきたものの、私からみればそのグラフィックの質は少しも失われていない。色分けの仕方や明快でシンプルなところがたまらなく好きだ。そしてもちろん、美しいジョンソンのタイプフェイスも。

今はデザイナーにとって興味深く、面白い時代だ。ニューメディアはインフォメーション・デザインに新しい面だけでなく、新たな挑戦をももたらした。複雑な構造を説明したり、プロセスを明確にするのに、アニメーションやインタラクティビティがどう使われているのかに私は魅了されている。しかし、私たちがどんどん新しい手法を取り入れ、絶えまなく変化するファッション・スタイルを探究している最中にも、ひとつだけ変わらないことがある。インフォメーション・デザインはユーザのためにあるということだ。A地点からB地点までどう行けばいいのかを教えてくれるのに役立つ。それがすべてなのだ。

プロフィール
ギルマー・ベントは、ロンドンを拠点にするコーポレイト・デザイン・カンパニー、SASのクリエイティブ・ディレクター。SASは15年間にわたり、様々な一流企業のクライアントが、出資者や取引先、従業員などとより効果的なコミュニケーションが取れるように支援している。
www.sasdesign.co.uk

EDITORIAL NOTES

CREDIT FORMAT　クレジットフォーマット

■Caption　作品説明文

■Country from which submitted / Year of completion　制作国／制作年

■Creative staff　制作スタッフ

CD: Creative Director（クリエイティブディレクター）

AD: Art Director（アートディレクター）

D: Designer（デザイナー）

P: Photographer（カメラマン）

I: Illustrator（イラストレーター）

CW: Copywriter（コピーライター）

DF: Design Firm（デザイン事務所）

CL: Client（クライアント）

S: Submittor（作品提供者）

* Full names of all others involved in the creation / production of the work.
　上記以外の制作スタッフの呼称は略さずに記載しています。

* Please note that some credit data has been omitted at the request of the submittor.
　作品提供者の意向によりクレジット・データの一部を記載していないものがあります。

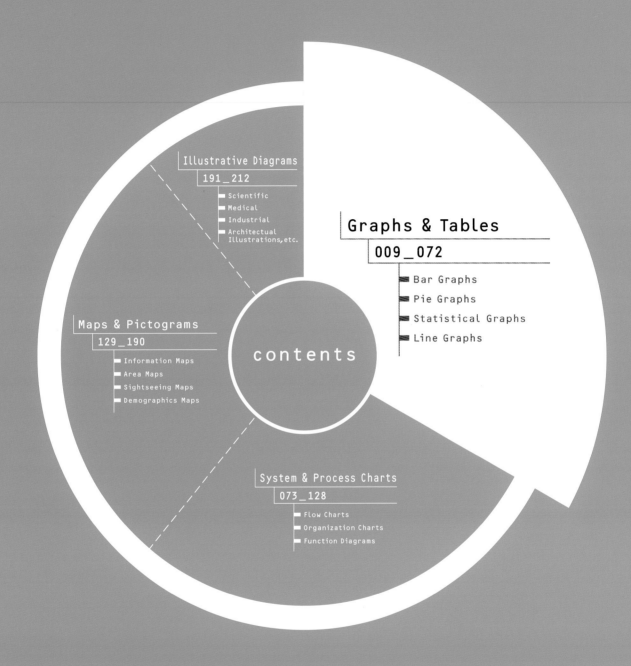

Daten und Fakten

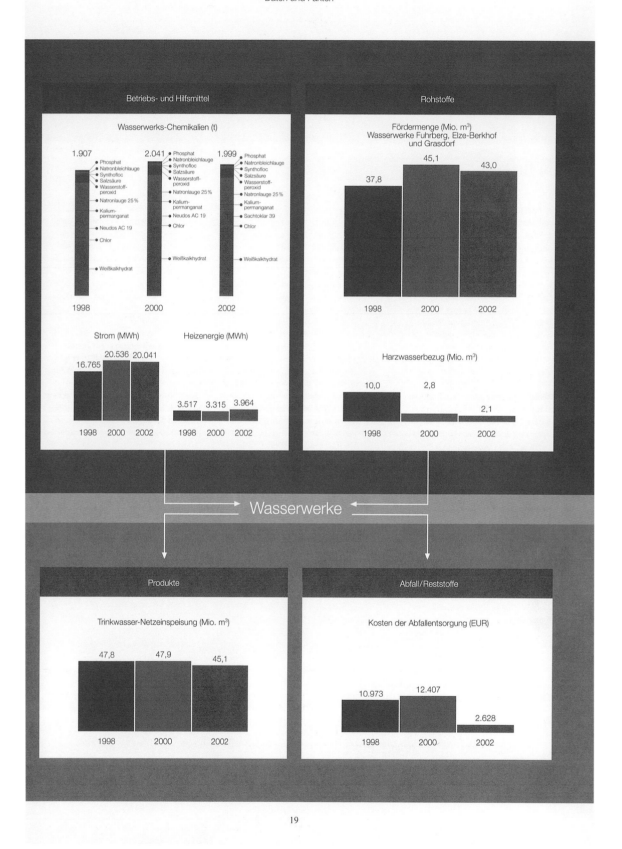

Graphs providing the information on environmental facts and figures of power stations and water companies.

発電所や水道会社の環境に関する情報を示すグラフ。

Germany 2003
CL, S: Stadtwerke Hannover AG

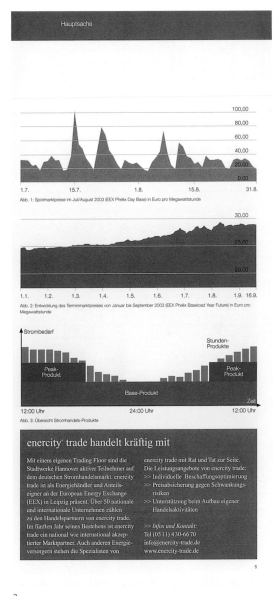

Hauptsache

Abb. 1: Spotmarktpreise im Juli/August 2003 (EEX Phelix Day Base) in Euro pro Megawattstunde

Abb. 2: Entwicklung des Terminmarktpreises von Januar bis September 2003 (EEX Phelix Baseload Year Future) in Euro pro Megawattstunde

Abb. 3: Übersicht Stromhandels-Produkte

enercity® trade handelt kräftig mit

Mit einem eigenen Trading Floor sind die Stadtwerke Hannover aktiver Teilnehmer auf dem deutschen Stromhandelsmarkt. enercity trade ist als Energiehändler und Anteilseigner an der European Energy Exchange (EEX) in Leipzig präsent. Über 50 nationale und internationale Unternehmen zählen zu den Handelspartnern von enercity trade. Im fünften Jahr seines Bestehens ist enercity trade ein national wie international akzeptierter Marktpartner. Auch anderen Energieversorgern stehen die Spezialisten von

enercity trade mit Rat und Tat zur Seite. Die Leistungsangebote von enercity trade:
>> Individuelle Beschaffungsoptimierung
>> Preisabsicherung gegen Schwankungsrisiken
>> Unterstützung beim Aufbau eigener Handelsaktivitäten

>> Infos und Kontakt:
Tel (05 11) 430-66 70
info@enercity-trade.de
www.enercity-trade.de

5

a

Arbeitswelt

Klimafreundlichkeit wird belohnt

Der Strom kommt aus der Steckdose, das weiß jeder. Was sich aber genau hinter der Abkürzung KWK oder den KWK-Gesetzen verbirgt und warum ökologisches Handeln belohnt wird, kann man hier nachlesen.

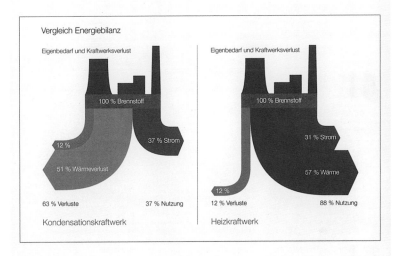

Vergleich Energiebilanz

Der Strom der Stadtwerke Hannover AG kommt zu gut zwei Dritteln aus Kraft-Wärme-Kopplungs-Anlagen. Diese Anlagen zeichnen sich durch eine umweltfreundliche Stromerzeugungstechnik aus und werden seit März 2000 durch die KWK-Gesetzgebung gefördert.

Was bedeutet KWK?
Bei Kraftwerken, die nur Strom erzeugen, den Kondensationskraftwerken, wird die Energie des eingesetzten Brennstoffes wie Kohle oder Erdgas in einem thermischen Prozess nur in mechanische Energie sprich Kraft umgewandelt. Mit dieser Kraft, dem Wasserdampf, wird ein Generator angetrieben, der dann das eigentliche Produkt, den Strom erzeugt. Ein großer Teil der durch die Verbrennung frei werdenden Wärme kann nicht genutzt werden

und muss als verlustige Abwärme an die Umgebung abgeführt werden.
Die Abkürzung KWK steht für Kraft-Wärme-Kopplung. In einem Heizkraftwerk werden eben diese beiden Produkte erzeugt. Gegenüber dem Kondensationskraftwerk verzichtet ein Heizkraftwerk auf einen kleinen Teil der Stromerzeugung und kann dafür den Teil der

b

Each graph showing the current of market price in July/August 2003, the option market price in September 2003, and the trade in a day. (a)
Graphs comparing the energy balance between the condensation power station and the combined heat and power station. (b)

それぞれ、2003年7～8月の市場価格、9月のオプション市場価格および1日あたりの取引の推移を示すグラフ。 (a)
蒸気凝縮方式の発電所と熱併給発電所のエネルギーのバランスを比較するグラフ。 (b)

011

Aantal gerechtigden AOW/Anw en AKW per vestiging

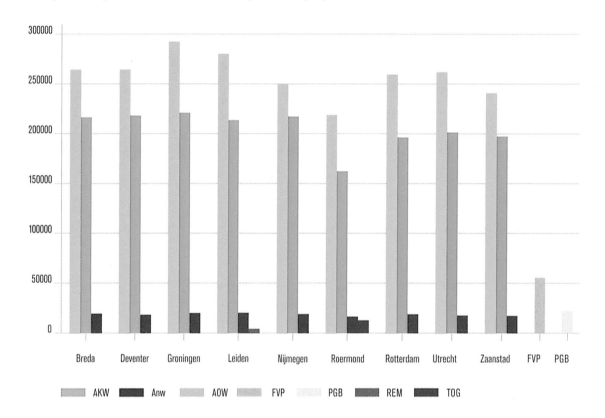

Aantal AOW-gerechtigden per leeftijdsklasse

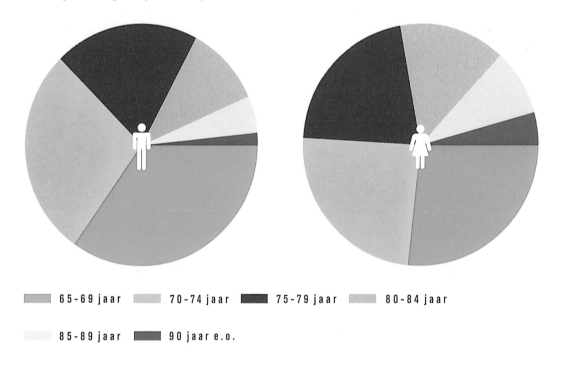

Charts from a social annual report which introduces the activities of the empoyees working in the bank. Showing not the financial status but the social aspects of the bank.

銀行の従業員の活動を紹介するソーシャルアニュアル・レポートより。銀行の財政状況ではなく、社会的な面を明らかにしている。

Netherlands 2001
CD, AD, D: Wout De Vringer   AD, I: Bob Van Dijk   CW: Corporate Communication SVB   DF, S: Faydherbe / De Vringer   CL: SVB (Sociale Verzekerings Bank)

**Sozialkapital:
Gesellschaft und
Gemeinsinn in Vorarlberg**

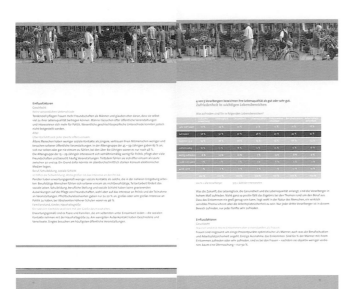

Graphs indicate social capital and life satisfaction in Austria.

オーストリアにおける社会資本や人生に対する満足度を表すグラフ。

Austria 2002
CD, AD: Sigi Ramoser   D, P, I: Sabine Sowieja   CW: Petra Zudrell   DF, S: Sägenvier   CL: Land Vorarlberg

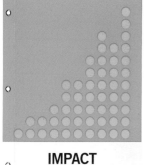

IMPACT
GLSEN 2003 ANNUAL REPORT

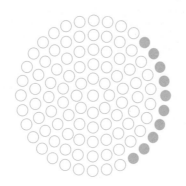

BEST OF TIMES
BY THE END OF THE 2002-2003 SCHOOL YEAR,
1,864 STUDENT CLUBS OR GAY-STRAIGHT
ALLIANCES (GSAs) HAD REGISTERED WITH
GLSEN — A 50% RISE OVER 2001-2002.
STUDENTS WHO SAY THEIR SCHOOLS HAVE A GSA
ARE MORE LIKELY TO FEEL SAFE IN THEIR SCHOOLS.*

* GLSEN'S 2001 National School Climate Survey

4

WORST OF TIMES
MORE THAN 90% OF AMERICA'S HIGH SCHOOLS
STILL HAVE NO GSA OR OTHER STUDENT CLUB
WORKING TO STOP ANTI-LGBT BIAS.

5

ONE STEP FORWARD
THE GLSEN LUNCHBOX WAS FIRST CREATED IN
2000 AS A COMPREHENSIVE TEACHER TRAINING
PROGRAM FOR ENDING ANTI-LGBT BIAS IN
SCHOOLS. THERE ARE CURRENTLY MORE THAN
1,000 LUNCHBOXES IN USE IN SCHOOLS AND
COMMUNITIES THROUGHOUT THE U.S.

6

SO MANY STEPS TO GO...
1,000 LUNCHBOXES CAN REACH
ONLY A MINUTE FRACTION OF THE
TEACHERS IN AMERICA'S SCHOOLS.
39.7% OF STUDENTS REPORT THAT THERE ARE
NO TEACHERS OR PERSONNEL WHO ARE SUPPORTIVE
OF LGBT STUDENTS AT THEIR SCHOOL.*

* GLSEN'S 2001 National School Climate Survey

7

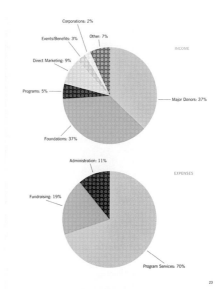

INCOME

Corporations: 2%
Events/Benefits: 3%
Other: 7%
Direct Marketing: 9%
Programs: 5%
Major Donors: 37%
Foundations: 37%

EXPENSES

Administration: 11%
Fundraising: 19%
Program Services: 70%

23

GLSEN is an organization devoted to building tolerance and acceptance for gay and transgender high school students. Charts represent the financial statements in 2003.

GLSENはゲイや性同一性障害の高校生に対する理解を深めるために活動している団体。2003年の決算報告を表すグラフ。

USA   2003
CD, AD, D, I: Brian Wong   DF, S: Suka Design   CL: GLSEN (Gay, Lesbian and Straight Education Network)

2

Recoletos en Cifras

Total ingresos EBITDA EBIT Resultado consolidado

Cuenta de explotación consolidada

Número medio de empleados

2002	1.588
2001	1.772
2000	1.812

Estado de flujo de caja consolidado

Balance

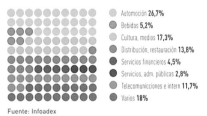

Desglose de ingresos 2002 / Desglose de margen bruto 2002

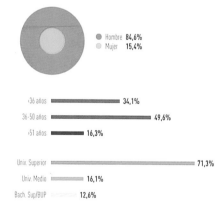

Sectores anunciantes de Expansión
(en % de páginas de publicidad)

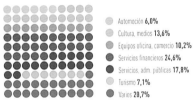

- Automoción **6,0%**
- Cultura, medios **13,6%**
- Equipos oficina, comercio **10,2%**
- Servicios financieros **24,6%**
- Servicios, adm. públicas **17,8%**
- Turismo **7,1%**
- Varios **20,7%**

Fuente: Infoadex

Sectores anunciantes de Marca
(en % de páginas de publicidad)

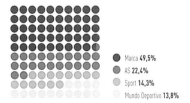

- Automoción **26,7%**
- Bebidas **5,2%**
- Cultura, medios **17,3%**
- Distribución, restauración **13,8%**
- Servicios financieros **4,5%**
- Servicios, adm. públicas **2,8%**
- Telecomunicaciones e intern **11,7%**
- Varios **18%**

Fuente: Infoadex

Expansión Perfil del lector

- Hombre **84,6%**
- Mujer **15,4%**

‹36 años	34,1%
36-50 años	49,6%
›51 años	16,3%
Univ. Superior	71,3%
Univ. Medio	16,1%
Bach. Sup/BUP	12,6%

Cuota de mercado
Difusión OJD 2002 preliminares a Junio

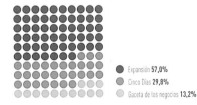

- Expansión **57,0%**
- Cinco Días **29,8%**
- Gaceta de los negocios **13,2%**

Cuota de mercado
Difusión OJD 2002 datos preliminares a junio 2002

- Marca **49,5%**
- AS **22,4%**
- Sport **14,3%**
- Mundo Deportivo **13,8%**

Various graphs and charts for an annual report of a media company providing market information.

市場に関する情報を提供する、メディア企業のアニュアル・レポートのためのグラフやチャート。

Spain 2002
CD: Emilio Gil   D: Ingrid Forbord   DF, S: Tau Diseño   CL: Recoetos Group

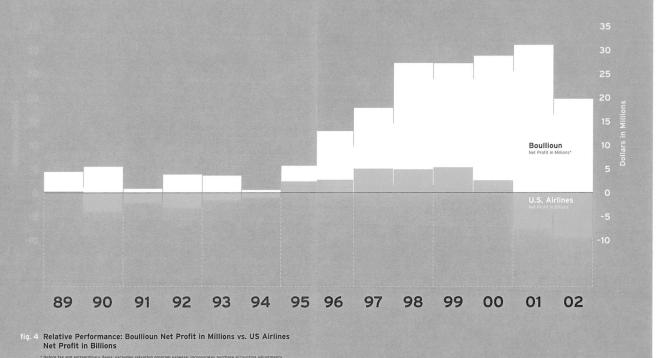

In 2002, Boullioun performed well ahead of the curve.

Boullioun
Net Profit in Millions*

U.S. Airlines
Net Profit in Billions

Dollars in Millions

35
30
25
20
15
10
5
0
-5
-10

89 90 91 92 93 94 95 96 97 98 99 00 01 02

fig. 4 Relative Performance: Boullioun Net Profit in Millions vs. US Airlines Net Profit in Billions

* Before tax and extraordinary items; excluding retention program expense; incorporates purchase accounting adjustments in 1994, 1998 and 2001.

p. 3

Metaphoric illustrations and charts are used in strong flat colors to show how risk is minimized in leasing, how global presence helps spread risk, and how the Boullioun team operates at the highest professional level.

強いフラットな色調を使用した隠喩的なイラストとグラフは、リースにおけるリスクを最小限にする方法、グローバルな企業が直面するリスク、最高の専門性を誇る航空機のリース企業がどのように経営されているかなどを示している。

USA 2003
AD: Jack Anderson AD, D: Katha Dalton D, I: Belinda Bowling D: Michael Brugman CW: John Koval DF, S: Hornall Anderson Design Works, Inc. CL: Boullioun Aviation Services

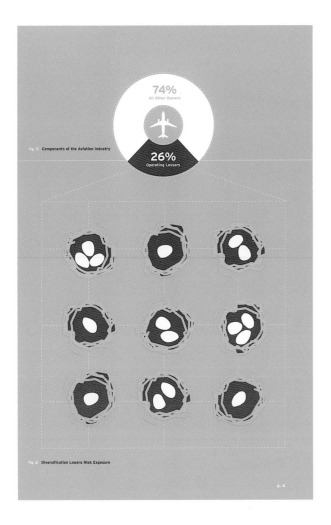

fig. 5　Components of the Aviation Industry

74%
All Other Owners

26%
Operating Lessors

fig. 6　Diversification Lowers Risk Exposure

fig. 7　Portfolio by Aircraft Type

Number of Planes

24　11　12　11　2　1　16

737-300　737-400　737-700　737-800　757-200　767-300　A320/A319

fig. 8　A Good Time To Invest

p. 6

p. 4

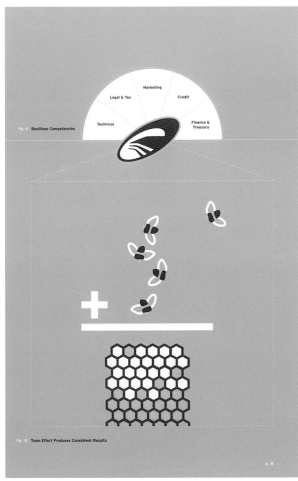

fig. 9　Boullioun Competencies

Marketing
Legal & Tax　　Credit
Technical　　Finance & Treasury

fig. 10　Team Effort Produces Consistent Results

p. 8

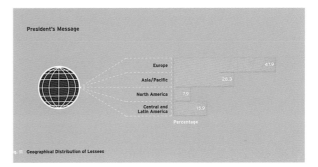

President's Message

Europe　47.9
Asia/Pacific　28.3
North America　7.9
Central and Latin America　15.9

Percentage

fig. 11　Geographical Distribution of Lessees

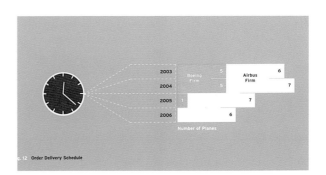

2003　Boeing Firm　5　Airbus Firm　6
2004　5　7
2005　1　7
2006　6

Number of Planes

fig. 12　Order Delivery Schedule

017

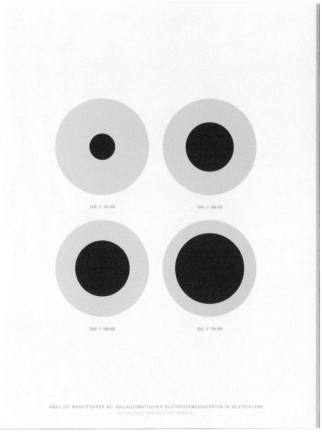

Graphs in simple but various forms indicating the market shares, increase of sales turnover, and business perspectives of a electronic devices distributor.

シンプルだが様々な形態で表したグラフは、電子機器販売会社のマーケット・シェア、販売額の増加、ビジネスの展望などを示している。

Germany 2002
CD: Jochen Rädeker   AD, D: Kirsten Dietz   D: Stephanie Zehender   CW: Eberhard Kaiser   DF, S: Strichpunkt GmbH   CL: 4MBO International Electronic AG

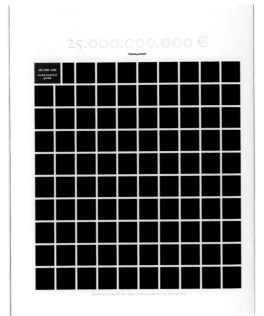

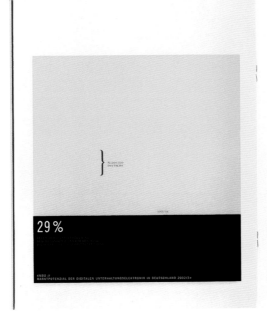

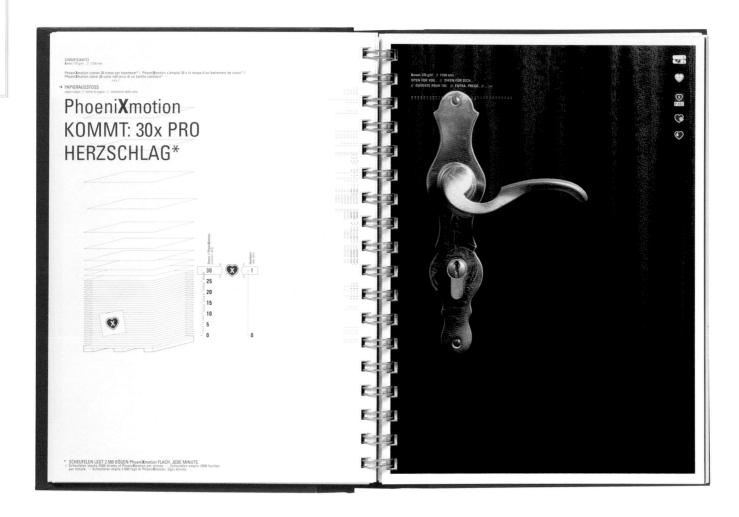

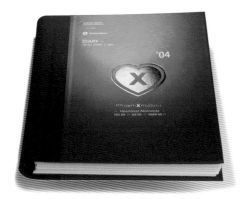

From a diary for a papermill using diagrams comparing the characteristics of the paper brand "Phoenixmotion:paper with heart" with the features of human heart.

製紙会社のために作成されたダイアリーから抜粋。「Phoenixmotion：ハートのこもった紙」という紙のブランドの特徴を、人間のハートの特徴と比較したダイアグラムを使用している。

Germany 2003
CD, AD, D: Kirsten Dietz   CD, CW: Jochen Rädeker   D: Tanja Günther / Felix Widmaier   P: Jan Steinhilber   DF, S: Strichpunkt GmbH   CL: Papierfabrik Scheufelen GmbH+Co. KG

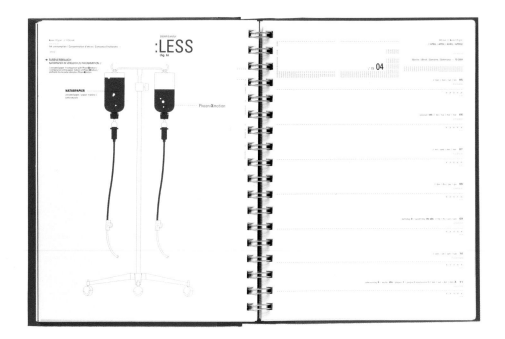

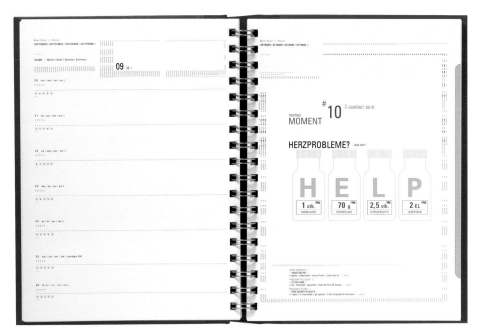

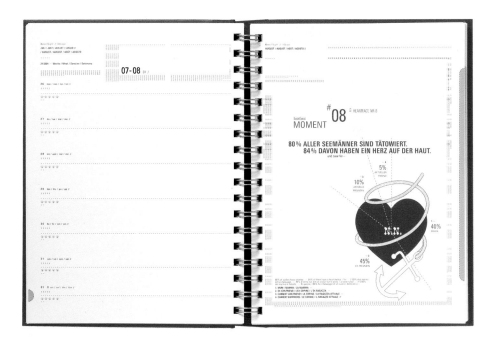

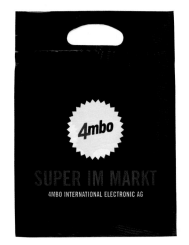

LAGEBERICHT DES 4MBO-KONZERNS

// GESCHÄFTSJAHR 2002

GESAMTWIRTSCHAFTLICHE ENTWICKLUNG

Entgegen vielen zu Beginn des Jahres 2002 abgegebenen Prognosen kam die weltweite Konjunktur auch 2002 nicht in Fahrt. So wuchs das Bruttoinlandsprodukt in den Industrieländern nach Angaben des Hamburgischen Welt-wirtschaftsarchivs (HWWA) lediglich um 1,5% und in der Euro-Zone sogar nur um 0,8%. In diesem schwierigen Umfeld ist das Wachstum in Deutschland im Jahr 2002 nahezu zum Stillstand gekommen. Real stieg das Brutto-inlandsprodukt um magere 0,2% – der schlechteste Wert seit 1993.

Ein Abrutschen in die Rezession verhinderte lediglich der starke Export, der einen Wachstumsbeitrag von 1,5% lieferte. Enttäuschend entwickelte sich hingegen der private Konsum – er war 2002 erstmals seit der Wiederverein-igung schwächer als im Jahr zuvor. Dies schlägt sich in Zahlen nieder: Nach Erhebungen des Statistischen Bundesamtes hat der Einzelhandel in Deutschland im Jahr 2002 nominal (in jeweiligen Preisen) 2,0% und real (in konstanten Preisen) 2,3% weniger umgesetzt als im Vorjahr. Einen Umsatzrückgang im Einzelhandel im Jahresvergleich gab es zuletzt 1997.

From an annual report of a hardware distributor. Using various graphics for visualization of the turnover and business development.
Annual report is placed inside a bag "SUPER IM MARKT."

ハードウェアの販売会社のアニュアル・レポートより。売上高やビジネスの成長度を視覚化するために様々なグラフィックを使用している。
このアニュアル・レポートは「SUPER IM MARKT」という袋に入れられている。

Germany   2003
CD, AD, D: Kirsten Dietz   CD, AD, CW: Jochen Rädeker   CW: Eberhard Kaiser   DF, S: Strichpunkt GmbH   CL: 4MBO International Electronic AG

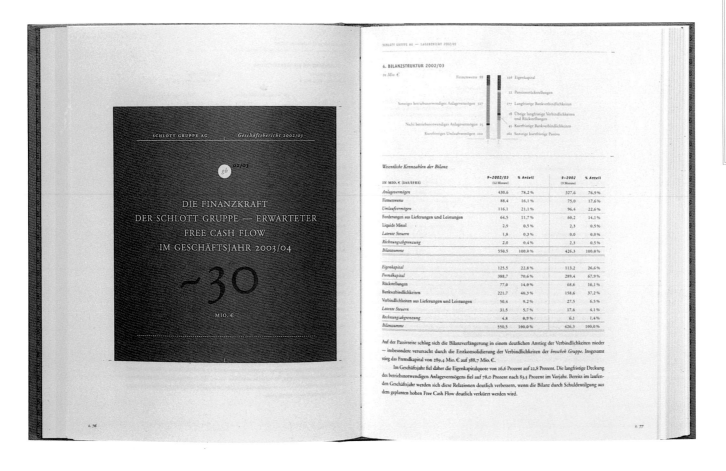

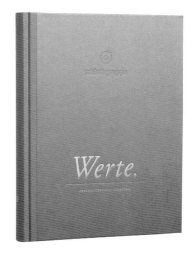

From an annual report of a printing company. Showing facts and figures of the fiscal year.

印刷会社のアニュアル・レポートより。本年度の売上などの情報を示している。

Germany　2003
CD, AD: Kirsten Dietz　CD: Jochen Rädeker　D: Stephanie Zehender / Gernot Walter　P: Andreas Langen / Kai Loges　CW: Pr + Co.
DF, S: Strichpunkt GmbH　CL: Schlott Gruppe AG

A pie chart showing the state of being of typical Diesel individuals.

典型的なディーゼル愛好者の性格を示す円グラフ。

Netherlands 2003
AD: Pim Van Nunen P: Luiz Sanchez CW: Lorenzo De Rita DF, S: Kesselskramer CL: Diesel

Graphs showing the result of market research
to provide a better understanding of the Diesel individuals
around the world and establish the impact
and percentage of effectiveness of Diesel's clothing
in making their life successful.

世界中のディーゼル愛好者を良く理解し、彼らの人生を成功に導いた同社の
洋服の効果や、影響の度合いを立証するマーケット・リサーチの結果を
示すグラフ。

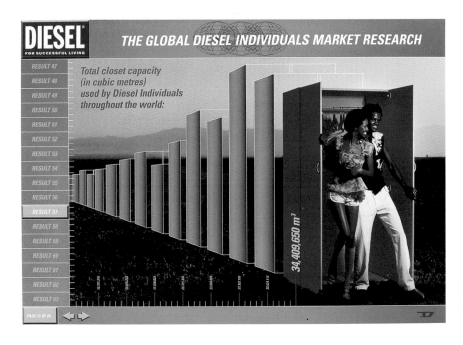

A graph illustrating total closet capacity (in cubic meters)
used by Diesel individuals throughout the world.

世界中のディーゼル愛好者が使用しているクローゼットの広さの
合計（立方平方メートル）を表すグラフ。

A graph showing a number of sand castles accidentally
destroyed by Diesel swimsuit wearers during the summer.

夏の間、ディーゼルの水着を着た人に偶然壊されてしまった砂の城の数
を示すグラフ。

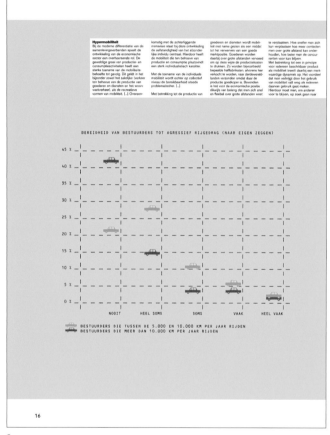

a

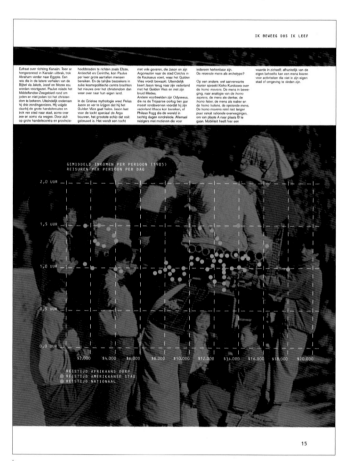

b

Diagram showing the aggressive behavior in traffic:drivers who drive between 5,000 and 10,000km versus those who drive more than 10,000km per year. (a)
Diagram showing average income per person versus travelling time per person per day in Africa, USA, and the Netherlands. (b)

渋滞における攻撃的な行動を示すダイアグラム。年間5,000～10,000キロを運転するドライバーと年間10,000キロ以上運転するドライバーの比較。 (a)
アフリカ、アメリカおよびオランダの個人の平均収入と1日の移動時間を比較したダイアグラム。 (b)

Netherlands 2003
CD, AD: André Toet   CD: Jan Sevenster   D: Bas Meulendijks   CW: Paul Van Koningsbruggen   DF, S: Samenwerkende Ontwerpers   CL: Grafische Cultuurstichting

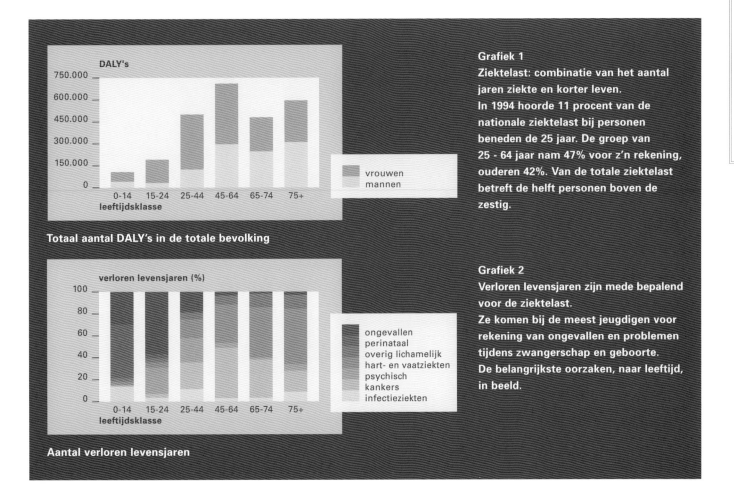

Totaal aantal DALY's in de totale bevolking

Aantal verloren levensjaren

Grafiek 1
Ziektelast: combinatie van het aantal jaren ziekte en korter leven.
In 1994 hoorde 11 procent van de nationale ziektelast bij personen beneden de 25 jaar. De groep van 25 - 64 jaar nam 47% voor z'n rekening, ouderen 42%. Van de totale ziektelast betreft de helft personen boven de zestig.

Grafiek 2
Verloren levensjaren zijn mede bepalend voor de ziektelast.
Ze komen bij de meest jeugdigen voor rekening van ongevallen en problemen tijdens zwangerschap en geboorte.
De belangrijkste oorzaken, naar leeftijd, in beeld.

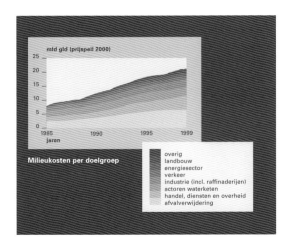

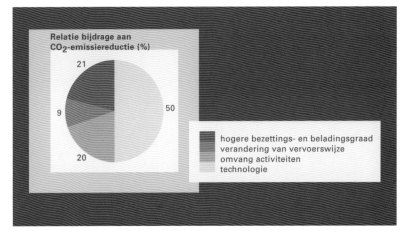

Various diagrams showing studies and statistics on environmental issues : population, CO2 emission, temparature, and etc.

人口、二酸化炭素排出量、気温など、環境問題に関する研究と統計を示す様々なグラフ。

Netherlands   2001
CD: Annemieke Later   D: Edwin Van Praet   DF, S: TelDesign   CL: RIVM

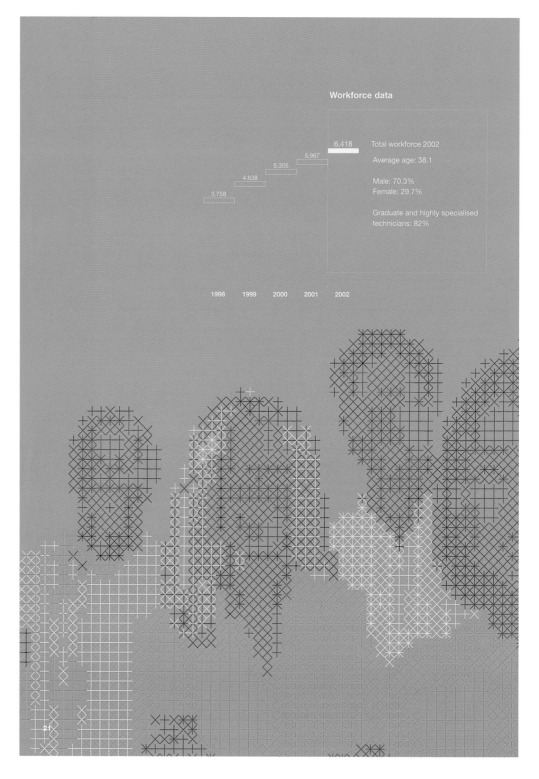

Workforce data

3,758 — 4,638 — 5,305 — 5,967 — 6,418

Total workforce 2002

Average age: 38.1

Male: 70.3%
Female: 29.7%

Graduate and highly specialised technicians: 82%

1998 1999 2000 2001 2002

From an annual report of a telecommunication company. Graphs showing average daily trading volume per month, workforce data, average share value, and profit and revenues.

テレコミュニケーション会社のアニュアル・レポートより。1ヶ月あたりの平均的な日常の取引高、従業員数のデータ、平均的な株価、利益と収入を示すグラフ。

Spain 2003
CD: Emilio Gil   AD: Jorge García   CW: Angel Alloza   DF, S: Tau Diseño   CL: Indra

General Evolution

A weak economy that performed below initial expectations and the slowdown in growth had an adverse impact on overall confidence in 2002. The information technologies industry, in which the majority of Indra's operations take place, has not been immune to these circumstances, growth rates having declined with respect to 2001 in all markets, including Spain.

Despite this scenario, Indra has again fulfilled its permanent medium-term goal of rapid growth in turnover and profitability, significantly above the Spanish and European markets, in a year of negative results for many industry companies.

All objectives set for 2002 have been met, even though the general economic outlook at the end of 2001, when the company's aims were defined, was not as adverse as the situation that unfolded during the year:

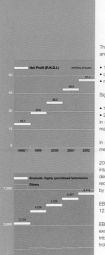

	Initial objectives	Year end
Growth in IT revenues (ex balloting projects)	12%-15%	15%
Growing in SIM/ATS + DEE revenues	15%	17%
Operating profitability (EBIT margin as % of sales)	10.8%	11%
Net profit growth	**15%**	**20%**

Total revenues for 2002 reached €873.6m, entailing a rise of 13% on 2001 (15% ex balloting projects).

Order intake amounted to €927.3m, a figure 6% higher than total revenues for the year and similar to the total for 2001, when order intake grew 29%.

At the year end the order backlog totalled €1,177m or 1.35 times revenues for the year, ensuring a good coverage level for coming years.

The IT business performed well despite the industry scenario previously referred to. Total revenues of €669.4m represent 12% year-on-year growth (15% ex balloting projects). The following issues should be noted:

• 15% growth (20% ex balloting projects) was achieved in the three institutional markets (accounting for 62% of revenues), the two most significant being Defence & Security Forces and Transport & Traffic. Balloting projects declined in 2002 as no elections were held in Indra's habitual markets, although business was secured in new regions;

• as regards the remaining vertical markets, significant progress was made in Industry & Commerce (18%) and Finance & Insurance (10%). In spite of the general weak performance in this market in 2002, Indra's Telecommunications & Utilities business grew 3% on 2001, when it rose 50% compared with the previous year.

IT Revenues by market	2002 (€M)	2001 (€M)	Variation
Transport & Traffic	189.0	156.9	20%
Defence & Security Forces	177.2	142.7	24%
Telecommunications & Utilities	157.9	153.2	3%
Public Administration & Healthcare	47.5	44.5	7%
Public Administration Balloting Projects	3.6	19.9	-82%
Finance & Insurance	52.0	47.1	10%
Industry & Commerce	42.2	35.7	18%
Total IT Revenues	**669.4**	**600.1**	**12%**

The following should be noted in relation to the Simulation and Automatic Test Systems (SIM/ATS) and Defence Electronics Equipment (DEE) businesses, where turnover totalled €204.2m:

• 17% overall rise in revenues, SIM/ATS having grown 30%;
• continued high visibility and a large order backlog equal to 2.6 times 2002's turnover;
• major projects have been identified that should generate new contracts as from 2004.

Significant developments relating to total revenues by geographical areas are as follows:

• 19% growth in the Spanish market, which accounts for 70% of total revenues;
• 20% growth in international markets, not including Latin America, which has offset the decline in revenues in this area caused by a decrease in balloting projects and the depreciation of the main currencies.

In general, Indra's international business has again helped to support the company's development, representing 30% of total revenues.

2002 has been a positive year from a commercial viewpoint, in terms of revenues and order intake; profitability has also improved, despite price pressures accompanied by slow growth in demand and stricter customer requirements, factors that have caused a reduction in profits recorded by the industry's leading European companies, whose operating margins have declined by an average of 37%.

EBITDA has risen 18% to reach €113.6m, totalling 13% of revenues in 2002 compared with 12.4% in 2002.

EBIT has increased to €96.0m, amounting to 11% of revenues in 2002 versus 10.8% in 2001 and exceeding the initial target for the year. This growth in profitability is explained by a rise in the contribution from added value products, a flexible funding structure and ongoing measures to control costs and optimise production.

Net profit totals €57.4m, entailing a rise of 20% on the figure for 2001.

Indra also continues to generate a substantial cash flow, which amounted to €86m in 2002, 22% up on 2001. This factor, coupled with a considerable rise in working capital, has resulted in a net cash position of €36.5m at the year end after investing €100m, of which €73m relates to acquisitions (a 49% stake in Indra EWS and 60% of the Portuguese company CPC).

ROCE (return on capital employed) and ROE (return on equity) stand at 51% and 29%, respectively (excluding financial coverage for option plans in both cases).

Indra's stock has performed above average in 2002 thanks in part to sound economic and financial figures, as described above, and the company's sustained growth since the IPO, all yearly targets having been fulfilled and even exceeded.

During the year, stock markets have been highly volatile due to the loss of confidence in an economic recovery. The major indices have registered substantial losses, particularly IT industry indices.

2002 was a poor year from an economic viewpoint and this is also true in the financial markets, the world's stock exchanges having suffered for the third year running as a result of the recession in the real economy.

In this adverse context, Indra's performance was clearly above average, even though the stock fell 32% over the year. The European IT services sector lost 67%, the main Spanish index (IBEX-35) closed at a loss for the third consecutive year (28%) and the technological indices have shown no signs of recovering: the Nasdaq fell 33% and Spain's New Market lost 47%.

The following graph shows the evolution of Indra's share price, the IBEX 35 and the average share prices for the main European IT services companies in 2002 (base 100):

This above-average market performance becomes even clearer based on Indra's performance since the IPO in March 1999. While Indra's stock has risen in value by 45%, the average share value for the principal European IT companies has fallen 80% and the IBEX 35 has lost 39%, as shown in the following graph (base 100):

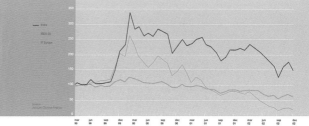

We may therefore conclude that Indra's position has improved both in absolute terms and, more importantly, in comparison with the rest of the industry, following three years of unfavourable and even crisis conditions (2000-2002). This has been possible thanks to a number of specific features that may be identified in the company's business model, including:

• selective growth policy as regards retaining customers, securing new business and providing services.
• strong commitment to project execution and delivery.
• focus on cost control and production optimisation.
• major emphasis on cash generation by projects and working capital management.
• all the above is supported by a selective acquisitions policy, alliances forged to access wider markets and a proven capacity to generate projects in emerging markets.

Meggitt PLC Report and Accounts 2003

Around 3,700 employees.
Four integrated divisions.
One Meggitt.

Meggitt is more than the responsible custodian of first-class, operationally independent businesses.

Within or across the four divisions through which we manage them, you'll find Meggitt's operating units increasingly marching in step; sharing research,

engineering, operational and marketing expertise; and orchestrating technical solutions of increasingly high value to customers—in ways they want them delivered.

Aerospace Systems

90% of the world's aircraft carry the engine vibration monitoring systems we have developed over half a century. Today, we enjoy a wider diagnostic capability, evidenced by our recent launch of the world's first, comprehensive, on-engine condition monitoring unit for the A380 Airbus. With our electronics, this unit adds parameters of temperature, pressure and speed from digital engine control systems to our oil debris and vibration analysis tools, sharpening maintenance scheduling and enhancing the readiness of mission critical aerospace applications.

The division's electronic cockpit displays are compact, information-rich yet optically-clear, and function in extreme conditions. With 2002's acquisition of best-in-class air data computers, specialised avionics sensors and data acquisition units, discrete flight instrumentation is now being integrated into comprehensive, higher value systems for military aircraft.

£124.1m
Turnover 2003

31%
Percentage of group turnover

2003 126.1
2002 102.7
2001 107.7
2000 96.7
1999 77.5

Defence Systems

43 countries favour our aerial targets, electronic scoring systems and unmanned air vehicles, which are used to train personnel and develop and evaluate anti-aircraft weapon systems. Turnkey systems and services add value to these products. Our aero-mechanical launch and recovery systems—deploying targets or towed decoys to foil missile threats—are installed on numerous military aircraft the world over. These innovative proprietary technologies are protected and developed through total systems control, guaranteeing a high degree of customisation for each client.

Two acquisitions in 2003 widened the scope of the division's offer. Caswell International extended our targetry expertise to ground-based stationary and mobile target equipment for small arms and armour training. Meggitt Western Design enhanced our weapons systems development capability with its world class, automated ammunition handling technology and environmental control systems.

£52.0m
Turnover 2003

13%
Percentage of group turnover

2003 50.6
2002 36.9
2001 37.1
2000 29.7
1999 26.6

Aerospace Equipment

The flight time of our fire detection systems, which have never missed a true fire warning, exceeds one billion hours. Our high speed fuel control and shut-off valves operate in less than 50 milliseconds at extreme temperatures. Our unique Blood Air Leak Detection system is now on the C5 jet and Aermacchi M346 jet trainer and our tank pressurisation ducts on the Space Shuttle. Our quick disconnect products, used on interconnecting lines involving corrosive and other exotic fluids found on military aircraft and space vehicles, are made to the highest specifications, ready to be uncoupled at speed with zero leakage and air inclusion.

When you consider that our products transmit signals, help control engine clearance, regulate

de-icing, cool avionics, select landing gear, manage fuel and control cabin pressure and temperature, you can see why our products and systems—also repaired and replaced by us over the average 30-year life of an aircraft—are on virtually every aircraft flying today. We work on the ground, too: on transfer cooling solutions involving proprietary printed circuit heat exchange technology, and fire and gas detection systems for industrial applications.

The newly acquired, high performance products of Meggitt Airdynamics will increase the military-grade content of the division's environmental control systems. In turn, with access to complementary products across the division, Meggitt Airdynamics will advance its systems offer.

£151.4m
Turnover 2003

38%
Percentage of group turnover

2003 151.4
2002 149.3
2001 173.6
2000 155.4
1999 95.2

Electronics

We design and manufacture high-value, active sensors for mission critical applications. Our markets are characterised by the need for absolute measurement from high performance products that function in demanding environments.

Our customers, who operate in regulated business sectors of the medical, flight, military and transportation safety markets, demand the highest standards of product reliability. After all, life can depend on the integrity of systems that include Meggitt technology. At one end of the spectrum, our sensor technology developments support new ideas in human condition monitoring like in vitro drug delivery systems and blood pressure monitoring and, at the other, networked intelligent sensors that guide orbiting satellites.

The division also produces high volume, position sensors, potentiometers and encoders for a diverse range of automotive and domestic applications including audio volume and tuning control, climate management and airflow distribution, and equipment positioning and mode switching.

£71.2m
Turnover 2003

18%
Percentage of group turnover

2003 71.2
2002 68.6
2001 67.4
2000 64.5
1999 62.0

...leading to record profits—
the highest in Meggitt's history.

In 2003, we delivered another set of outstanding results.

We did this by maintaining investment in new products—even in depressed markets there are always customers for innovation.

We continued to take a balanced approach to market diversification within our chosen niches with a portfolio designed to offset demand changes in our primary aerospace and defence markets.

And we supported customers in other sectors hungry for the aerospace quality which characterises Meggitt's engineering-rich, information-oriented products.

We continued to integrate our divisions so that we can, as a group, manage the select core of customers that drive many of our businesses.

We realised intrinsic value from current operations and, through another year of

astute acquisitions, positioned ourselves to refresh core technologies, deliver new products and exploit new markets.

And that's how we will continue to deliver value to our customers—and the kind of returns to which Meggitt shareholders have become accustomed.

£75.5m
Profit before tax, exceptional items and goodwill amortisation

2003 75.5
2002 70.3
2001 72.4
2000 66.1
1999 49.1

£81.7m
Cash flow from operating activities

2003 81.7
2002 81.6
2001 88.3
2000 81.6
1999 49.8

18.3p
Earnings per share (MMT basis)

2003 18.3
2002 17.1
2001 17.4
2000 16.2
1999 13.2

7.5p
Dividends per share

2003 7.5
2002 7.0
2001 6.8
2000 6.4
1999 5.7

Cash generation (£m)

2003 83.7
2003 81.7
2002 78.4
2002 81.6
2001 84.5
2001 88.3
2000 80.6
2000 81.6
1999 56.0
1999 49.8

■ Operating profit before   □ Cash flow from
goodwill amortisation   operations

Turnover by geographical destination (%)

■ UK: 15%
   (2002: 16%)
■ Continental Europe: 23%
   (2002: 21%)
■ North America: 52%
   (2002: 52%)
■ Rest of World: 10%
   (2002: 11%)

Exchange rates effective for 2003

	Balance Sheet Year end rate		Profit & Loss Account Weighted average	
	2003	2002	2003	2002
US dollar	1.79	1.61	1.63	1.46
Euro	1.42	1.53	1.45	1.57
Swiss franc	2.21	2.23	2.21	2.34

Currency profile of net debt (£m)

	2003	2002
Sterling	(22.8)	(29.4)
US dollar	141.2	144.8
Euro	(3.2)	(6.3)
Swiss franc	25.7	31.3
Other	(0.4)	(0.7)
Total net debt	**140.5**	**139.7**

Gearing (%)

1999 118.6
2000 83.1
2001 60.7
2002 54.2
2003

Graphs indicating data on employees and analysis of turnover for 2001-2003.

2001年から2003年の売上高の分析や従業員に関するデータを表すグラフ。

UK 2004
CD: David Stocks / Gilmar Wendt   AD, D, I: Rachael Godfrey   DF, S: SAS   CL: Meggit PLC

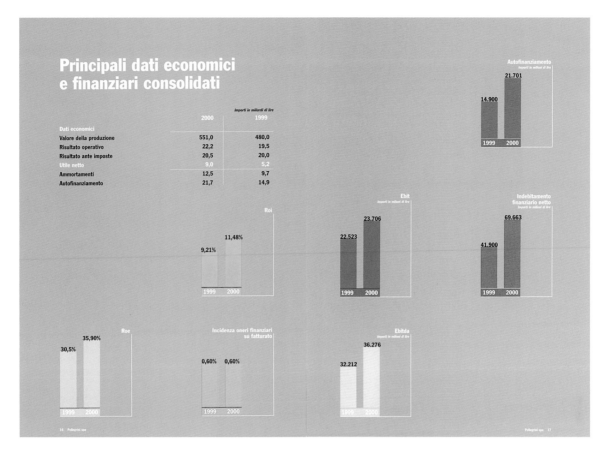

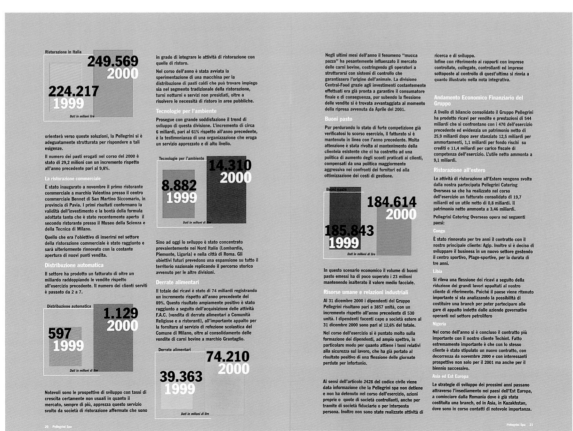

From an annual report of a catering company. Graphs detail various costs in the catering industry in Italy.

外食企業のアニュアル・レポートより。イタリアの外食産業における様々なコストを表すグラフ。

Italy   2001
CD, I: Guido Grognola   AD, D: Andrea Fanji   P: Industrial & Corporate Profiles Srl-Fiorenza Cicogna
CW: Andrea Di Gregorio   DF, S: Industrial & Corporate Profiles Srl   CL: Pellegrini Spa

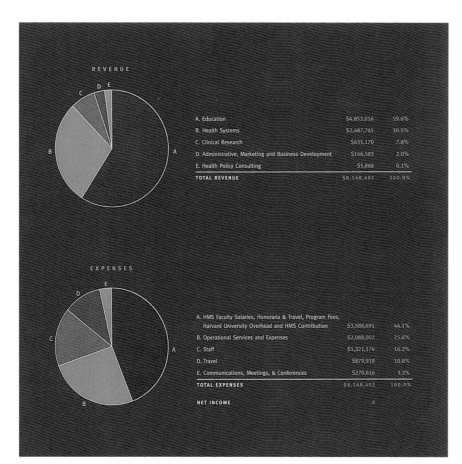

REVENUE

A. Education	$4,853,016	59.6%
B. Health Systems	$2,487,765	30.5%
C. Clinical Research	$635,170	7.8%
D. Administrative, Marketing and Business Development	$166,583	2.0%
E. Health Policy Consulting	$5,868	0.1%
TOTAL REVENUE	$8,148,402	100.0%

EXPENSES

A. HMS Faculty Salaries, Honoraria & Travel, Program Fees, Harvard University Overhead and HMS Contribution	$3,588,691	44.1%
B. Operational Services and Expenses	$2,088,002	25.6%
C. Staff	$1,321,174	16.2%
D. Travel	$879,919	10.8%
E. Communications, Meetings, & Conferences	$270,616	3.3%
TOTAL EXPENSES	$8,148,402	100.0%
NET INCOME	0	

Pie charts itemizing the revenus and expenses.
From an annual report for a non-profit unit of
Harvard Medical School.

収益と費用の内訳を示す円グラフ。
ハーバード大学医学部内の非営利部門のアニュアル・レポートより。

USA 2002
CD, AD, D: Natalie Pangaro / Shannon Beer
DF, S: Pangaro Beer   CL: Harvard Medical International

Industry Classification

Summary of the Funds' investment portfolio by industry and by type of ownership as of December 31, 2003.

Based on Investment Cost

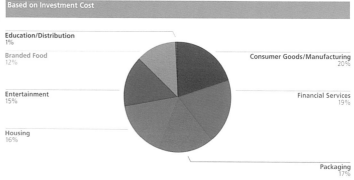

Education/Distribution 1%
Branded Food 12%
Entertainment 15%
Housing 16%
Consumer Goods/Manufacturing 20%
Financial Services 19%
Packaging 17%

Type of Ownership

Based on Number of Investments

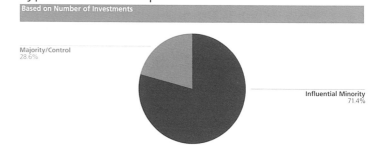

Majority/Control 28.6%
Influential Minority 71.4%

Graphs to communicate financial results for ZN Mexico Funds,
an investment fund focusing on Mexico. From an annual report.

メキシコに焦点をあてた投資ファンド、ZN Mexico Fundsの決算報告を伝えるグラフ。
アニュアル・レポートより。

USA 2004
CD, D: Graham Hanson   D: Pilar Freire   CW: Mariel Creo
DF, S: Graham Hanson Design   CL: Zephyr Management

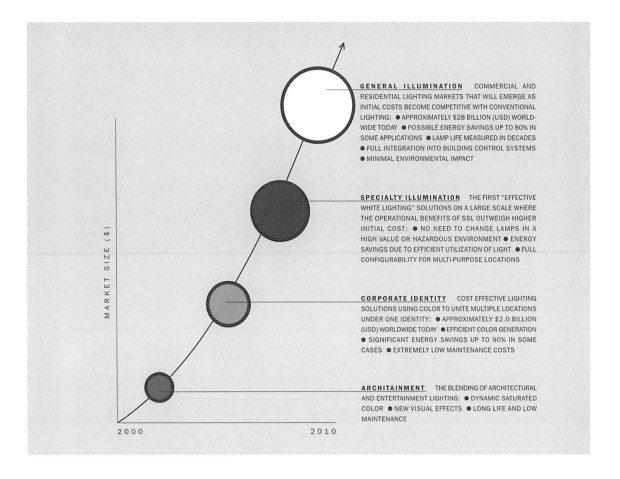

GENERAL ILLUMINATION COMMERCIAL AND RESIDENTIAL LIGHTING MARKETS THAT WILL EMERGE AS INITIAL COSTS BECOME COMPETITIVE WITH CONVENTIONAL LIGHTING: ● APPROXIMATELY $28 BILLION (USD) WORLD-WIDE TODAY ● POSSIBLE ENERGY SAVINGS UP TO 80% IN SOME APPLICATIONS ● LAMP LIFE MEASURED IN DECADES ● FULL INTEGRATION INTO BUILDING CONTROL SYSTEMS ● MINIMAL ENVIRONMENTAL IMPACT

SPECIALTY ILLUMINATION THE FIRST "EFFECTIVE WHITE LIGHTING" SOLUTIONS ON A LARGE SCALE WHERE THE OPERATIONAL BENEFITS OF SSL OUTWEIGH HIGHER INITIAL COST: ● NO NEED TO CHANGE LAMPS IN A HIGH VALUE OR HAZARDOUS ENVIRONMENT ● ENERGY SAVINGS DUE TO EFFICIENT UTILIZATION OF LIGHT ● FULL CONFIGURABILITY FOR MULTI-PURPOSE LOCATIONS

CORPORATE IDENTITY COST EFFECTIVE LIGHTING SOLUTIONS USING COLOR TO UNITE MULTIPLE LOCATIONS UNDER ONE IDENTITY: ● APPROXIMATELY $2.0 BILLION (USD) WORLDWIDE TODAY ● EFFICIENT COLOR GENERATION ● SIGNIFICANT ENERGY SAVINGS UP TO 90% IN SOME CASES ● EXTREMELY LOW MAINTENANCE COSTS

ARCHITAINMENT THE BLENDING OF ARCHITECTURAL AND ENTERTAINMENT LIGHTING: ● DYNAMIC SATURATED COLOR ● NEW VISUAL EFFECTS ● LONG LIFE AND LOW MAINTENANCE

MARKET SIZE ($)

2000   2010

A graph showing the market growth of solid state lighting.

半導体照明のマーケットの成長を示すグラフ。

USA 2001
CD, AD, D: Dave Mason   AD, D: Pamela Lee   D: Nancy Willett   P: Victor John Penner   DF, S: Samata Mason   CL: TIR Systems Ltd.

(2) Market share and position
We hold the leading position in the key fixed and mobile systems markets

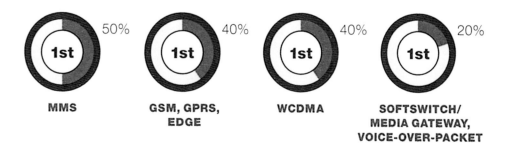

50%   40%   40%   20%

1st   1st   1st   1st

MMS   GSM, GPRS,   WCDMA   SOFTSWITCH/
            EDGE   MEDIA GATEWAY,
                                  VOICE-OVER-PACKET

Pie charts showing market share and position.

マーケットシェアと市場を示す円グラフ。

UK 2004
CD, AD: Gilmar Wendt   CD: David Stocks   D, I: John-Paul Sykes   P: Peter Hoelstad   CW: Tim Rich / Mats Thoren   DF, S: SAS   CL: Ericsson

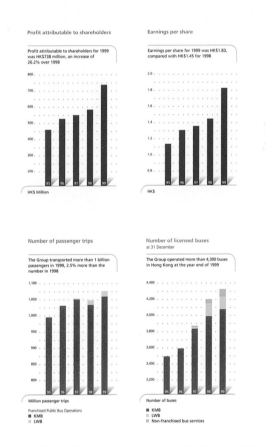

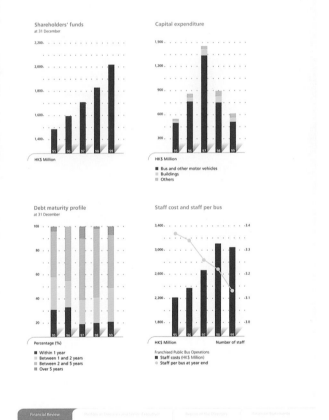

A series of graphs showing corporate profitability, number of passengers and buses. From an annual report.

企業の収益性、乗客やバスの数を示す一連のグラフ。アニュアル・レポートより。

Hong Kong 2000

CD, AD, D: Freeman Lau Siu Hong   AD, D: Eddy Yu   DF, S: Kan & Lau Design Consultants   CL: The Kowloon Motor Bus Holdings Ltd.

Performance Highlights—Non-Consolidated (Fiscal 2002)

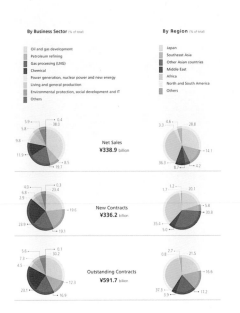

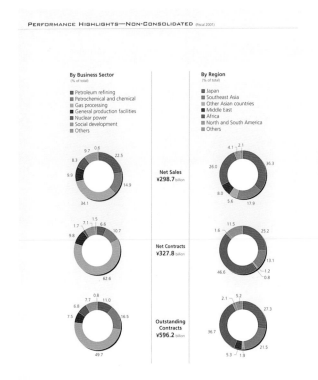

a

b

c

d

Pie charts showing sales, orders and backlog by region and business type. (a, b)
Pie charts showing sales, orders and backlog by sector and business type. (c, d)

事業分野別・地域別の売上高、受注高、受注残高を表す円グラフ。 (a, b)
セクターごとの事業分野別売上高、受注高、受注残高を表す円グラフ。 (c, d)

Japan   2003 (a) / 2002 (b) / 1999 (c, d)
D: Ayano Sasaki (a) / Shinji Suzuki (b) / Mayumi Noguchi (c, d)   CL: JGC Corporation   S: The IR Corporation

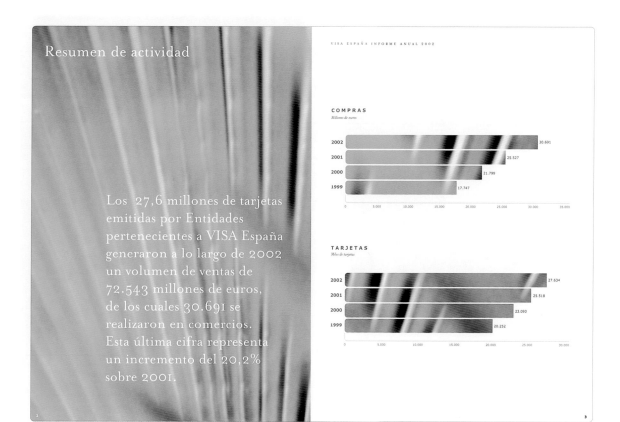

A series of financial chart for annual reports of the VISA Group.

VISAグループ各社のアニュアル・レポートから抜粋した、財務関連のチャートのシリーズ。

Spain 2003
CD: Emilio Gil   D: Ingrid Forbord   DF, S: Tau Diseño   CL: Sermepa

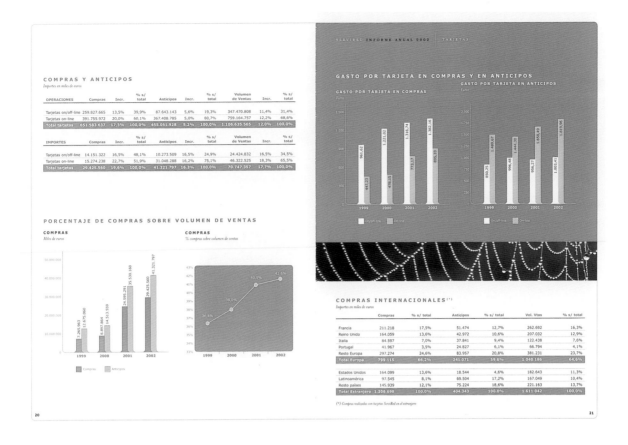

COMPRAS Y ANTICIPOS
Importes en miles de euros

OPERACIONES	Compras	Incr.	% s/ total	Anticipos	Incr.	% s/ total	Volumen de Ventas	Incr.	% s/ total
Tarjetas on/off-line	259.827.665	13,5%	39,9%	87.643.143	5,6%	19,3%	347.470.808	11,4%	31,4%
Tarjetas on-line	391.755.972	20,0%	60,1%	367.408.785	5,0%	80,7%	759.164.757	12,2%	68,6%
Total tarjetas	**651.583.637**	**17,3%**	**100,0%**	**455.051.928**	**5,2%**	**100,0%**	**1.106.635.565**	**12,0%**	**100,0%**

IMPORTES	Compras	Incr.	% s/ total	Anticipos	Incr.	% s/ total	Volumen de Ventas	Incr.	% s/ total
Tarjetas on/off-line	14.151.322	16,5%	48,1%	10.273.509	16,5%	24,9%	24.424.832	16,5%	34,5%
Tarjetas on-line	15.274.238	22,7%	51,9%	31.048.288	16,2%	75,1%	46.322.525	18,3%	65,5%
Total tarjetas	**29.425.560**	**19,6%**	**100,0%**	**41.321.797**	**16,3%**	**100,0%**	**70.747.357**	**17,7%**	**100,0%**

PORCENTAJE DE COMPRAS SOBRE VOLUMEN DE VENTAS

COMPRAS
Miles de euros

COMPRAS
% compras sobre volumen de ventas

GASTO POR TARJETA EN COMPRAS Y EN ANTICIPOS

GASTO POR TARJETA EN COMPRAS
Euros

GASTO POR TARJETA EN ANTICIPOS
Euros

COMPRAS INTERNACIONALES (*)
Importes en miles de euros

	Compras	% s/ total	Anticipos	% s/ total	Vol. Vtas	% s/ total
Francia	211.218	17,5%	51.474	12,7%	262.692	16,3%
Reino Unido	164.059	13,6%	42.972	10,6%	207.032	12,9%
Italia	84.597	7,0%	37.841	9,4%	122.438	7,6%
Portugal	41.967	3,5%	24.827	6,1%	66.794	4,1%
Resto Europa	297.274	24,6%	83.957	20,8%	381.231	23,7%
Total Europa	**799.115**	**66,2%**	**241.071**	**59,6%**	**1.040.186**	**64,6%**
Estados Unidos	164.099	13,6%	18.544	4,6%	182.643	11,3%
Latinoamérica	97.545	8,1%	69.504	17,2%	167.049	10,4%
Resto países	145.939	12,1%	75.224	18,6%	221.163	13,7%
Total Extranjero	**1.206.698**	**100,0%**	**404.343**	**100,0%**	**1.611.042**	**100,0%**

(*) *Compras realizadas con tarjeta ServiRed en el extranjero*

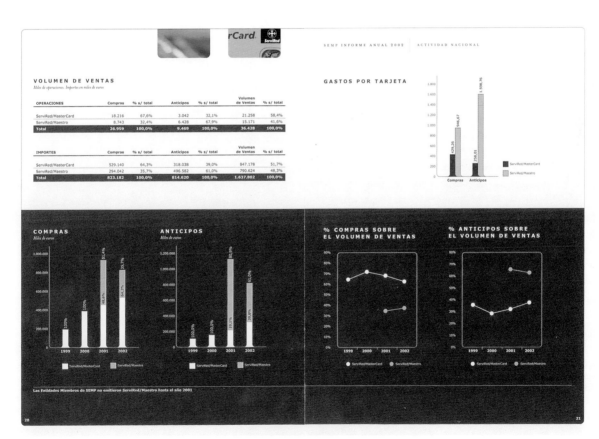

VOLUMEN DE VENTAS
Miles de operaciones. Importes en miles de euros

OPERACIONES	Compras	% s/ total	Anticipos	% s/ total	Volumen de Ventas	% s/ total
ServiRed/MasterCard	18.216	67,6%	3.042	32,1%	21.258	58,4%
ServiRed/Maestro	8.743	32,4%	6.428	67,9%	15.171	41,6%
Total	**26.959**	**100,0%**	**9.469**	**100,0%**	**36.428**	**100,0%**

IMPORTES	Compras	% s/ total	Anticipos	% s/ total	Volumen de Ventas	% s/ total
ServiRed/MasterCard	529.140	64,3%	318.038	39,0%	847.178	51,7%
ServiRed/Maestro	294.042	35,7%	496.582	61,0%	790.624	48,3%
Total	**823.182**	**100,0%**	**814.620**	**100,0%**	**1.637.802**	**100,0%**

GASTOS POR TARJETA

COMPRAS
Miles de euros

ANTICIPOS
Miles de euros

% COMPRAS SOBRE EL VOLUMEN DE VENTAS

% ANTICIPOS SOBRE EL VOLUMEN DE VENTAS

Las Entidades Miembros de SEMP no emitieron ServiRed/Maestro hasta el año 2001

ホットライン・サービスが受けた電話相談の詳細と統計を示すグラフ。アニュアル・レポートのタイトルが「聴くこと：耳は心に通じる道」であるので、「心」を象徴する色として赤を使用している。

Statistik 2003	**Telefonseelsorge Notruf 142**	Anrufe gesamt: 11.909

Anrufe

26 %	Männer
74 %	Frauen
60 %	Anonym
40 %	Namentlich
22 %	ErstanruferInnen *
78 %	MehrfachanruferInnen *

Alter *

38 %	0 – 19 Jahre
11 %	20 – 39 Jahre
15 %	40 – 59 Jahre
3 %	60 – 79 Jahre
1 %	über 80 Jahre
32 %	nicht erfasst

* Konnte nur zum Teil oder ungenau erhoben werden.

Lebensform

15 %	Alleinlebend
3 %	In Partnerschaft
4 %	Alleinerzieher
20 %	Familie
1 %	Heim / WG
57 %	nicht erfasst

Problembereich

23 %	Psychische Themen
25 %	Partnerschaft, Familie
16 %	Soziales Umfeld
36 %	sonstige Themen

Tagesbereich

17 %	Vormittag
37 %	Nachmittag
34 %	Abend
12 %	Nacht

Statistik 2003	**Details Jugendliche**	Anrufe gesamt: 4.618

Anrufe

39 %	Burschen
61 %	Mädchen
87 %	Anonym
13 %	Namentlich
28 %	ErstanruferInnen *
72 %	MehrfachanruferInnen *

Alter *

4 %	0 – 10 Jahre
68 %	11 – 15 Jahre
28 %	16 – 20 Jahre

Anlässe für Anrufe

8 %	Familienprobleme
22 %	Freundschaft, Liebe
5 %	Probleme mit Gruppen
2 %	Probleme in der Schule
3 %	Gewalt
2 %	Sucht
6 %	Psychische Probleme
5 %	Lebenssituation
9 %	Fachauskünfte
35 %	Anrufe ohne spezielles Thema
1 %	Schweigeanrufe

Tagesbereich

14 %	Vormittag
44 %	Nachmittag
35 %	Abend
7 %	Nacht

Telefonseelsorge
Vorarlberg
Jahresbericht 2003

Graphs showing details and statistics on telephone calls received by hotline services.
The title of the annual report is : "Listening—The ear is the way to the heart," so the color red is chosen as it symbolizes the heart.

ホットライン・サービスが受けた電話相談の詳細と統計を示すグラフ。アニュアル・レポートのタイトルが「聴くこと：耳は心に通じる道」であるので、「心」を象徴する色として赤を使用している。

Austria 2004
AD, D: Peter Felder   CW: Dr. Albert Lingg   DF, S: Felder Grafikdesign   CL: Telefonseelsorge Vorarlberg (the samaritans on phone Vorarlberg)

Statistik

	Notruf 142	Internet-Beratung www.142online.at
Männer	22 %	24 %
Frauen	60 %	76 %
Unbekannt	18 %	
Anonym	58 %	35 %
Namentlich	42 %	65 %
ErstanruferInnen*	24 %	54 %
MehrfachanruferInnen*	76 %	46 %

Alter*
00 – 19 Jahre	31 %	31 %
20 – 39 Jahre	13 %	21 %
40 – 59 Jahre	15 %	07 %
60 – 79 Jahre	03 %	
über 80 Jahre	01 %	
unbekannt	37 %	41 %

Lebensform*
Alleinlebend	15 %	07 %
In Partnerschaft	03 %	03 %
Alleinerziehend	04 %	03 %
Familie	16 %	32 %
Heim	01 %	01 %
unbekannt	61 %	54 %

Problembereiche
Psychische Themen	23 %	30 %
Partnerschaft/Familie	21 %	47 %
Soziales Umfeld	07 %	10 %
Sonstige Themen	49 %	13 %

Tagesbereich
Vormittag	17 %	20 %
Nachmittag	39 %	30 %
Abend	24 %	30 %
Nacht	20 %	20 %

Anrufe: Anzahl gesamt: 13.441   Mailberatung: 159

* Konnte nur zum Teil oder
ungenau erhoben werden.

Bar graphs from an annual report show details and statistics on telephone calls received by hotline services. Each diagram is depicted in different colors depending on the topic.

アニュアル・レポートから抜粋した、ホットライン・サービスが受けた相談電話の詳細と統計を示す棒グラフ。それぞれテーマごとに色分けされている。

Austria 2002

AD, D: Peter Felder   D: René Dalpra   CW: Elisabeth Tos / Sepp Grofler   DF, S: Felder Grafikdesign   CL: Telefonseelsorge Vorarlberg (the samaritans on phone Vorarlberg)

GRAPHS & TABLES SYSTEMS & PROCESS CHARTS MAPS & PICTOGRAMS ILLUSTRATIVE DIAGRAMS

FINANCIAL HIGHLIGHTS

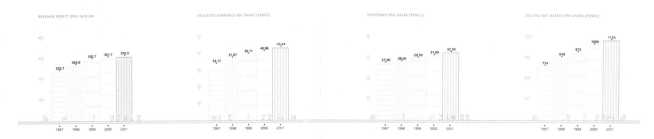

REVENUE PROFIT (PRE-TAX) £M	ADJUSTED EARNINGS PER SHARE (PENCE)	DIVIDENDS PER SHARE (PENCE)	DILUTED NET ASSETS PER SHARE (PENCE)

	31 March 2001	31 March 2000	Change %	Ten Year Compound Growth %
NET PROPERTY INCOME	£497.5m	£457.2m	+8.8	+4.6
*REVENUE PROFIT (PRE-TAX)	£308.9m	£301.7m	+2.4	+3.7
PRE-TAX PROFIT	£314.6m	£327.7m	−4.0	+3.5
*ADJUSTED EARNINGS PER SHARE	43.44p	40.86p	+6.3	+3.5
EARNINGS PER SHARE	44.57p	45.44p	−1.9	+3.5
DIVIDENDS PER SHARE	32.50p	31.00p	+4.8	+5.1
*ADJUSTED DIVIDEND COVER (times)	1.34	1.37		
DIVIDEND COVER (times)	1.37	1.52		
DILUTED NET ASSETS PER SHARE	1154p	1090p	+5.9	+5.6
PROPERTIES	£8,229.0m	£7,453.7m		
BORROWINGS	£1,757.1m	£1,556.3m		
EQUITY SHAREHOLDERS' FUNDS	£6,150.9m	£5,781.8m		
†GEARING (net)	28.1%	24.5%		
†INTEREST COVER (times)	3.04	3.11		

*Excludes results of property sales and bid costs.
†See glossary (page 72).

HIGHLIGHTS

- concluded our strategic review and restructured the Group into Portfolio Management and Development business units
- completed the acquisition of Trillium and created our Total Property Services business unit
- broadened our skill base by appointing three new executive directors
- invested £577.8m on acquisitions and developments for the investment property business
- increased the development programme spend to £2bn
- accelerated the portfolio rationalisation by selling 72 properties for £431.2m
- appointed preferred bidder for BBC property partnership contract

Since the year end

- appointed preferred bidder for BT property partnership contract
- completed acquisition of Whitecliff Properties for £63.4m

PORTFOLIO MANAGEMENT SHOPS AND SHOPPING CENTRES

VALUATION
31 MARCH 2001

£2,687.0m

% OF GROUP VALUATION

34.0%

RENTAL INCOME
YEAR ENDED 31 MARCH 2001

£178.7m

% OF GROUP
RENTAL INCOME

35.8%

VALUATION BY LOCATION

Total £2,687.0m

WEST END & VICTORIA
£597.2m | 22.2%

CITY & MIDTOWN
£66.7m | 2.5%

GREATER LONDON & HOME COUNTIES
£289.2m | 10.8%

E. & W. MIDLANDS & E. ANGLIA
£324.8m | 12.1%

NORTH, N.W., YORKSHIRE & HUMBERSIDE
£552.3m | 20.5%

WALES & SOUTH WEST
£331.0m | 12.3%

SCOTLAND & N. IRELAND
£525.8m | 19.6%

VALUATION %

50.2	25.1	24.7
SHOPPING CENTRES	OTHER IN-TOWN SHOPS	CENTRAL LONDON SHOPS

RENTAL INCOME %

50.0	28.2	21.8
SHOPPING CENTRES	OTHER IN-TOWN SHOPS	CENTRAL LONDON SHOPS

% VOIDS BY RENTAL VALUE	▸ 1.2
% REVERSIONARY	▸ 11.4
AVERAGE UNEXPIRED LEASE TERM (years) ▸	11

Bar charts explaining the financial highlights of Land Securities between 1997 and 2001, and diagrams indicating the portforio valuation by location. From an annual report.
Land Securities社の1997年から2001年までの業績の推移を説明する棒グラフと、土地別の資産評価を示すダイアグラム。アニュアル・レポートより。

UK 2001
CD: Gilmar Wendt / Nick Austin   AD, D, I: Mike Hall   P: Chris Mouse / Marcus Lyon   DF, S: SAS   CL: Land Securities

a

b

Graphs showing the financial overview in easily understandable way. From an annual report of an insurance mutual company. (a)
A pie chart illustrates percentage investment of fixed income securities by quality. (b)

決算の概要を簡単に分かりやすく表したグラフ。保険相互会社のアニュアル・レポートより。 (a)
確定所得証券への投資額のランク別内訳を示した円グラフ。 (b)

Canada 2004
CD, AD: Frank Viva   D: Sarah Wu   P: Christopher Wahl / Gloria Baker   I: Mark Summers / Ken Perkins   CW: Paul Goldman
DF, S: Viva Dolan Communications & Design Inc.   CL: New York Life Insurance Company

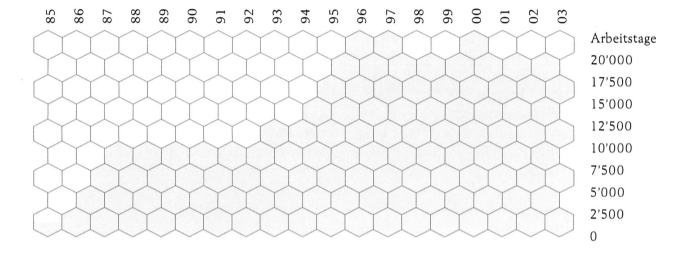

From an annual report for an environmental protection foundation. Diagrams describe how the foundation helps to maintain the high altitude meadows and farmland by fighting erosion and growing bush land.

環境保護団体のアニュアル・レポートより。高地にある牧草地や農地を侵食や増大する低木地から守るという財団の活動を説明するダイアグラム。

Switzerland 2004
CD, AD, D: Heinz Wild   D: Dan Petter   P: Pascal Wüest   I: Dan Petter   CW: Christine Loriol / Marianne Hassenstein / Christoph Müller
DF, S: Heinz Wild Design   CL: Stiftung Umwelt-Einsatz Schweiz SUS

As of March 31, 2003
Units in Millions

Outside Japan

Hardware

Software

A graph showing the consolidated total units of Nintendo hardware and software sold in abroad.

国外における任天堂のハードウェアとソフトウェアの連結累計販売台数を表すグラフ。

Japan 2003
CD: Shin Kojo   AD, D: Takashi Maeda   CL, S: Nintendo Co., Ltd.

Der Mittelstand – eine Säule der deutschen Wirtschaft

ANTEIL MITTELSTAND AN DER GESAMTWIRTSCHAFT, 2000

43,2 %	*37,2 %*	*48,8 %*
Umsatz*	Bruttoinvestitionen	Bruttowertschöpfung
72,2 %	*83 %*	*99,7 %*
Beschäftigung von Erwerbstätigen**	Ausbildung von Lehrlingen	Anzahl Unternehmen***

* MwSt.-pflichtiger Umsatz.   ** Vollzeitkräfte.   *** Mindestens 16,6 Tsd. Euro steuerpflichtiger Jahresumsatz.
Quelle: IfM Bonn, Presseartikel, McKinsey

Eigenkapitalquote im Vergleich

DURCHSCHNITTLICHE EIGENKAPITALQUOTE DES DEUTSCHEN MITTELSTANDES / in Prozent der Bilanzsumme

INTERNATIONAL*

USA	45 %
Spanien	41 %
Großbritannien	40 %
Frankreich	34 %
Italien	22 %
Japan	22 %
Deutschland **	21 %

NATIONAL

TecDax	50 %
M-Dax	29 %
Dax	23 %
Mittelstand **	20 %

* Durchschnitt 1995–1999 (EU bis 40 Mio. Euro Umsatz, USA bis 25 Mio. US-Dollar)   ** Deutschland / Mittelstand: 2,5–50 Mio. Euro Umsatz
Quelle: Deutsche Bundesbank, Europäische Kommission, McKinsey

These graphs showing the economic situation. From a corporate magazine of Säl. Oppenheim, one of leading private banks in Europe.
経済状況を示すグラフ。ヨーロッパでも有数の個人銀行、Sal. Oppenheim社のコーポレイト・マガジンより。

Germany   2003
AD, D: Bernd Vollmöller   D: Volker Weinmann   CW: Ulrich Mattwer   DF, S: Simon & Goetz Design   CL: SAL, Oppenheim jr. & Cie. KGaA

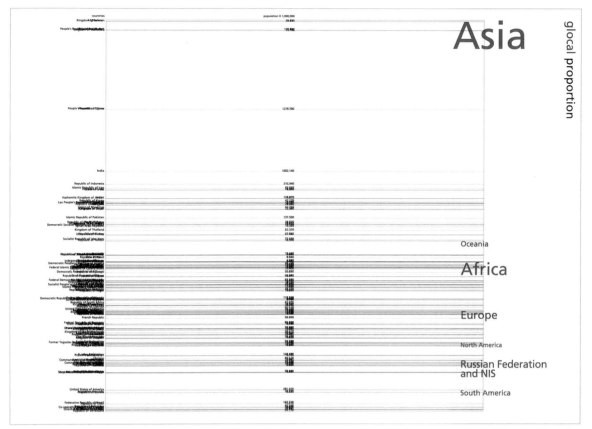

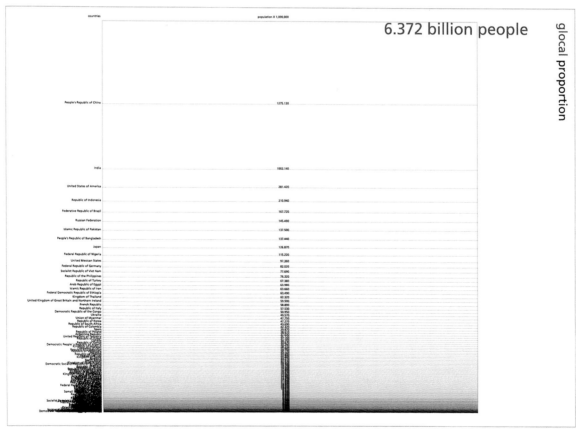

Number of countries graphed geometrically by continent according to population. (a)
Number of countries graphed geometrically according to population. (b)

人口順、大陸別に国の数を幾何学的にグラフ化。 (a)
人口順に国の数を幾何学的にグラフ化。 (b)

Japan   2003
AD, D: Shinnoske Sugisaki   DF, S: Shinnoske Inc.   CL: Inter Medium Institute

Financial Highlights

Systemwide Sales(a) (in millions of U.S. Dollars)

12,500
10,000
7,500
5,000
2,500

96 97 98 99 00

Revenues (in millions of U.S. Dollars)

12,000
10,000
8,000
6,000
4,000
2,000

96 97 98 99 00

Operating Margin(b) (in millions of U.S. Dollars)

350
300
250
200
150
100
50

96 97 98 99 00

(a) Represents total sales of Company-owned branches and franchises.
(b) Represents Operating profit excluding nonrecurring items in 1999 and 1998.

a

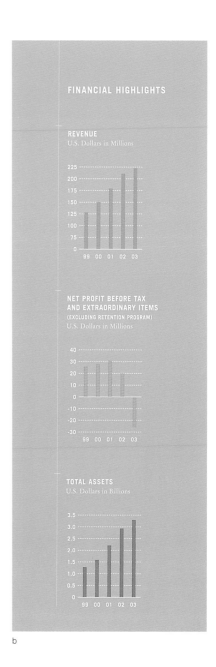

b

From the 2000 annual report of Manpower Inc.
Graphs showing financial highlights (Sales, revenues, operating margin). (a)

Manpower社の2000年度のアニュアル・レポートより。
グラフは主な財政状況（売上、収益、営業利益率）を示している。 (a)

USA 2001
CD, AD: Greg Samata   D: Beth May   CW: Tracy Shilobrit   DF, S: Samata Mason
CL: Manpower, Inc.

Graphs for the annual report of an airplane leasing company. (b)

航空機リース会社のアニュアル・レポートのためのグラフ。 (b)

USA 2004
AD: Jack Anderson   AD, D: Katha Dalton   D, I: Holly Craven / Michael Brugman
P: Jeff Corwin   CW: John Koval   DF, S: Hornall Anderson Design Works, Inc.
CL: Boullioun Aviation Services

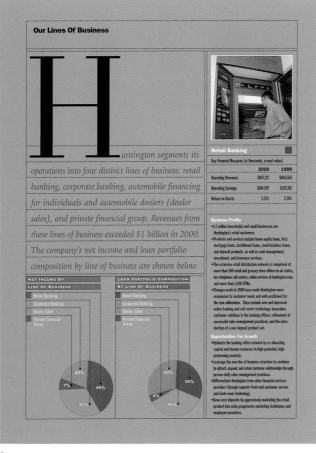

a

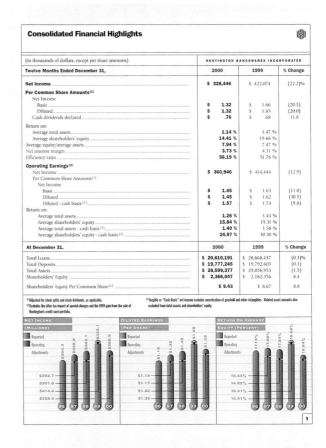

b

Pie charts illustrate the bank's net income and loan portforio composition by line of business. (a)
Graphs show revenues of a banking company over the past 5 years. From an annual report. (b)

銀行の純利益と貸出債権の内訳を業務別に示した円グラフ。 (a)
銀行の過去5年間の収益を示すグラフ。アニュアル・レポートより。 (b)

USA 2001
CD, AD, D: Eric Rickabaugh   P: George Anderson / Stock   CW: Nancy Flynn   DF, S: Rickabaugh Graphics   CL: Huntington Banks

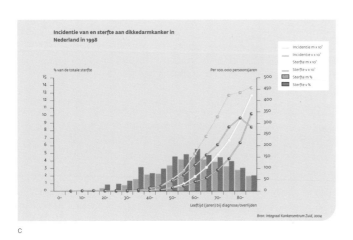

c

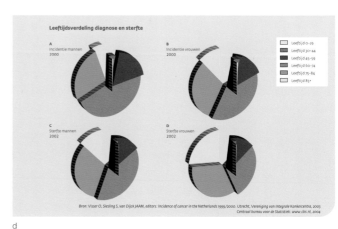

d

Graphs showing the diagnosis and mortaliy of the large intestine cancer by age. (c, d)
年齢別の大腸癌の診断と死亡率を示すグラフ。 (c, d)

Netherlands 2004
CD: Annemieke Later   D: René de Jong   DF, S: TelDesign   CL: KWF-Kankerbestrijding

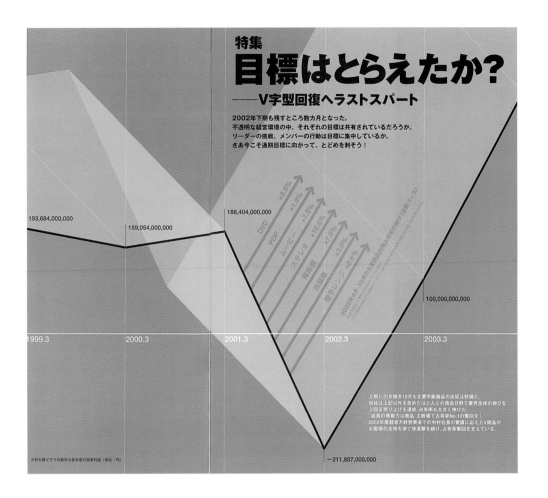

特集
目標はとらえたか？
——V字型回復へラストスパート

2002年下期も残すところ数カ月となった。
不透明な経営環境の中、それぞれの目標は共有されているだろうか。
リーダーの挑戦、メンバーの行動は目標に集中しているか。
さあ今こそ通期目標に向かって、とどめを刺そう！

193,684,000,000

159,054,000,000

188,404,000,000

DVD +9.6%
PDP +1.9%
ムービー +7.6%
ステレオ +10.0%
携帯電 +7.5%
冷蔵庫 +3.0%
電子レンジ +8.6%
2002年4月～10月の主要販売商品出荷構成比と占有率（台数ベース）

100,000,000,000

1999.3　2000.3　2001.3　2002.3　2003.3

上期に引き続き10月も主要市販商品の出足は好調だ。
当社は上記以外を含めたほとんどの商品分野で業界全体の伸びを
上回る売り上げを達成、占有率も大きく伸びた。
「成長の原動力は商品、主戦場で占有率No.1の奪回を」
2002年度経営方針発表会での中村社長の要請に応えたV商品が
お客様の支持を得て快進撃を続け、占有率奪回を支えている。

−211,807,000,000

※折れ線グラフの数字は各年度の営業利益（単位：円）

Graph showing the growth of businness profit
and market share of primary goods shipment.

営業利益と主要商品出荷占有率の伸びを表すグラフ。

Japan 2002-2003
AD, D: Shinnoske Sugisaki   D: Jun Itadani   DF, S: Shinnoske Inc.
CL: Matsushita Electric Industrial Co., Ltd.

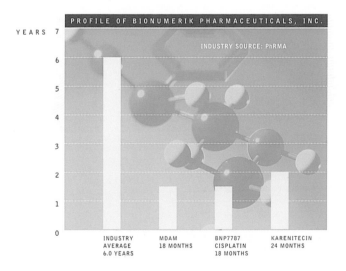

PROFILE OF BIONUMERIK PHARMACEUTICALS, INC.

YEARS 7

INDUSTRY SOURCE: PhRMA

6
5
4
3
2
1
0

INDUSTRY   MDAM   BNP7787   KARENITECIN
AVERAGE   18 MONTHS   CISPLATIN   24 MONTHS
6.0 YEARS   18 MONTHS

The graph explaining the power of a pharmaceutical company's approach.

製薬会社の開発力を表すグラフ。

USA 2000
CD, AD, D: Wing Chan   I: Jared Schneidman (JSD)
DF, S: Wing Chan Design, Inc.   CL: BioNumerik Pharmaceuticals, Inc.

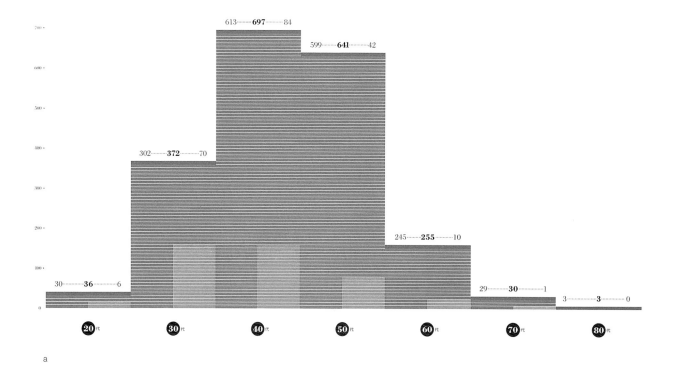

a

JAGDA地区・地域別正会員総数 —— **2,034**人

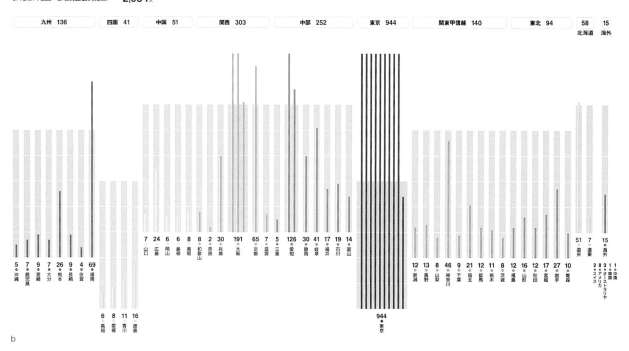

b

A bar graph expressing number of members by area and region. The graph as a whole forms a map of Japan.　(a)
A graph showing male-female ratio of members by age.　(b)

年代別の会員数を男女比で構成したグラフ。　(a)
地区、地域別会員数を棒グラフで表現。グラフ全体が日本地図にもなっている。　(b)

Japan　2000
CD, AD, D, S: Tetsuya Ota　CL: JAGDA

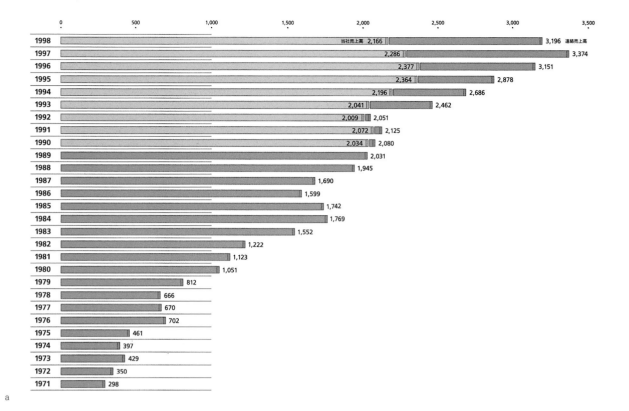

a

	0	500	1,000	1,500	2,000	2,500	3,000	3,500

1998　当社売上高 2,166　　3,196 連結売上高
1997　2,286　3,374
1996　2,377　3,151
1995　2,364　2,878
1994　2,196　2,686
1993　2,041　2,462
1992　2,009　2,051
1991　2,072　2,125
1990　2,034　2,080
1989　2,031
1988　1,945
1987　1,690
1986　1,599
1985　1,742
1984　1,769
1983　1,552
1982　1,222
1981　1,123
1980　1,051
1979　812
1978　666
1977　670
1976　702
1975　461
1974　397
1973　429
1972　350
1971　298

アメリカ
14,143 千t

ドイツ
7,993 千t

日本
1,169 千t

フランス
5,808 千t

イギリス
7,411 千t

中国
5,422 千t

b

Sales statistics expressed as a bar graph. (a)
Paper imports of major world nations shown in an arrow bar graph. (b)

売上高の推移を棒グラフで表現。 (a)
世界主要国の紙の輸入高を矢印の棒グラフで表現。 (b)

Japan 1999
CD, AD, D, S: Tetsuya Ota   CL: Nippon Electric Glass (a) / Nippon Paper Industries (b)

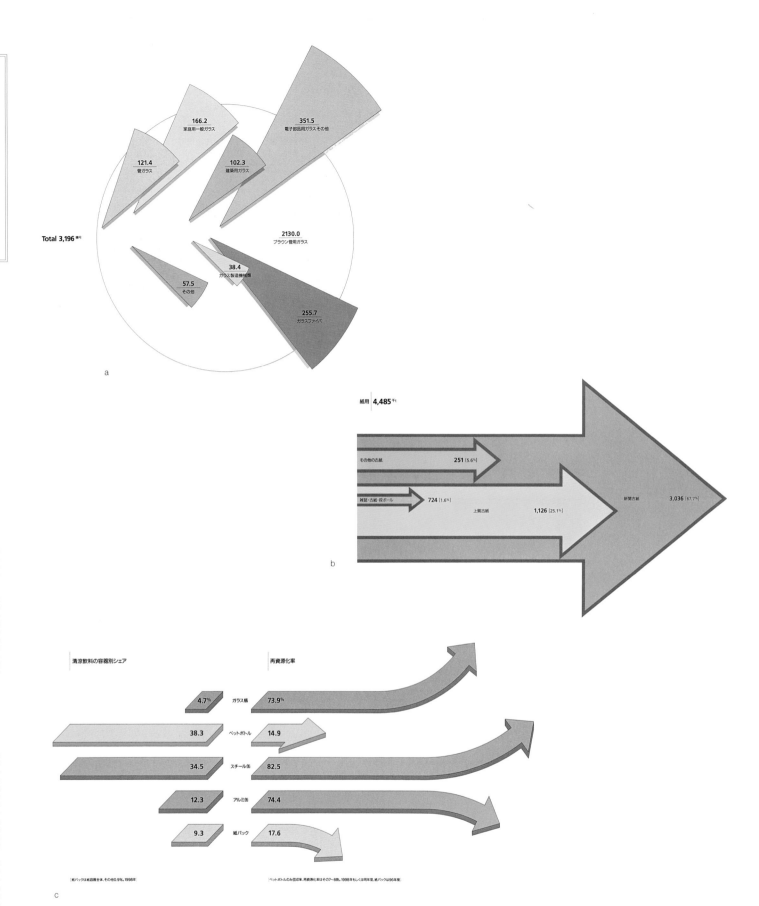

Total 3,196 億円

121.4
管ガラス

166.2
家庭用一般ガラス

102.3
建築用ガラス

351.5
電子部品用ガラスその他

2130.0
ブラウン管用ガラス

38.4
ガラス製造機械類

57.5
その他

255.7
ガラスファイバ

a

紙用 4,485 千t

その他の古紙　251 [5.6%]

雑誌・古紙・段ボール　724 [1.6%]

上質古紙　1,126 [25.1%]

新聞古紙　3,036 [67.7%]

b

清涼飲料の容器別シェア　　　　　再資源化率

4.7%　ガラス瓶　73.9%

38.3　ペットボトル　14.9

34.5　スチール缶　82.5

12.3　アルミ缶　74.4

9.3　紙パック　17.6

「紙パックは紙容器全体、その他0.9%。1998年」　　「ペットボトルのみ回収率。再資源化率はその7〜8割。1998年もしくは同年度、紙パックは96年度」

c

Distribution ratio (sales) by product shown as a pie graph. (a)
Market share of soft drinks by container and recycling ratio expressed as a bar graph using arrows. (b)
The use of arrow-like forms to express a comparison by paper grade of used paper consumption creates a dynamic visual effect. (c)

製品別構成比（売上）を円グラフでみせる。(a)
清涼飲料の容器別シェアと再資源化率を、矢印を用いた棒グラフで表現。(b)
主要古紙の紙別消費高の量の比較を相似形の矢印で動きのある視覚的効果で表現。(c)

Japan　1999
CD, AD, D, S: Tetsuya Ota　CL: Nippon Electric Glass (a) / Asahi Shinbun (b) / Japan Paper Association (c)

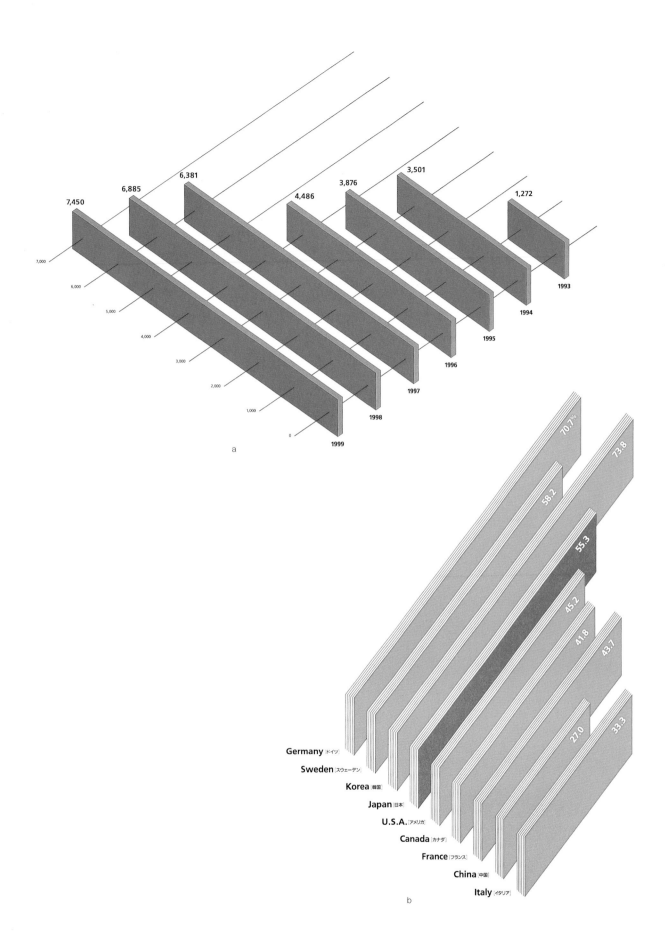

Oblique bar graph emphasizing fluctuations in company sales. (a)
A bar graph imaged after paper, expressing paper-recycling ratios of nine countries. (b)

斜め棒グラフで企業の売上の変化を強調。 (a)
世界9カ国の古紙の回収率を棒グラフで紙をイメージして作成。 (b)

Japan 1999
CD, AD, D, S: Tetsuya Ota   CL: NTT-DO (a) / Nippon Paper Industries (b)

図01 | 2002年度のスチール缶のリサイクル量

817,000t

=東京タワー200基分

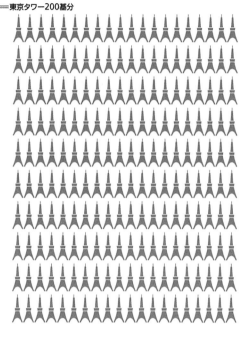

Source：スチール缶リサイクル協会

A

Aki-can [空き缶]
日本のスチール缶リサイクル率は世界一です。それは鉄が磁石にくっつくという性質を利用して、一度に大量選別しているからです。リサイクルされた鉄はさまざまな製品に生まれ変わります。まさに「鉄の七変化」です。[図01]

Asia [アジア]
現在、東アジアは1960年代の日本のように急激な工業化を実現し、「東アジア経済圏」を形成しつつあります。一方でCO₂の大量発生や酸性雨、砂漠化などの環境問題を抱えています。環境技術先進国である日本はアジアとの連携を深めて、地球温暖化や環境保全に取り組んでいます。

B

Biomass Energy [バイオマスエネルギー]
バイオマスエネルギーは、今までは捨てられていた廃材木などを化石燃料（石油や石炭）の代わりに使うことにより、化石燃料の使用量やCO₂の発生量を削減することができます。

C

CO₂ [二酸化炭素]
二酸化炭素CO₂はダイオキシンやSOxとは異なりそれ自体が有害ではありません。しかしオゾン、フロンガスなどと同様に太陽エネルギーを透過する一方、地表から再放射される赤外線の熱を放射しない温室効果があり、地球温暖化の原因といわれています。世界中で温暖化防止のための技術開発や政策が実施されていますが、国や企業の取り組みだけでは不十分です。生活者一人ひとりの意識と行動が基本です。

図02 | 日本の二酸化炭素排出量の内訳 [2001年度]
Source：地球温暖化対策推進本部

廃棄物 2.0%
工業プロセス 4.2%
エネルギー転換部門 6.4%
産業部門 37.2%
運輸部門 22.0%
民生部門 28.2%
事務所、ビル等 15.5%
家庭 12.7%

図03 | 各部門ごとの二酸化炭素排出量の増減率
Source：地球温暖化対策推進本部

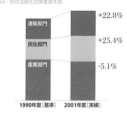

運輸部門 +22.8%
民生部門 +25.4%
産業部門 -5.1%

1990年度 [基準]　2001年度 [実績]

D

Datsu-genpatsu [脱原発]
CO₂を出さないエネルギーとして期待されている原子力発電ですが、ヨーロッパ各国を中心に「脱原発へ」という方向転換がみられます。確かに原発は核燃料廃棄物の処理や安全性の確保など解決すべき課題は多いのですが、エネルギーセキュリティ（確保）と温暖化防止という視点からは有効です。

From a pamphlet on global warming. 38 key words defined using easy-to-understand comments and illustrations.

地球温暖化に関するパンフレットより。38のキーワードを分かりやすい解説と図で説明。

Japan　2004
CD: Reiji Oshima　AD: Kenzo Nakagawa　D: Satoshi Morikami / Infogram　I: Kumiko Nagasaki　CW: Yasuko Seki　DF, S: NDC Graphics Inc.
CL: The Japan Iron and Steel Federation

図10 | 国別のエネルギー起源二酸化炭素排出量

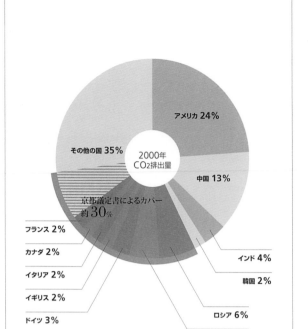

図12 | 製鉄所内の緑化総面積

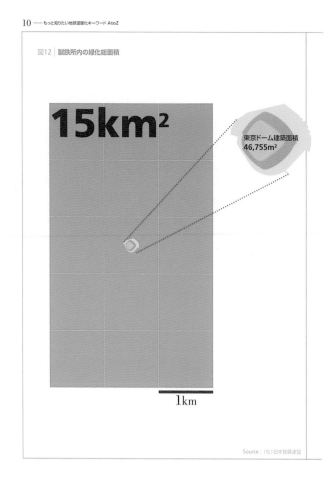

図13 | コークス炉ガスの改質による水素増幅

水 蒸 気

900℃
コークス炉ガス廃熱

水素

水素増幅

メタン

一酸化炭素

コークス炉ガス

水素

メタン

一酸化炭素

水素増幅後

外からの
エネルギーを加えないで
燃料電池自動車
100万台に供給

🚗 = 1万台

図15 | 鉄鋼業のエネルギー消費量削減目標

1990年

-10%

2010年 [目標]

数字で見るインターネットの最新動向

N^et Impre^ssions | Volume 02

Edited by 小橋 昭彦 ＋ インターネットマガジン 編集部　Designed by © Infogram

電子商取引市場［BtoC］のセグメント構成変化

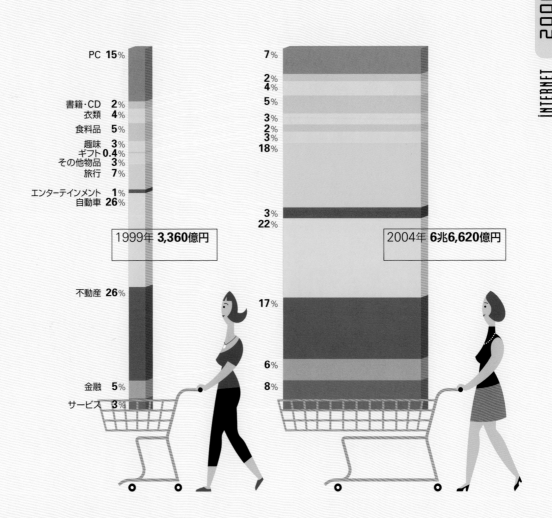

PC **15**%

書籍·CD **2**%
衣類 **4**%

食料品 **5**%

趣味 **3**%
ギフト **0.4**%
その他物品 **3**%
旅行 **7**%

エンターテインメント **1**%
自動車 **26**%

1999年 **3,360**億円

不動産 **26**%

金融 **5**%
サービス **3**%

7%
2%
4%
5%
3%
2%
3%
18%

3%
22%

2004年 **6兆6,620**億円

17%

6%
8%

Source:「日本の消費者向け（BtoC）電子商取引市場」電子商取引実証推進協議会・アンダーセン コンサルティング

From "Internet magazine", graphs showing results of a survey on internet user trends.

『インターネットマガジン』より。インターネット利用者の動向調査結果をグラフで表している。

Japan 2000-2002
AD: Kenzo Nakagawa / Akiyuki Okada　D: Satoshi Morikami / Norika Nakayama / Infogram　I: Hiroyasu Nobuyama　DF, S: NDC Graphics Inc.
CL: Impress Corporation

数字で見るインターネットの最新動向
Net Impressions Volume 05

Edited by 小橋 昭彦 ＋ インターネットマガジン 編集部 Designed by © Infogram

主な耐久消費財の普及状況 [*]

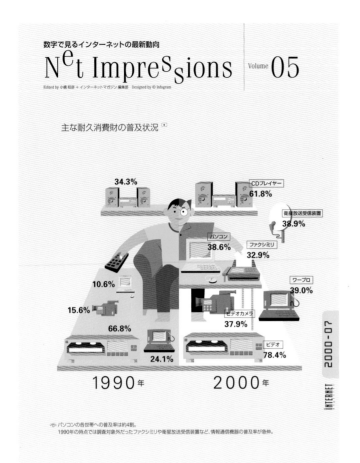

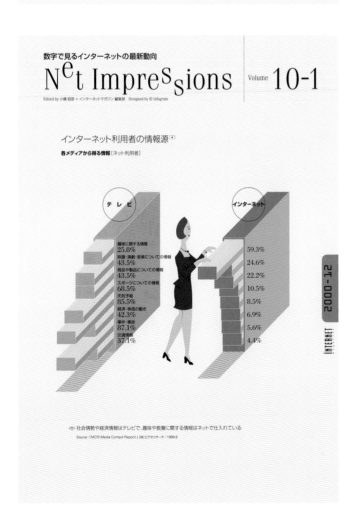

- CDプレイヤー 61.8%
- 34.3%
- 衛星放送受信装置 38.9%
- パソコン 38.6%
- ファクシミリ 32.9%
- 10.6%
- ワープロ 39.0%
- 15.6%
- ビデオカメラ 37.9%
- 66.8%
- ビデオ 78.4%
- 24.1%

1990年   2000年

2000-07 INTERNET

[*] パソコンの各世帯への普及率は約4割。
1990年の時点では調査対象外だったファクシミリや衛星放送受信装置など、情報通信機器の普及率が急伸。

Source 『消費動向調査』経済企画庁／2000.3

数字で見るインターネットの最新動向
Net Impressions Volume 13-1

Edited by 小橋 昭彦 ＋ インターネットマガジン 編集部 Designed by © Infogram

インターネット利用によるメディア消費時間への影響 [*]

ネット利用・非利用者のメディア消費時間

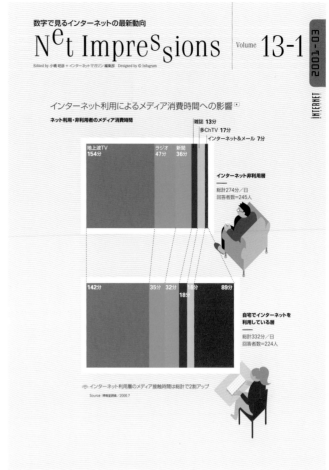

雑誌 13分
多ChTV 17分
インターネット&メール 7分

- 地上波TV 154分
- ラジオ 47分
- 新聞 36分

インターネット非利用層
総計274分／日
回答者数=245人

- 142分
- 35分 32分 18分 16分
- 89分

自宅でインターネットを利用している層
総計332分／日
回答者数=224人

[*] インターネット利用層のメディア接触時間は総計で2割アップ

Source 『情報室調査』／2000.7

2002-03 INTERNET

数字で見るインターネットの最新動向
Net Impressions Volume 10-1

Edited by 小橋 昭彦 ＋ インターネットマガジン 編集部 Designed by © Infogram

インターネット利用者の情報源 [*]

各メディアから得る情報 [ネット利用者]

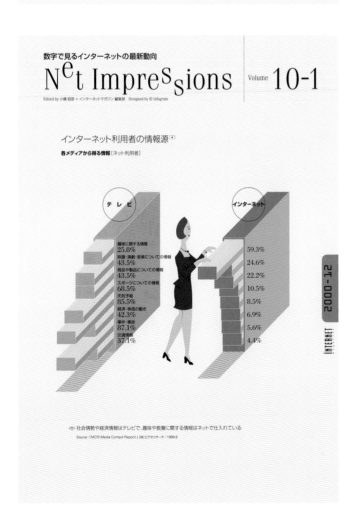

テレビ　　　　　　インターネット

	テレビ	インターネット
趣味に関する情報	25.8%	59.3%
映画・演劇についての情報	43.5%	24.6%
商品や製品についての情報	43.5%	22.2%
スポーツについての情報	68.5%	10.5%
天気予報	85.5%	8.5%
経済・株価の動き	42.3%	6.9%
事件・事故	87.1%	5.6%
交通情報	37.1%	4.4%

[*] 社会情勢や経済情報はテレビで、趣味や教養に関する情報はネットで仕入れている

Source TMCR (Media Contact Report) [株]ビデオリサーチ／1999.6

2000-12 INTERNET

数字で見るインターネットの最新動向
Net Impressions Volume 14-2

Powered by Nielsen//NetRatings

Edited by 衣袋 宏美 [ネットレイティングス株式会社] ＋ インターネットマガジン 編集部 Designed by © Infogram

携帯電話からのウェブ利用者、900万人規模に [*]

インターネット利用可能携帯電話の所有者数とウェブ利用者数

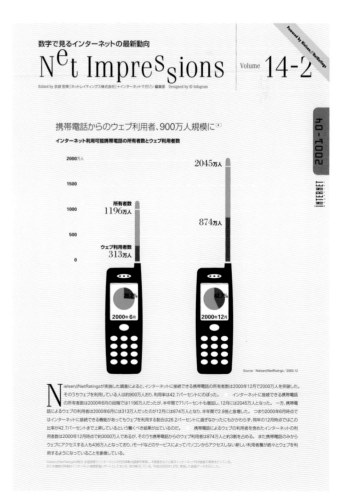

2000万人
1500
1000
500
0

2045万人

所有者数
1196万人

874万人

ウェブ利用数
313万人

26.2%　　　42.7%

2000年6月　　2000年12月

Source Nielsen//NetRatings／2000.12

Nielsen//NetRatingsが実施した調査によると、インターネットに接続できる携帯電話の所有者数は2000年12月で2000万人を突破した。そのうちウェブを利用している人は約900万人おり、利用率は42.7パーセントにのぼった。　　インターネットに接続できる携帯電話の所有者数は2000年6月の段階では1196万人だったのが、半年間で71パーセントも増加し、12月には2045万人となった。一方、携帯電話によるウェブの利用者は2000年6月には313万人だったのが12月には874万人となり、半年間で2.8倍と急増した。つまり2000年6月時点ではインターネットに接続できる機能があってもウェブを利用する割合は26.2パーセントに過ぎなかったにもかかわらず、同年の12月時点ではこの比率が42.7パーセントまで上昇しているという驚くべき結果が出ているのだ。　　携帯電話によるウェブの利用者を含めたインターネットの利用者数を2000年12月時点で約3000万人であるが、そのうち携帯電話からのウェブ利用者は874万人と約3割を占める。また携帯電話のみからウェブにアクセスする人も436万人となっており、iモードなどのサービスによってパソコンからアクセスしない新しい利用者層が続々とウェブを利用するようになっていることを実証している。

Nielsen//NetRatingsとは……（以下小さく判読困難）

2001-04 INTERNET

2000-03

INTERNET magazine

数字で見るインターネットの最新動向

N^{e}t Impre^s$_s$ions | Volume 01

Edited by 小橋 昭彦 ＋ インターネットマガジン 編集部　Designed by © Infogram

インターネットの普及率と英語能力

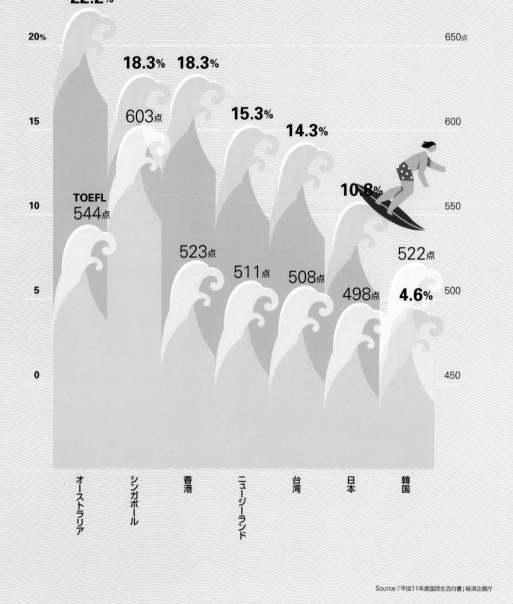

インターネット普及率
22.2%

20%

18.3% **18.3%**

603点

15

15.3%

14.3%

TOEFL
544点

10

523点

511点　508点

10.8%

522点

5

498点　**4.6%**

0

オーストラリア　シンガポール　香港　ニュージーランド　台湾　日本　韓国

650点

600

550

500

450

Source:「平成11年度国民生活白書」経済企画庁

From "Internet magazine", graphs showing results of a survey on internet user trends.

『インターネットマガジン』より。インターネット利用者の動向調査結果をグラフで表している。

Japan 2000-2002
AD: Kenzo Nakagawa / Akiyuki Okada   D: Satoshi Morikami / Norika Nakayama / Infogram   I: Hiroyasu Nobuyama   DF, S: NDC Graphics Inc.
CL: Impress Corporation

数字で見るインターネットの最新動向
N^et Impre^s_sions | Volume 15-1

Edited by 小橋 昭彦 ＋ インターネットマガジン 編集部　Designed by © Infogram

電子商取引市場規模

モバイルコマースの市場規模

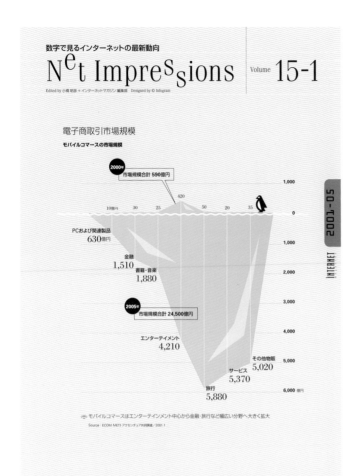

2000年 市場規模合計 590億円

420　10億円　30　25　50　20　35

1,000
0

PCおよび関連製品
630億円

金融
1,510

書籍・音楽
1,880

2005年 市場規模合計 24,500億円

エンターテイメント
4,210

その他物販
5,020

サービス
5,370

旅行
5,880

6,000 億円

モバイルコマースはエンターテインメント中心から金融・旅行など幅広い分野へ大きく拡大

Source：ECOM/METI・アクセンチュア共同調査／2001-1

2001-05　INTERNET

数字で見るインターネットの最新動向
N^et Impre^s_sions | Volume 14-1

Edited by 小橋 昭彦 ＋ インターネットマガジン 編集部　Designed by © Infogram

起業家精神ランキング

現在、会社設立中ないしは設立後42か月以内の会社運営に携わっている人の割合

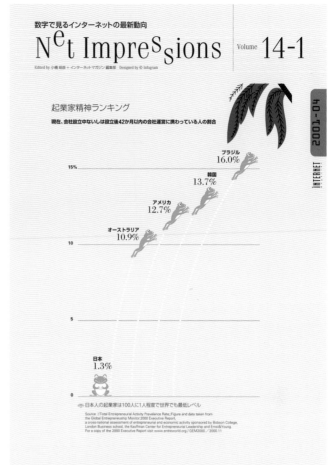

15%

ブラジル
16.0%

韓国
13.7%

アメリカ
12.7%

オーストラリア
10.9%

10

5

日本
1.3%

日本人の起業家は100人に1人程度で世界でも最低レベル

Source：「Total Entrepreneurial Activity Prevalence Rate」Figure and data taken from the Global Entrepreneurship Monitor:2000 Executive Report, a cross-national assessment of entrepreneurial and economic activity sponsored by Babson College, London Business school, the Kauffman Center for Entrepreneurial Leadership and Ernst&Young. For a copy of the 2000 Executive Report visit www.entreworld.org／GEM2000／2000.11

2001-04　INTERNET

数字で見るインターネットの最新動向
N^et Impre^s_sions | Volume 18-2

Edited by 衣袋 宏幸［ネットレイティングス株式会社］＋インターネットマガジン 編集部　Designed by © Infogram

自宅以外のPCユーザーのネット接続比率は関東が約5割 [*]

自宅以外でのパソコン利用率｜インターネット利用率［地域別］

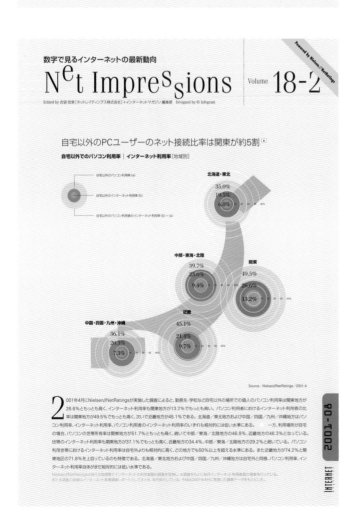

自宅以外のパソコン利用率（a）
自宅以外のインターネット利用率（b）
自宅以外のパソコン利用者のインターネット利用率（b）÷（a）

北海道・東北
35.0%
19.5%
6.8%

中部・東海・北陸
39.7%
23.6%
9.4%

関東
49.5%
26.0%
13.2%

近畿
45.1%
21.4%
9.7%

中国・四国・九州・沖縄
36.1%
20.3%
7.3%

Source：Nielsen//NetRatings／2001.4

2 001年4月にNielsen//NetRatingsが実施した調査によると、勤務先・学校など自宅以外の場所での個人のパソコン利用率は関東地方が26.6%ともっとも高く、インターネット利用率も関東地方が13.2%でもっとも高い。パソコン利用者におけるインターネット利用者の比率は関東地方が49.5%でもっとも高く、次いで近畿地方が45.1%である。北海道／東北地方および中国／四国／九州／沖縄地方はパソコン利用率、インターネット利用率、パソコン利用者のインターネット利用率のいずれも相対的には低い水準にある。　一方、利用場所が自宅の場合、パソコンの世帯所有率は関東地方が51.7%ともっとも高く、続いて中部／東海／北陸地方の46.8%、近畿地方の46.3%となっている。世帯のインターネット利用率も関東地方が37.1%でもっとも高く、近畿地方の34.4%、中部／東海／北陸地方の29.2%と続いている。パソコン利用世帯におけるインターネット利用率も相対的に高く、どの地方でも50%以上を超える水準にある。また近畿地方が74.2%と関東地区の71.8%を上回っているのも特徴である。北海道／東北地方および中国／四国／九州／沖縄地方は自宅以外と同様、パソコン利用率、インターネット利用率自体がまだ相対的には低い水準である。

Nielsen//NetRatingsは行動観察型でインターネットの利用動態の調査を実施し、web上でインターネット利用者の発表を行っている。また、従来の調査ではインターネット利用者数はパネルによるものを発表していたが、取引現に、今回は2001年4月に実施した調査データをもとにした。

2001-08　INTERNET

数字で見るインターネットの最新動向
N^et Impre^s_sions | Volume 07

Edited by 小橋 昭彦 ＋ インターネットマガジン 編集部　Designed by © Infogram

世界におけるデジタルデバイド

地域別インターネット普及率

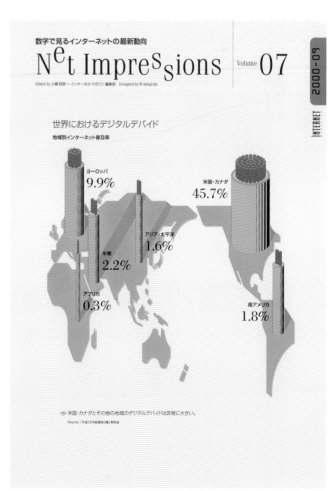

ヨーロッパ
9.9%

米国・カナダ
45.7%

中東
2.2%

アジア・太平洋
1.6%

アフリカ
0.3%

南アメリカ
1.8%

米国・カナダとその他の地域のデジタルデバイドは非常に大きい。

Source：「平成12年通信白書」郵政省

2000-09　INTERNET

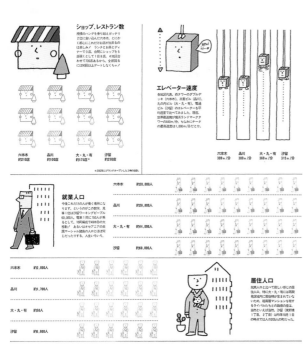

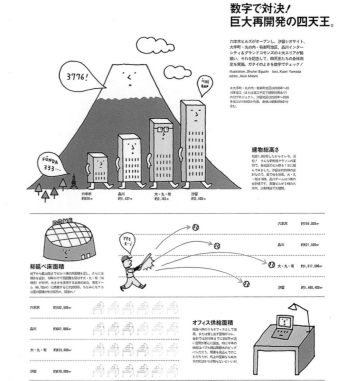

Comparative graphs related to Tokyo's urban development expressed with illustrations.
東京の都市開発についての各種比較グラフをイラストレーションで表した。

Japan 2003
AD: Yasushi Fujimoto(Cap)　D: Youichi Iwamoto　I: Shuhei Eguchi　S: Magazinehouse, Ltd.

I wanna Watch !

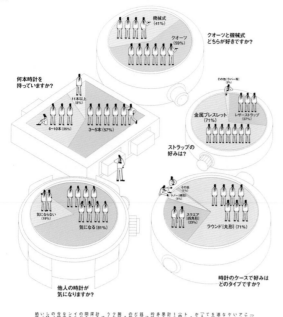

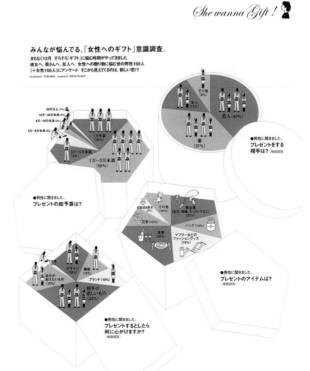

a

She wanna Gift !

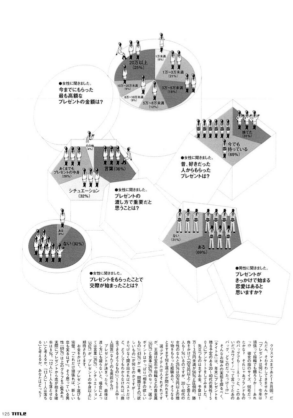

b

An opinion poll of 300 men and women aged 20 through 50 on wrist watches from the magazine "TITLe." (a)
An opinion poll of 150 men aged 20 through 50 on gifts for women from the magazine "TITLe." (b)

雑誌『TITLe』より。20代〜40代の男女300人の、腕時計に対する意識調査。 (a)
雑誌『TITLe』より。20代〜40代の男性150人の女性へのギフトに対する意識調査。 (b)

Japan 2003
AD: Tetsushi Kawamura   I: Tokuma   DF: Atmosphere, Ltd.   CL: Bungeishunju Ltd.   S: bowlgraphics

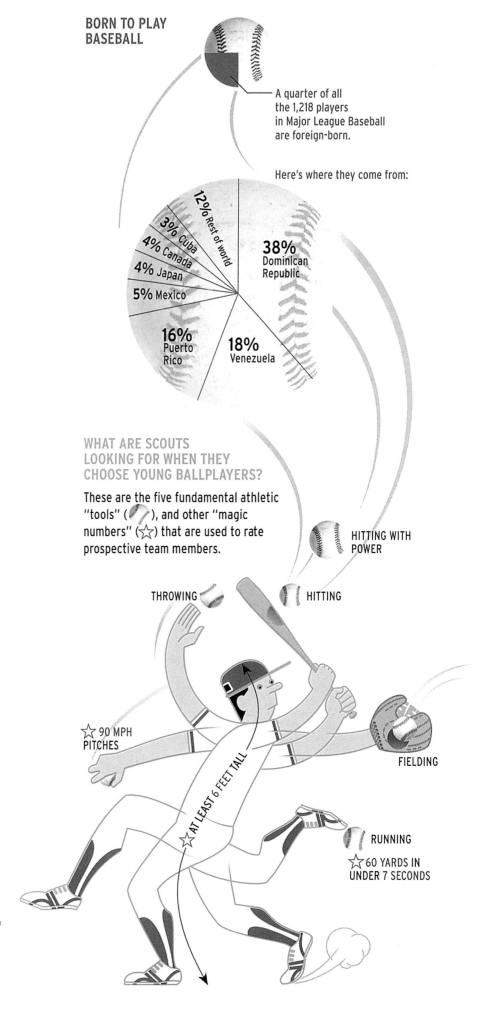

BORN TO PLAY BASEBALL

A quarter of all the 1,218 players in Major League Baseball are foreign-born.

Here's where they come from:

- 12% Rest of world
- 3% Cuba
- 4% Canada
- 4% Japan
- 5% Mexico
- 38% Dominican Republic
- 18% Venezuela
- 16% Puerto Rico

WHAT ARE SCOUTS LOOKING FOR WHEN THEY CHOOSE YOUNG BALLPLAYERS?

These are the five fundamental athletic "tools" ( ), and other "magic numbers" (☆) that are used to rate prospective team members.

HITTING WITH POWER

THROWING

HITTING

☆ 90 MPH PITCHES

AT LEAST 6 FEET TALL

FIELDING

RUNNING

☆ 60 YARDS IN UNDER 7 SECONDS

Illustration explaining how baseball scouts choose young baseball players.

野球のスカウトが若い野球選手を選ぶポイントなどを
説明するイラストレーション。

USA 2004
AD: Holly Holliday   D, I, S: Nigel Holmes
DF: Explanation Graphics   CL: Attaché Magazine

7.700 Gigawattstunden

8.690 Gigawattstunden

9.180 Gigawattstunden
ohne Aktionsplan

8.670 Gigawattstunden
mit Aktionsplan

Energieverbrauch
Vorarlberg 1990

Energieverbrauch
Vorarlberg 2000

Energieverbrauch
Vorarlberg 2010

1 Gigawattstunde = 1 Million Kilowattstunden

Graphs showing the government's plan of energy consumption, CO2 sources, etc. up through 2010.

2010年までのエネルギーの消費量やCO2の放出量などに関する政府の計画を示すグラフ。

Austria   2001
CD, AD: Sigi Ramoser   D, P, I: Klaus Österce   CW: Elke Burtscher   DF, S: Sägenvier   CL: Land Vorarlberg

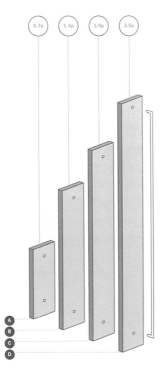

DIVIDEND PER SHARE

Ⓐ 52 weeks to April 1999
Ⓑ 52 weeks to December 1999 pro-forma
Ⓒ 52 weeks to December 2000
Ⓓ 52 weeks to December 2001

0.7p 1.4p 1.9p 2.5p

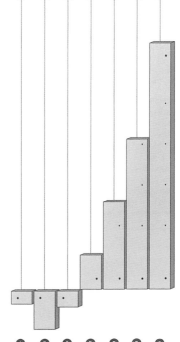

5 HOWDEN JOINERY OPERATING PROFITS

Ⓐ 52 weeks to December 1995 pro-forma
Ⓑ 52 weeks to December 1996 pro-forma
Ⓒ 52 weeks to December 1997 pro-forma
Ⓓ 52 weeks to December 1998 pro-forma
Ⓔ 52 weeks to December 1999 pro-forma
Ⓕ 52 weeks to December 2000
Ⓖ 52 weeks to December 2001

£-1.3m £-3.7m £-1.6m £3.6m £8.9m £15.3m £24.5m

Ⓐ Ⓑ Ⓒ Ⓓ Ⓔ Ⓕ Ⓖ

Graphs explaining financial highlights,
dividend per share,
operating profits, and so on.

財務概要、1株当たりの配当金、
営業利益などを説明するグラフ。

UK   2002
CD: David Stocks   AD, D: Gilmar Wendt
I: Emma Slater / Roger Taylor
DF, S: SAS   CL: MFI Group

Growing profits
The chart below shows the contribution of gross profits from biotechnology products (PICmarq™) to the Company's gross profits over the last three years.

Graph showing the growth of profits from biotechnology products over the last three years.

バイオテクノロジー製品に関する過去3年間での利益の伸びを示すグラフ。

UK   2002
CD: Tor Pettersen   AD, D, CW: David Brown   D: Craig Johnson
DF, S: Tor Pettersen & Partners   CL: Sygen International

2000 £0.2m   2001 £2.1m   2002 £3.2m

APPLYING BIOTECHNOLOGY
PROMOTES GROWTH

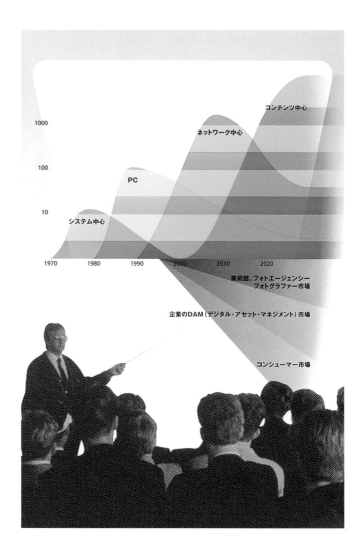

Above, the movement and numbers centered around the computer market; below, the market share and market Celartem Technology has expanded.

上はコンピュータ市場の中心の動きとその数、
下はセラーテムテクノロジー社が広げてきた販売シェア数と市場を表している。

Japan   2001
AD: Shinnoske Sugisaki   D: Chiaki Okuno / Shinsuke Suzuki
/ Seiji Minato (CID Lab. Inc.)   CW: Hiroshi Iida (NCP Agency)
DF, S: Shinnoske Inc.   CL: Celartem Technology Inc.

transfor ming

our costs...

Kingfisher is a customer-driven business with a simple aim – to give people the inspiration, confidence and product solutions with which they can create better homes.

The booming popularity of home improvement has coincided with a fundamental shift in the customer profile – fewer families, more female shoppers, more time-pressured, more affluent, highly value-conscious.

Group brands now offer products that are easier to use, with more comprehensive instruction and less preparation and finishing. Products with detailed explanation and a greater focus on colour, design and the end result. Ranges combining leading edge design with seasonal flexibility.

Kingfisher has also pursued new and innovative ways of delivering exceptional value for money. EDLP – 'every day low pricing' – was launched in 1998 and it quickly became clear that low retail prices every day required low supplier costs every day.

The Cost Price Reduction Programme (CPR) was created specifically to deliver a reduction in the cost of goods and drive the bottom line. The programme aims to forge mutually-beneficial long term partnerships with key suppliers – relationships that benefit both sides of the retailer-supplier equation. For Kingfisher, lower product costs and commonality where the real benefit lies – at the product, component or formulation level.

For suppliers, growing volumes and the associated opportunity to reduce costs and invest in their operations. Today, an increasing number of suppliers are transforming their business and driving long term growth through partnership with Kingfisher.

CPR was introduced in Castorama France towards the end of 2002. Initial results have been encouraging and the programme will underpin delivery of this year's targeted integration benefits. It will create similar opportunities for long term partnerships, including suppliers working across the Group with both B&Q and Castorama.

Today, Kingfisher is working with suppliers to longer time horizons than ever before – three, five, even seven years – with agreement on capacity, cost reduction and product innovation. This is creating a truly world class supplier base.

*For more information on Kingfisher visit www.kingfisher.com

No other home improvement retailer in the world operates a comparable, systematic programme of cost reduction with such significant benefits for the business, its shareholders, suppliers and, of course, customers. CPR is entirely customer focused – the people who shop at Kingfisher's Home Improvement brands experience the CPR saving as lower prices, improved service and more and better stores.

...and our prices

Driving down the cost of home improvement B&Q's 'Price Reverse' campaign – an initiative enabled by CPR – has reduced the price of many products to levels lower than ten years ago

1992

THANK YOU FOR SHOPPING WITH B&Q

Crown Emulsion Matt White 5 litres	£13.98
Gainsborough 9.5kw Shower 1000X	£159.99
Bacho 244 Saw	£11.49
B&Q Value Silk Magnolia Paint 5 litres	£20.96
Dehumidifier WDH-101P	£219.00
Avon 6 Panel Door	£34.95
TOTAL	**£460.37**

2002*

*Note: actual prices, not adjusted for inflation. RPI over the period was 20.5%.

THANK YOU FOR SHOPPING WITH B&Q

Crown Emulsion Matt White 5 litres	£6.98
Gainsborough 9.5kw Shower 1000X	£89.98
Bacho 244 Saw	£6.88
B&Q Value Silk Magnolia Paint 10 litres	£8.98
Dehumidifier WDH-101P	£99.00
Avon 6 Panel Door	£16.94
TOTAL	**£228.76**

A comparative table in the form of two checkout receipts showing the cost saving on home improvement products over 10 years from B&Q stores.

2枚のレシートの形をした比較表。B&Qの店舗において日曜大工関連の製品の価格がここ10年間でどの程度下がったかを表している。

UK 2003
CD: Tor Pettersen   AD, D: Jeff Davis   D: Nick Kendall   DF, S: Tor Pettersen & Partners   CL: Kingfisher plc

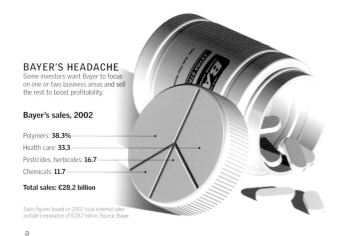

BAYER'S HEADACHE
Some investors want Bayer to focus on one or two business areas and sell the rest to boost profitability.

Bayer's sales, 2002

Polymers: **38.3%**
Health care: **33.3**
Pesticides, herbicides: **16.7**
Chemicals: **11.7**

Total sales: €28.2 billion

Sales figures based on 2002 total external sales outside corporation of €28.2 billion. Source: Bayer

a

Hermès sales, 2002: €1.2 billion

Leather goods: **31%**
Ready-to-wear: **14**
Art of Living*: **12**
Watches: **9**
Silk scarves: **7**
Perfumes: **5**
Other: **22**

*Lifestyle and home products. Source: Hermès

Clothes horse Analysts say Gaultier's designs should boost ready-to-wear, Hermès's second-biggest category.

b

Pie chart illustrating Bayer's sales by category. (a)
Pie chart illustrating Hermes' sales by category. (b)

バイエル社の業務別の売上を示す円グラフ。(a)
エルメスの商品別の売上を示す円グラフ。(b)

USA 2003 (a) **/ 2004** (b)
AD: Carol Macrini   D, I, S: Eliot Bergman   CL: Bloomberg Markets Magazine

BUND
CA. 245 000 WOHNEINHEITEN

BUNDESLÄNDER
CA. 340 000 WOHNEINHEITEN

KOMMUNEN
CA. 2 200 000 WOHNEINHEITEN

Wohnungsvermögen im Eigentum der öffentlichen Hand
QUELLE: BUNDESMINISTERIUM FÜR VERKEHR, BAU- UND WOHNUNGSWESEN

555,7   1.117,9   5.392,4   22.480,0*
1991   1994   1997   2000

Gesamtprivatisierungserlöse des Bundes in Millionen DM
QUELLE: BUNDESMINISTERIUM FÜR FINANZEN

Die Privatisierungspotenziale der Städte und Gemeinden

Diagrams show the potentials of privatization within cities and communities in Germany.
The pictures of flowers represent the prosperous economic development due to privatization.

ドイツの町とコミュニティの民営化の可能性を示すダイアグラム。花の写真で、民営化による将来的な経済発展を表現している。

Germany 2004
AD, D: Bernd Vollmöller   DF, S: Simon & Goetz Design   CL: Sal. Oppenheim jr. & Cie. KGaA

Educação
Education

Revolução escolar

Confira a evolução das notas das crianças que participam do projeto Criança Futuro Esperança (% de crianças de acordo com nível de desempenho).

A radical transformation at school

Check the improvement of the grades gotten by the children participating in Criança Futuro Esperança project (percentage of children according to the corresponding performance level).

1998	2002
33	178

Crianças participantes
Number of participants

65%

44%

25%
8%

31%   27%

Não satisfatório
Poor

Satisfatório
Satisfactory

Plenamente Satisfatório
Fully satsfactory

As crianças aprendem a importância do cooperativismo
Children learning the importance of cooperative endeavors

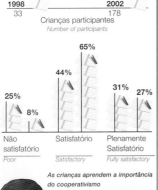

a

Responsabilidade Social
Social Responsibility

Onde a ABB faz e distribui o Sopão?

(em litros produzidos por dia)

Where does ABB prepare and distribute the Sopão?

(In liters produced per day)

200

80

40

20

Blumenau   Betim   Osasco   Guarulhos

b

Saúde
Health

Quem deixou de fumar?

(entre aqueles que participaram do programa em cada ano, em %)

Percentage of those who have quit smoking

(% of ABB employees that stopped smoking)

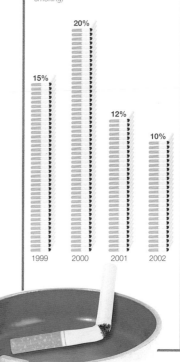

20%

15%

12%

10%

1999   2000   2001   2002

c

Graphs showing improvement of the grades achieved by the children participating in the project. (a)
Graphs indicating the amount of a product produced per a day. (b)
Graphs showing the percentage of those who have quit smoking. (c)

プロジェクトに参加した児童の成績の向上を示すグラフ。(a)
一日に生産される製品の量を示すグラフ。(b)
タバコをやめた人のパーセンテージを示すグラフ。(c)

Brazil   2003
CD: Meire Kanno   AD: Vanessa Soares   DF, S: Azul Publicidade e Propaganda   CL: ABB Ltda.

SCALE

Size matters. In distribution.

In production. In marketing.

Indeed, in just about every single link in the food processing chain.

Which means that growth is no longer just an option for your cooperative: it has become an imperative.

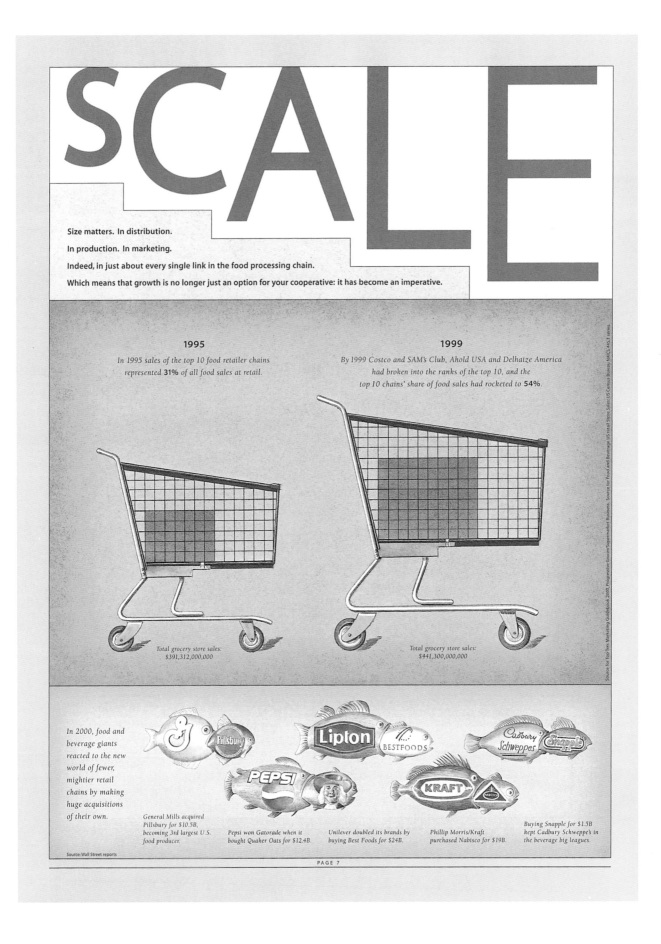

1995

In 1995 sales of the top 10 food retailer chains represented **31%** of all food sales at retail.

Total grocery store sales:
$391,312,000,000

1999

By 1999 Costco and SAM's Club, Ahold USA and Delhaize America had broken into the ranks of the top 10, and the top 10 chains' share of food sales had rocketed to **54%**.

Total grocery store sales:
$441,300,000,000

In 2000, food and beverage giants reacted to the new world of fewer, mightier retail chains by making huge acquisitions of their own.

Source: Wall Street reports

General Mills acquired Pillsbury for $10.5B, becoming 3rd largest U.S. food producer.

Pepsi won Gatorade when it bought Quaker Oats for $12.4B.

Unilever doubled its brands by buying Best Foods for $24B.

Phillip Morris/Kraft purchased Nabisco for $19B.

Buying Snapple for $1.5B kept Cadbury Schweppe's in the beverage big leagues.

PAGE 7

Illustrated charts and graphs using a warm palette to soften the news of tough industry trends in a straightforward, appealing way.
From an apple juice company's annual report.

アップルジュース・メーカーのアニュアル・レポートより。イラストを使用したチャートやグラフ。温かみのある色を使うことで具体的な数値の印象をやわらげた。
業界の厳しい動向に関するニュースを率直に訴えている。

USA 2001
AD, D: Katha Dalton   D: Jana Nishi / Michael Brugman   I: Rodica Prato   CW: Evelyne Rozner   DF, S: Hornall Anderson Design Works, Inc.   CL: Tree Top

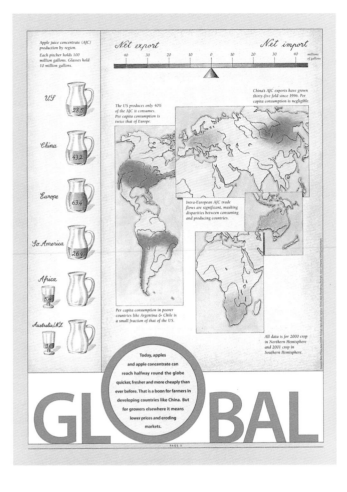

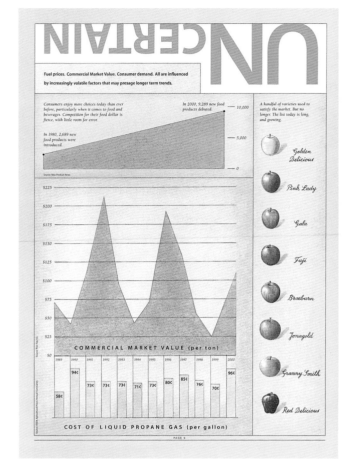

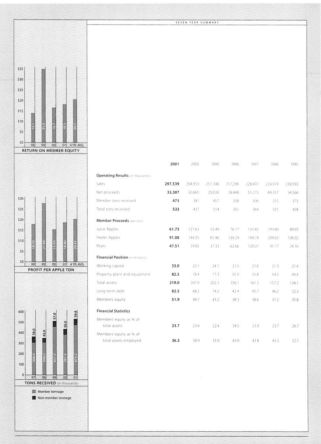

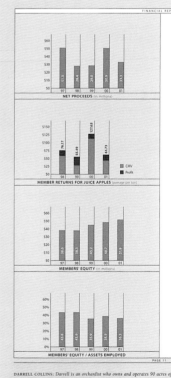

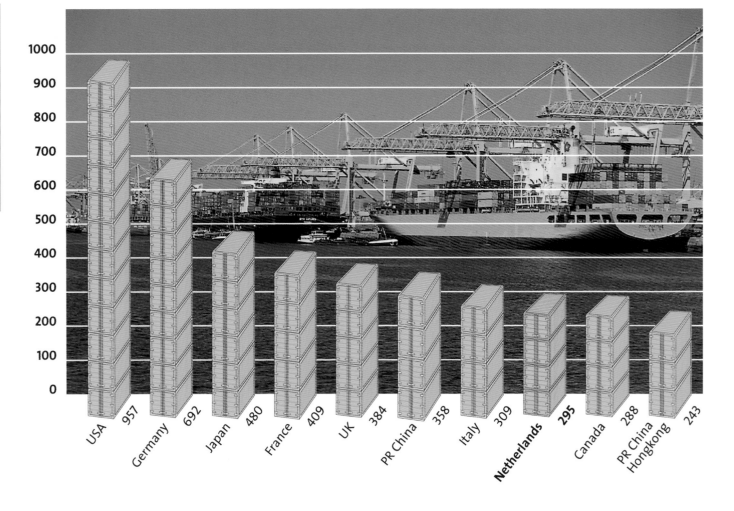

1000
900
800
700
600
500
400
300
200
100
0

USA 957　Germany 692　Japan 480　France 409　UK 384　PR China 358　Italy 309　**Netherlands 295**　Canada 288　PR China Hongkong 243

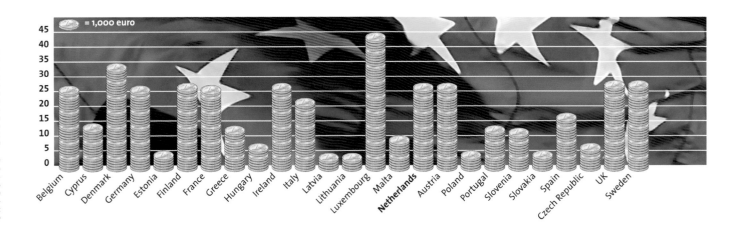

= 1,000 euro

45
40
35
30
25
20
15
10
5
0

Belgium　Cyprus　Denmark　Germany　Estonia　Finland　France　Greece　Hungary　Ireland　Italy　Latvia　Lithuania　Luxembourg　Malta　**Netherlands**　Austria　Poland　Portugal　Slovenia　Slovakia　Spain　Czech Republic　UK　Sweden

Graphs from a book on the Netherlands providing various data.

オランダを紹介する本より。様々なデータを表すグラフ。

Netherlands 2004
CD: Paul Vermijs　D: Toon Tesser　DF, S: TelDesign　CL: Ministry of Foreign Affairs

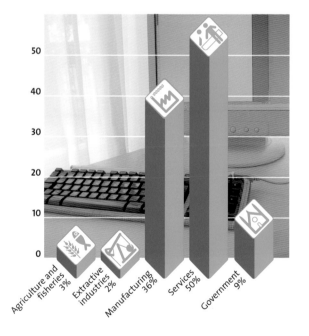

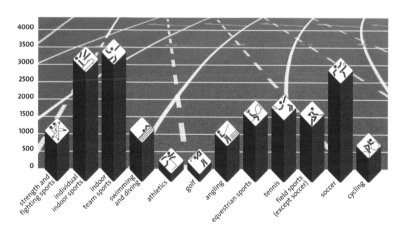

A Graph indicating statistical figures of black people
in Salvador city, Brazil.

ブラジルのサルバドルに住む黒人に関する統計的数値を示すグラフ。

Brazil 2003
D, S: Douglas Okasaki   P: Cassio Alves   CW: Nadja Vladi
CL: A Tarde Newspaper

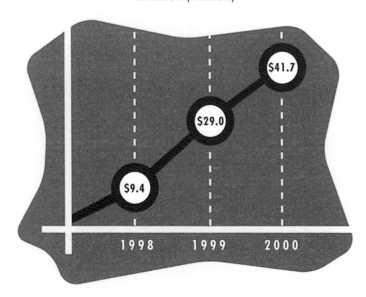

A Graph shows the revenue of a consulting company. From an annual report.

コンサルティング会社の収益を示すグラフ。アニュアル・レポートより。

USA 2000
CD, AD, D: Gordon Mortensen   D: Michael McDaniel   I: Jonathan Carlson   CW: Words By Design
DF, S: Mortensen Design Inc.   CL: Zamba Corporation

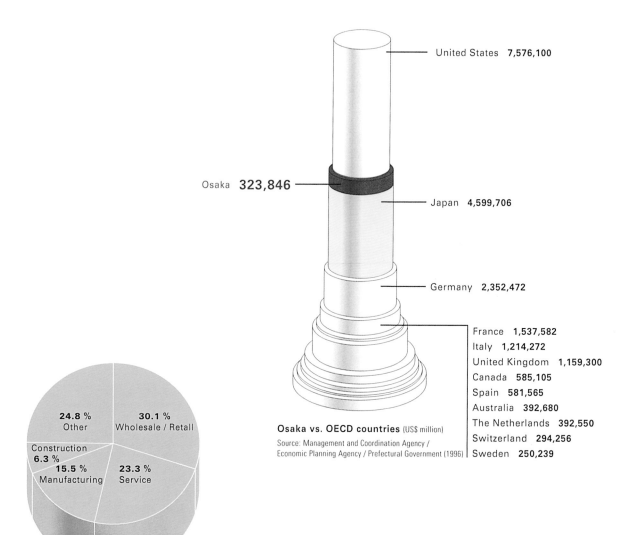

United States **7,576,100**

Osaka **323,846**

Japan **4,599,706**

Germany **2,352,472**

France **1,537,582**
Italy **1,214,272**
United Kingdom **1,159,300**
Canada **585,105**
Spain **581,565**
Australia **392,680**
The Netherlands **392,550**
Switzerland **294,256**
Sweden **250,239**

Osaka vs. OECD countries (US$ million)
Source: Management and Coordination Agency /
Economic Planning Agency / Prefectural Government (1996)

24.8 %
Other

30.1 %
Wholesale / Retail

Construction
6.3 %

15.5 %
Manufacturing

23.3 %
Service

Percentage of businesses by industry sector
Source: Annual Report of Prefectural Accounts 1996 (Economic Research Institute, Economic Planning Agency) /
Establishment Census (Statistics Bureau, Management and Coordination Agency) /
Report of Number of Establishments (Osaka Prefectural Government) (1996)

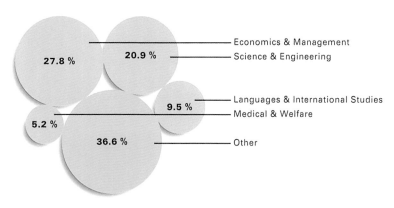

27.8 %

20.9 %

Economics & Management
Science & Engineering

9.5 %

Languages & International Studies
Medical & Welfare

5.2 %

36.6 %

Other

Ratio of fields of specialization at institutes of higher education
Source: School Basic Survey, conducted by the Ministry of Education (1998)

Diagrams used in a pamphlet to attract foreign business to Osaka expressing the GDP of different countries and the employment and schooling categories in Osaka.
大阪への海外企業誘致のためのパンフレットに使用されたダイアグラム。それぞれ各国のGDP、大阪での就業・就学カテゴリーを表現している。

Japan 2000
AD: Shinnoske Sugisaki   D: Chiaki Okuno / Reika Kusaka   DF, S: Shinnoske Inc.   CL: Osaka Prefecture

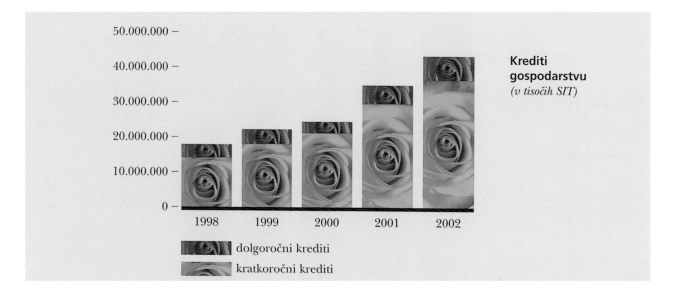

**Krediti
gospodarstvu**
(v tisočih SIT)

dolgoročni krediti

kratkoročni krediti

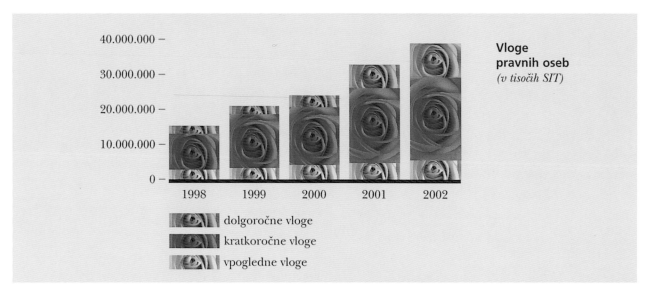

**Vloge
pravnih oseb**
(v tisočih SIT)

dolgoročne vloge

kratkoročne vloge

vpogledne vloge

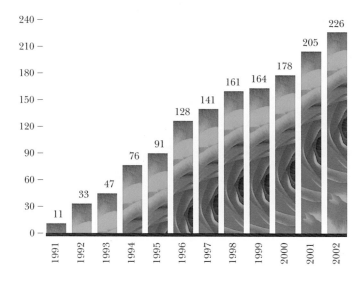

**Število zaposlenih
v banki na dan 31. 12.**

Bar graphs displaying the growth of financial services from 1998 to 2002.

1998年から2002年までの金融サービスの伸びを表した棒グラフ。

Slovenia 2003
AD, D, S: Edi Berk   P: Dragan Arrigler   DF: KROG, Ljubljana   CL: Probanka, Maribor

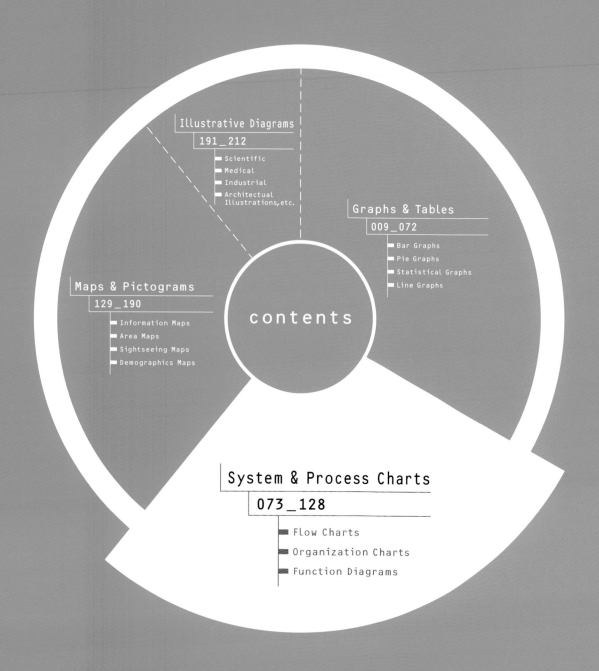

Genealogy of Speed
1966-

Speed is our obsession. Since the mid '60s, we have been designing and creating products specifically for speed. Designs from one have contributed to another - racing flats have influenced basketball, football has influenced cycling and sprinting has helped shape speed skating. Along the way, we have enlisted the help of some of the greatest athletes in the world. We have analyzed how their feet work, scrutinized their old shoes, probed their minds, and studied their bodies for any hint of how to make them go faster by fractions of a second. We have dug into our archives, interviewed our designers and uncovered the stories you see here. They are the stories that make us who we are. This is our family history. This is our genealogy of speed.

A genealogical expression of the many products developed as a collaboration between Nike technology and the world's top athletes in pursuit of "Speed."

「Speed」を追求するために、ナイキ社の持つ最高の技術と世界トップレベルのアスリートの協力により開発された数々のプロダクトを家系図化したもの。

Japan 2004
CD: Paul Tew   AD: Jeff Dey   CW: Dennie Wendt   DF: Big Giant   S, CL: NIKE, Inc.

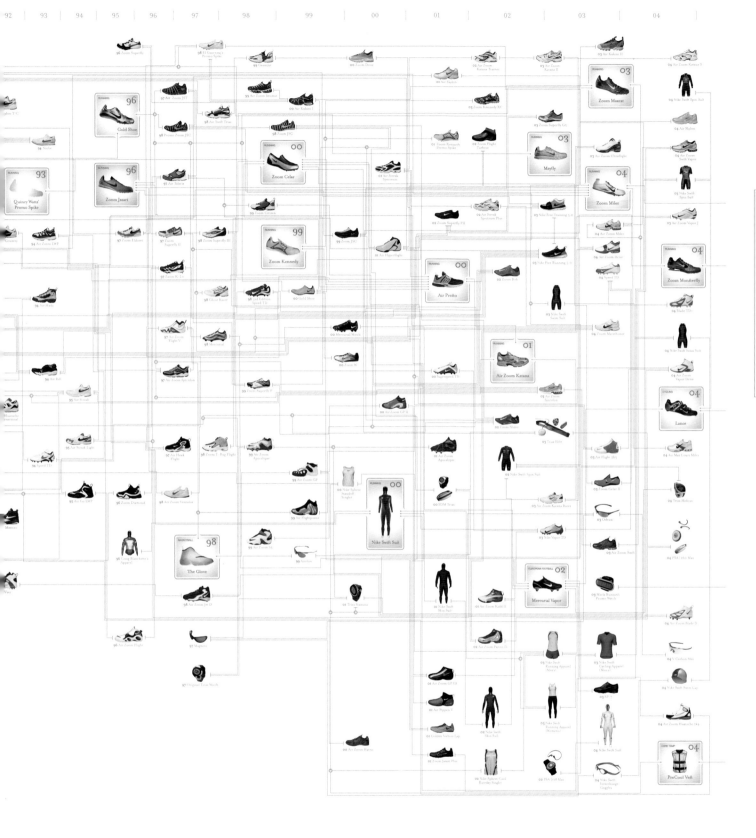

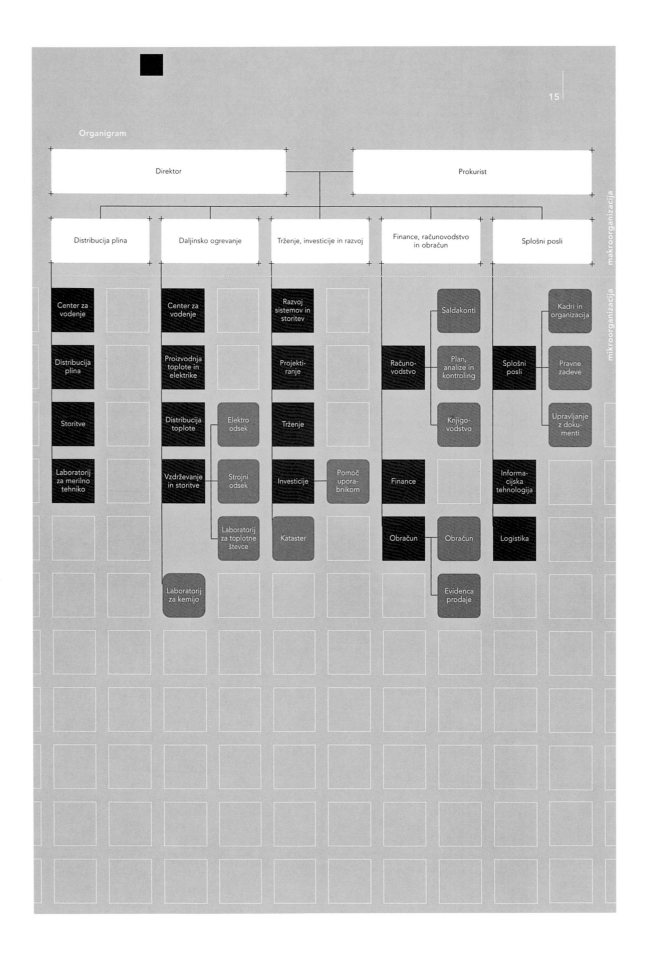

Organigram

Organaization chart of the Energetika Ljubljana, a public-service company in Slovenia.

スロベニアの公共事業、Energetika Ljubljana社の組織図。

Slovenia 2002
CD: Ladeja Godina Kosir   AD, D: Sašo Urukalo   P: Klemen Lajevec   I: Arhiv E.L. / Tadej Brate   CW: Medeja Lončar / Jana Bogdanovski / Tadeja Bular
DF, S: Agencija Imelda   CL: Energetika Ljubljana

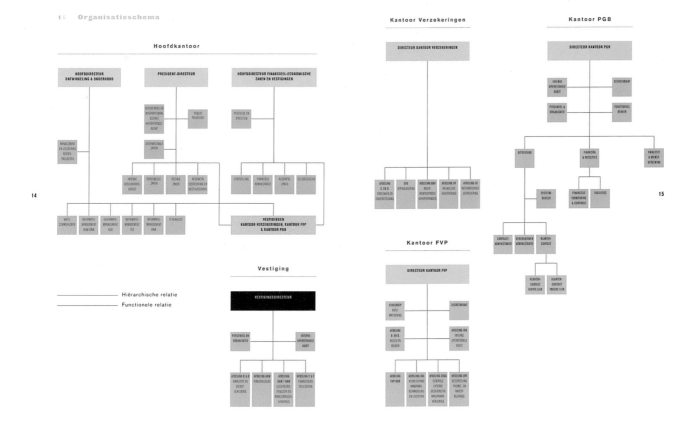

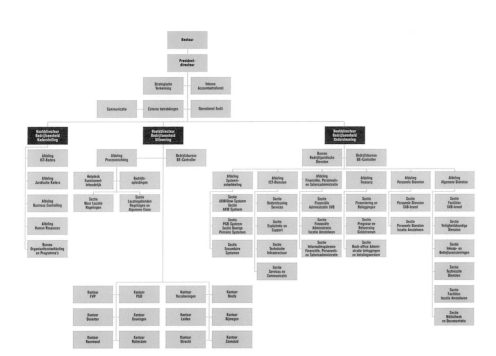

Organizational charts of a bank. From an annual report.

銀行の組織図。アニュアル・レポートより。

Netherlands 2001
CD, AD, D, P: Wout De Vringer   CD, AD: Bob Van Dijk   CW: Corporate Communication / SVB   DF, S: Faydherbe / De Vringer   CL: SVB (Sociale Verzekerings Bank)

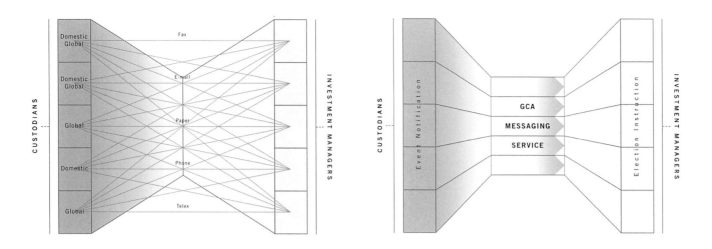

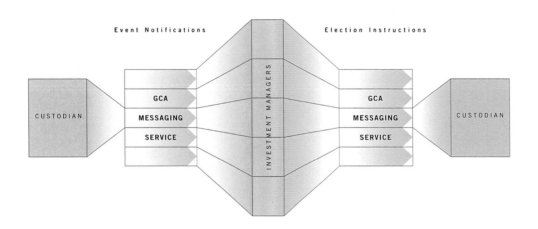

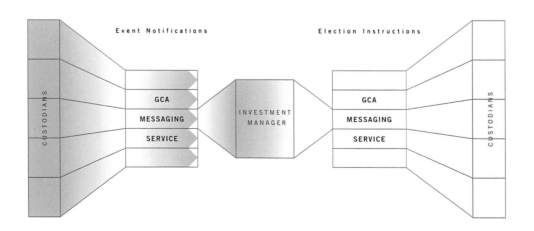

Charts explain the complex communications connections between parties communicating vital corporate financial information.

重要な企業の財政情報をやりとりする際の複雑なコミュニケーション関係を説明するチャート。

USA 2004
CD: Steve Ferrari   D, I: Kurt Finkbeiner   DF, S: Graphic Expression, Inc.   CL: Depository Trust & Clearing Corp.

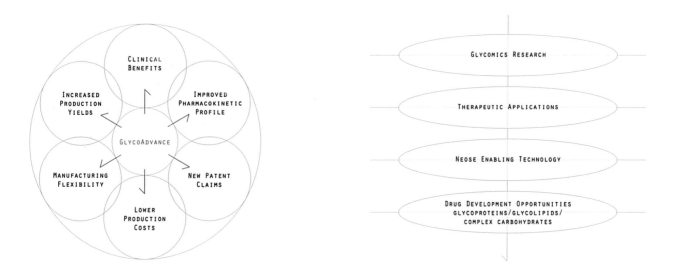

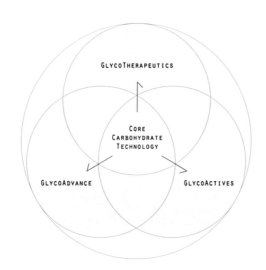

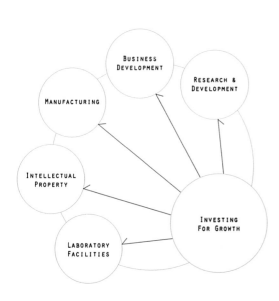

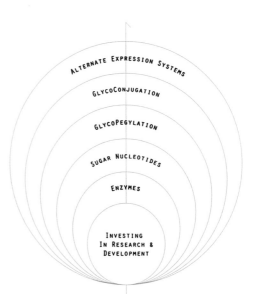

Charts illustrating the relationship between Neose's technology and its products and business strategy.

Neose社のテクノロジーと同社の製品やビジネス戦略の関連性を表したチャート。

USA 2001
CD: Steve Ferrari   D, I: Kurt Finkbeiner   DF, S: Graphic Expression, Inc.   CL: Neose Technologies, Inc.

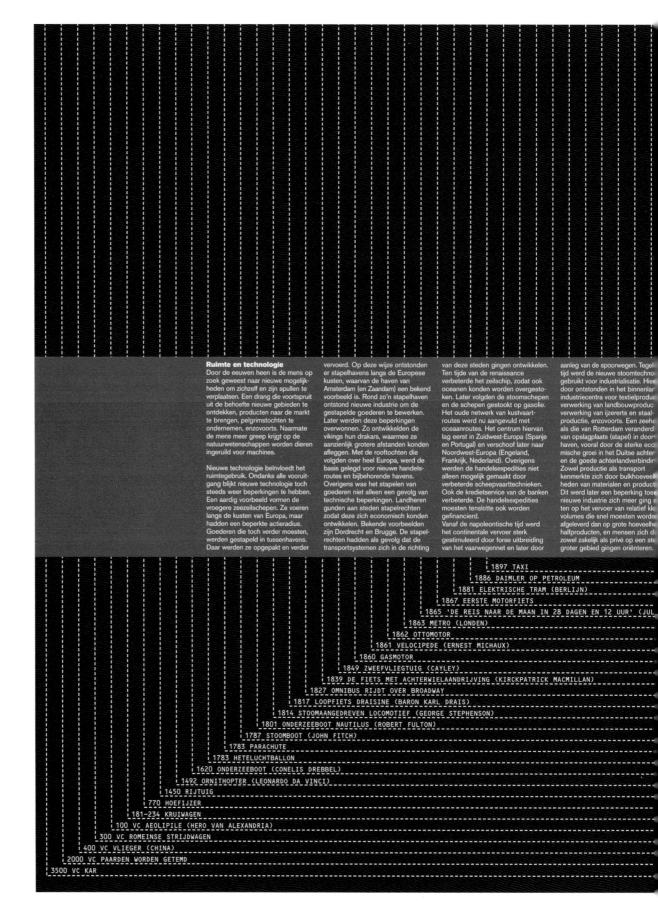

Ruimte en technologie
Door de eeuwen heen is de mens op zoek geweest naar nieuwe mogelijkheden om zichzelf en zijn spullen te verplaatsen. Een drang die voortspruit uit de behoefte nieuwe gebieden te ontdekken, producten naar de markt te brengen, pelgrimstochten te ondernemen, enzovoorts. Naarmate de mens meer greep krijgt op de natuurwetenschappen worden dieren ingeruild voor machines.

Nieuwe technologie beïnvloedt het ruimtegebruik. Ondanks alle vooruitgang blijkt nieuwe technologie toch steeds weer beperkingen te hebben. Een aardig voorbeeld vormen de vroegere zeezeilschepen. Ze voeren langs de kusten van Europa, maar hadden een beperkte actieradius. Goederen die toch verder moesten, werden gestapeld in tussenhavens. Daar werden ze opgepakt en verder

vervoerd. Op deze wijze ontstonden er stapelhavens langs de Europese kusten, waarvan de haven van Amsterdam (en Zaandam) een bekend voorbeeld is. Rond zo'n stapelhaven ontstond nieuwe industrie om de gestapelde goederen te bewerken. Later werden deze beperkingen overwonnen. Zo ontwikkelden de vikings hun drakars, waarmee ze aanzienlijk grotere afstanden konden afleggen. Met de rooftochten die volgden over heel Europa, werd de basis gelegd voor nieuwe handelsroutes en bijbehorende havens. Overigens was het stapelen van goederen niet alleen een gevolg van technische beperkingen. Landheren gunden aan steden stapelrechten zodat deze zich economisch konden ontwikkelen. Bekende voorbeelden zijn Dordrecht en Brugge. De stapelrechten hadden als gevolg dat de transportsystemen zich in de richting

van deze steden gingen ontwikkelen. Ten tijde van de renaissance verbeterde het zeilschip, zodat ook oceanen konden worden overgestoken. Later volgden de stoomschepen en de schepen gestookt op gasolie. Het oude netwerk van kustvaartroutes werd nu aangevuld met oceaanroutes. Het centrum hiervan lag eerst in Zuidwest-Europa (Spanje en Portugal) en verschoof later naar Noordwest-Europa (Engeland, Frankrijk, Nederland). Overigens werden de handelsexpedities niet alleen mogelijk gemaakt door verbeterde scheepvaarttechnieken. Ook de kredietservice van de banken verbeterde. De handelsexpedities moesten tenslotte ook worden gefinancierd. Vanaf de napoleontische tijd werd het continentale vervoer sterk gestimuleerd door forse uitbreiding van het vaarwegennet en later door

aanleg van de spoorwegen. Tegel... tijd werd de nieuwe stoomtechno... gebruikt voor industrialisatie. Hier... door ontstonden in het binnenlan... industriecentra voor textielproduc... verwerking van landbouwproduc... verwerking van ijzererts en staal... productie, enzovoorts. Een zeeha... als die van Rotterdam verander... van opslagplaats (stapel) in door... haven, vooral door de sterke eco... mische groei in het Duitse achter... en de goede achterlandverbindin... Zowel productie als transport kenmerkte zich door bulkhoeveel... heden van materialen en product... Dit werd later een beperking toe... nieuwe industrie zich meer ging... ten op het vervoer van relatief kle... volumes die snel moesten worde... afgeleverd op grote hoeveelhe... halfproducten, en mensen zich d... zowel zakelijk als privé op een st... groter gebied gingen oriënteren.

```
                                                      | 1897 TAXI
                                                   | 1886 DAIMLER OP PETROLEUM
                                                | 1881 ELEKTRISCHE TRAM (BERLIJN)
                                             | 1867 EERSTE MOTORFIETS
                                          | 1865 'DE REIS NAAR DE MAAN IN 28 DAGEN EN 12 UUR' (JUL
                                       | 1863 METRO (LONDEN)
                                    | 1862 OTTOMOTOR
                                 | 1861 VELOCIPEDE (ERNEST MICHAUX)
                              | 1860 GASMOTOR
                           | 1849 ZWEEFVLIEGTUIG (CAYLEY)
                        | 1839 DE FIETS MET ACHTERWIELAANDRIJVING (KIRCKPATRICK MACMILLAN)
                     | 1827 OMNIBUS RIJDT OVER BROADWAY
                  | 1817 LOOPFIETS DRAISINE (BARON KARL DRAIS)
               | 1814 STOOMAANGEDREVEN LOCOMOTIEF (GEORGE STEPHENSON)
            | 1801 ONDERZEEBOOT NAUTILUS (ROBERT FULTON)
         | 1787 STOOMBOOT (JOHN FITCH)
      | 1783 PARACHUTE
   | 1783 HETELUCHTBALLON
 | 1620 ONDERZEEBOOT (CONELIS DREBBEL)
 | 1492 ORNITHOPTER (LEONARDO DA VINCI)
 | 1450 RIJTUIG
 | 770 HOEFIJZER
 | 181-234 KRUIWAGEN
 | 100 VC AEOLIPILE (HERO VAN ALEXANDRIA)
 | 300 VC ROMEINSE STRIJDWAGEN
 | 400 VC VLIEGER (CHINA)
 | 2000 VC PAARDEN WORDEN GETEMD
 | 3500 VC KAR
```

Diagram indicating the development of mobility from 3500 B.C. till 2004.

紀元前3500年から2004年までの移動手段の発達を示すチャート。

Netherlands 2003
CD, AD: André Toet   CD: Jan Sevenster   D: Bas Meulendijks   CW: Paul Van Koningsbruggen
DF, S: Samenwerkende Ontwerpers   CL: Grafische Cultuurstichting

```
                                                                2004  ?
                                                          1994 CHUNNEL
                                                       1983 TGV
                                                    1981 SPACE SHUTTLE
                                                 1981 VLIEGTUIG OP ZONNEENERGIE
                                              1970 JUMBOJET
                                           1969 BEMANDE MAANMISSIE APOLLO
                                        1968 SUPERSONIC TRANSPORT (SST)
                                     1964 BULLET TRAIN
                                  1963 VALENTINA TERESJKOVA EERSTE VROUW IN DE RUIMTE
                               1961 JOERI GAGARIN EERSTE MAN IN DE RUIMTE
                            1958 REGENDRUPVORM ONDERZEEER (US)
                         1957 SPOETNIK 1
                      1956 HOVERCRAFT
                   1954 NUCLEAIRE ONDERZEEBOOT (USS NAUTILUS)
                1947 EERSTE VLUCHT SUPERSONISCH STRAALVLIEGTUIG
             1940 AUTOMATISCHE VERSNELLINGSBAK
          1939 EERSTE SUCCESVOLLE HELIKOPTERVLUCHT
       1924 AUTOSNELWEG ITALIE
    1914 VERKEERSLICHT
  1913 ZEILPLANK
 1908 FORD PRODUCEERT AAN DE LOPENDE BAND
 1907 TRANSATLANTISCHE PAKKETBOTEN
 1903 GEBROEDERS WRIGHT VLIEGEN MET HUN VLIEGTUIG
 1900 METRO PARIJS
 1899 ZEPPELIN
 1898 DICHTE AUTO MET VERSNELLINGSBAK (RENAULT)
 1895 AUTOBAND (MICHELIN)
1894 MOTORFIETS (HILDEBRAND & WOLFMULLER)
```

e periode tot de Tweede Wereld-
orlog kenmerkt zich dan ook door
e opkomst van de (vracht)auto, een
dividueel vervoermiddel bij uitstek.
a de Eerste Wereldoorlog groeit
et aantal autobezitters sterk, als
evolg van de seriefabricage van
uto's en het (tijdens WOII) bewezen
ut van snelle verplaatsingen met
racht)auto's. Vanaf de jaren vijftig
eemt het autogebruik pas echt een
rote vlucht. Het resultaat is dat de
frastructuur al snel begint te knellen.
e bestaande weginfrastructuur was
et resultaat van een evolutie over
e eeuwen heen. De eerste land-
egen in Nederland werden aan-
elegd op de 'dijken' langs de rivieren,
p de zandruggen en op de hoge
ronden in het midden en oosten
an het land. Met de opkomst van de
ligence in de napoleontische tijd
ntwikkelden de wegen zich verder.
ieuwe wegen werden aangelegd,

die nu nog vaak te herkennen zijn in
het landschap: lange rechten wegen
met aan weerszijden een bomenrij,
de as vaak zuiver gericht op een
kerktoren (Metzelaar). De auto vroeg
echter om meer ruimte, zowel in de
stad als op de verbindingen tussen de
steden. De inrichting van de steden
werd in de vijftiger en zestiger jaren
dan ook toegesneden op de auto.
Huizen, wijken en zelfs grachten en
singels maakten plaats voor grote
doorgangswegen en parkeerplaatsen
in de stad.
Tussen de steden werd uiteindelijk
het autosnelwegennet aangelegd.
Een netwerk dat zich kenmerkt door
ongelijkvloerse kruisingen, meerdere
rijstroken per rijbaan (rijrichting) en
keurig langs de steden geleide
wegen. Nieuwe constructietechnieken
zoals wegfundaties, asfalt en beton,
en de (stoom)wals maakten dit
mogelijk, doordat het aanleggen van

wegen minder afhankelijk werd van
de ondergrond.
De volgende beperking stond echter
al weer voor de deur in de vorm van
een te groot geworden aanslag op
het leefmilieu, verkeersveiligheid en
omgevingskwaliteit. De grootse
plannen voor de binnensteden werden
teruggedraaid, de groei van het autosnelwegennet stokte. Binnen de
steden wordt nu ruimte terug-
gewonnen op de auto. Tussen de
steden worden we geconfronteerd
met ernstige files die de roep om
bredere autosnelwegen weer doet
aanzwellen.
Na de Tweede Wereldoorlog groeit
ook de luchtvaart. Grote afstanden
kunnen veel sneller worden overbrugd,
waardoor de internationale netwerken
worden versterkt. Grote luchthavens
blijken een aanzuigende werking te
hebben op (hoofd)kantoren van
internationaal opererende bedrijven.

Er blijkt zelfs een geheel nieuw soort
stad te ontstaan, de luchthavenstad.
De evolutie zet zich door.

(Gebaseerd op: G. Abema, H.
Hartesema, L.W. van der Veen, M.
Schoor, K. Jansma, 10.000 jaar
Geschiedenis der Nederlanden.
Uitgeverij M.A. van Sijen,
Leeuwarden. TNO Beleidsstudies,
Universiteit Twente (1993),
Technische innovaties in het
Personenverkeer en -Vervoer, een
inventarisatie op zoek naar duurzame
mobiliteit. Apeldoorn. Metzelaar, W.
(1976), Nederland Deltaland. Stam
Technische Boeken, Culemborg.)

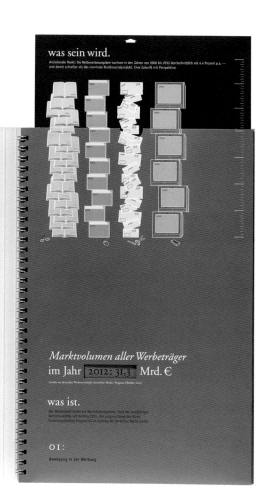

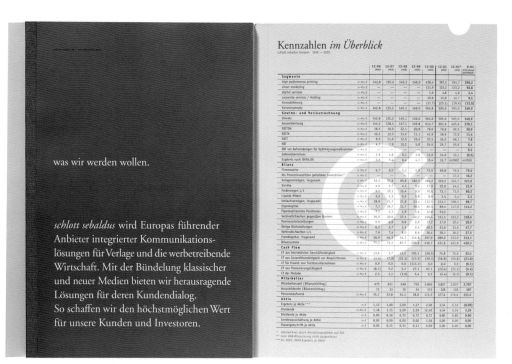

Interactive charts visualizing the change of European high volume printing market in the future and charts showing the current financial situation.
The latest future forecasts can be seen by pulling the inserts.

ヨーロッパの大量印刷市場の将来的な変化を視覚化したインタラクティブなチャートと、最近の財務状況を示すチャート。挿入された紙を引っ張ると将来の予測が現れる。

Germany 2002
CD, AD: Jochen Rädeker D, I: Gernot Walter CW: Norbert Hiller DF, S: Strichpunkt GmbH CL: Schlott Gruppe AG

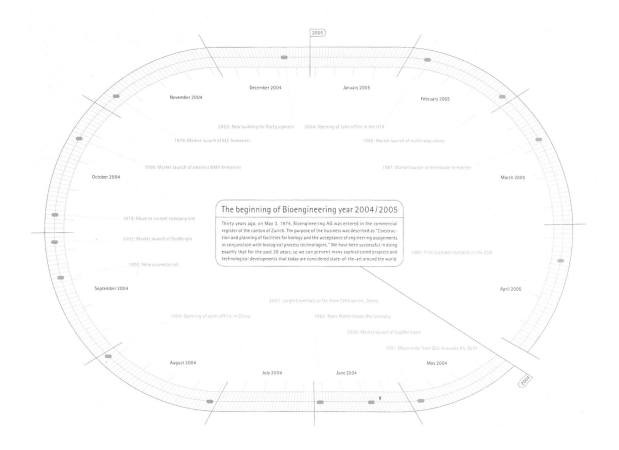

The beginning of Bioengineering year 2004/2005

Thirty years ago, on May 3, 1974, Bioengineering AG was entered in the commercial register of the canton of Zurich. The purpose of the business was described as "Construction and planning of facilities for biology and the acceptance of engineering assignments in conjunction with biological process technologies." We have been successful in doing exactly that for the past 30 years, so we can present many sophisticated projects and technological developments that today are considered state-of-the-art around the world.

30 Years Bioengineering AG

Diagrams showing important events and technological developments in the 30 years of corporate history.

30年におよぶ企業の歴史における重要な出来事や技術的な展開を示すチャート。

Switzerland 2004
CD, AD, D: Heinz Wild   D: Dan Petter   P: Michael Rast   CW: Kurt Schori / Erich Brandenberger   DF, S: Heinz Wild Design   CL: Bioengineering AG

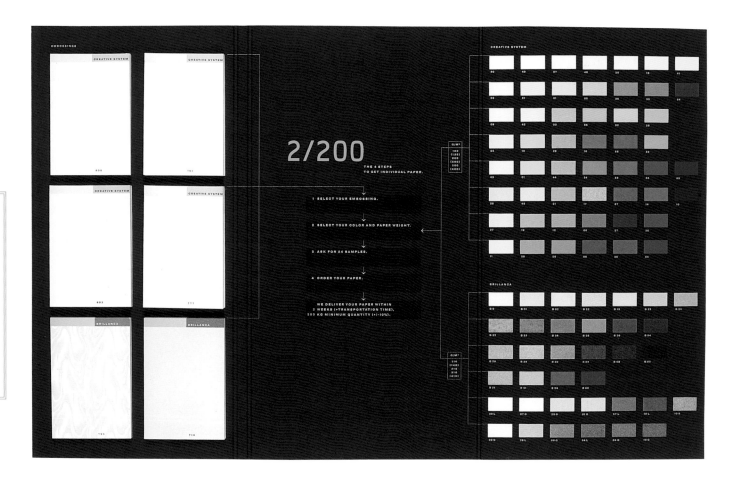

2/200 is the world's largest paper program with more than 100,000 possible combinations. Charts showing the selection process make the content easily accessible.

2/200は100,000以上もの組み合わせが可能な世界最大のペーパー・プログラム。選択プロセスを示すチャートによって簡単に利用できる。

Switzerland   2003-2004

CD, AD, D: Heinz Wild   CD: Florian Kohler   CW: Kurt Schori / Erich Brandenberger   DF, S: Heinz Wild Design   CL: Büttenpapierfabrik Gmund GmbH & Co. KG

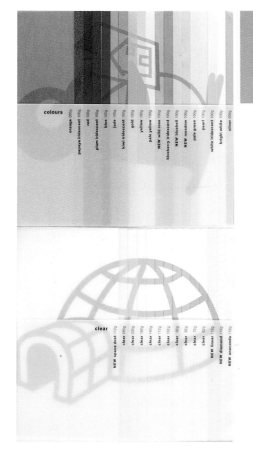

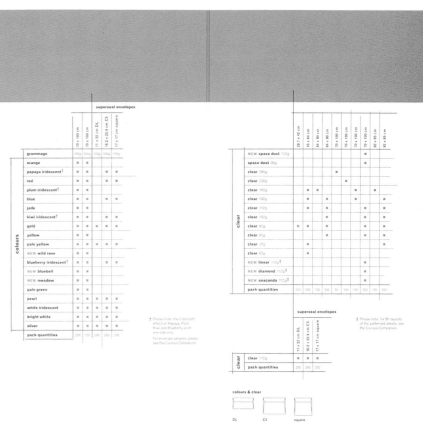

curious collection

Range charts designed to ensure that recipients could easily find and understand the availability, sheet dimension, weight, texture, and color of every paper of the "Curious" system.

"Curious"という紙のシリーズのためのチャート。入手可能かどうか、シートの寸法、斤量、テクスチャー、色を利用者が簡単に探したり理解することができる。

Canada 2004
CD, AD, D, I: Frank Viva   P: Ron Baxter Smith   I: Seth   CW: Doug Dolan   DF, S: Viva Dolan Communications & Design Inc.   CL: Arjomggins

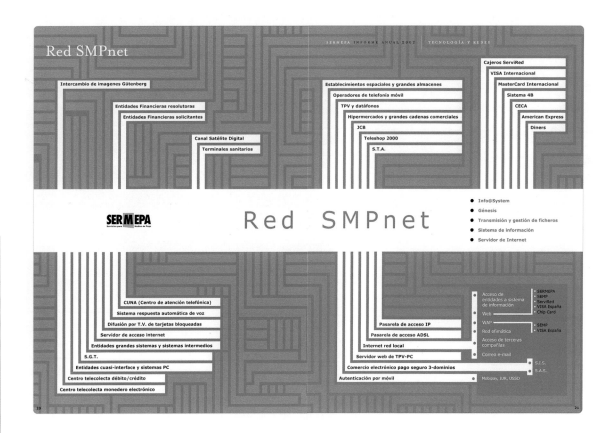

An organization chart showing affiliates of the VISA Group.

VISAグループのアニュアル・レポートから抜粋した、関連会社を示す組織図。

Spain　2003
CD: Emilio Gil　D: Ingrid Forbord　DF, S: Tau Diseño　CL: Sermepa

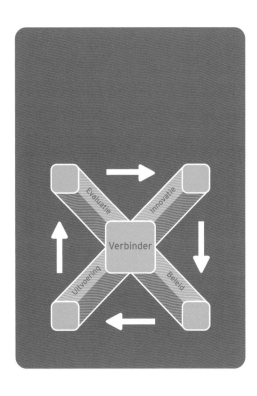
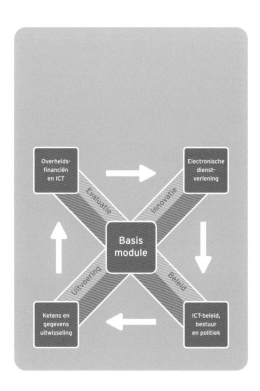

Diagrams explaining how information management works.

情報管理がどのように作用するかを説明する図。

Netherlands　2004
D: Toon Tesser　DF, S: TelDesign　CL: IMAC

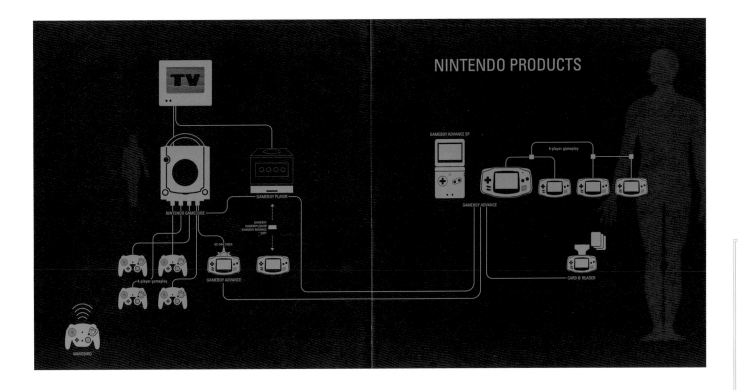

A diagram showing how to link and play Nintendo Game Cube and Game Boy Advance.

ニンテンドーゲームキューブとゲームボーイアドバンスをつなげて遊べることを表す図。

Japan   2003
CD: Shin Kojo   AD, D: Takashi Maeda   CL, S: Nintendo Co., Ltd.

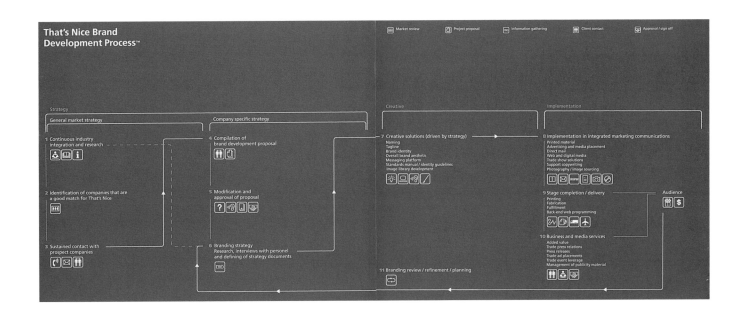

Charts showing "Brand Development Process" of That's Nice, an integrated marketing specialist.

総合的マーケティングのスペシャリスト、That's Nice社の「ブランド開発のプロセス」を示すチャート。

USA   2003
CD, CW: Mark Allen   AD: Nigel Walker   D: Beatriz Cifuentes   P: Brian Pierce   DF, CL, S: That's Nice LLC

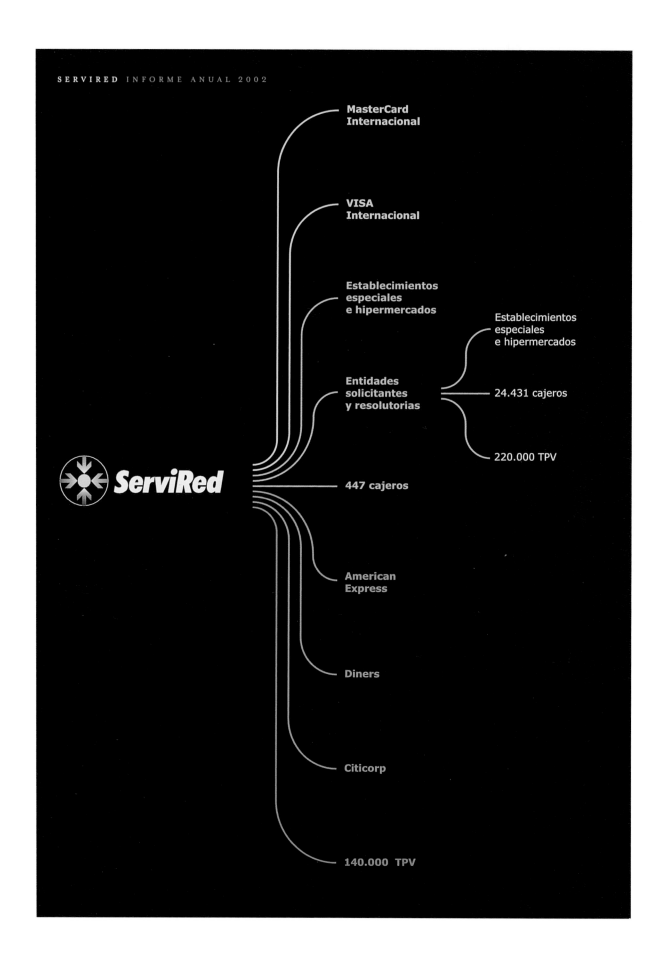

SERVIRED INFORME ANUAL 2002

ServiRed

MasterCard
Internacional

VISA
Internacional

Establecimientos
especiales
e hipermercados

Entidades
solicitantes
y resolutorias

Establecimientos
especiales
e hipermercados

24.431 cajeros

220.000 TPV

447 cajeros

American
Express

Diners

Citicorp

140.000 TPV

An organization chart showing business partners of ServiRed.

ServiRedの取引先企業を示す組織図。

Spain 2003
CD: Emilio Gil   D: Ingrid Forbord   DF, S: Tau Diseño   CL: Sermepa

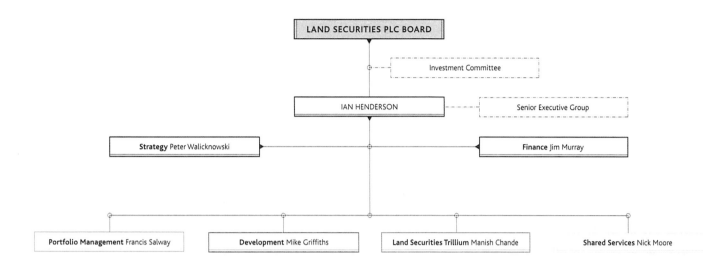

LAND SECURITIES BUSINESS MODEL

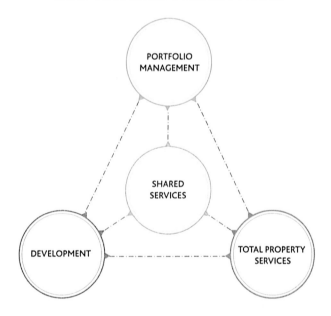

An organizational chart and business model chart for Land Securities.

Land Securities社の組織図およびビジネスモデルを説明するチャート。

UK 2001

CD: Gilmar Wendt / Nick Austin   AD, D, I: Mike Hall   P: Chris Mouse / Marcus Lyon   DF, S: SAS   CL: Land Securities

Business Software Implementation

Implementation Methodology

Implementation Project Workflow

Project Initiation	Design	Implementation	Post Conversion
Project definition	Preliminary design	System adjustments and tuning	Support users
System architecture review	Conference room pilot and GAP fit	Project configuration / Cut over	Tune system
Install application software	Detailed design	Build the application and operational reports	Post conversion review
Project team training and orientation		User testing and training	
Test server and production server		Prepare and finalize production environment	

Quality review and management approval / Quality review and management approval / Quality review and management approval / Quality review and management approval

Project management

Consulting & Information Solutions

1185 Avenue of the Americas
New York, NY 10036
212 372 1791
tbsny.cis.info@aexp.com
www.americanexpress.com/tbs

American Express Tax and Business Services Inc. is a wholly owned subsidiary of American Express, a publicly owned company. American Express employs CPAs but is not a licensed CPA firm.

Tax & Business Services

Offices throughout the United States

Not-for-Profit

Enterprise Resource Planning for Not-for-Profit Organizations (ERP/NFP)

Enterprise Component Model

The concept is simple — unity to achieve the mission. ERP/NFP enables the sharing of information efficiently, consistently and seamlessly for effective executive and managerial analysis, planning and operations.

Consulting & Information Solutions

1185 Avenue of the Americas
New York, NY 10036
212 372 1791
tbsny.cis.info@aexp.com
www.americanexpress.com/tbs

American Express Tax and Business Services Inc. is a wholly owned subsidiary of American Express, a publicly owned company. American Express employs CPAs but is not a licensed CPA firm.

Tax & Business Services

Offices throughout the United States

From the project sheets to support the management consulting unit of American Express. Charts outline the unit's services.

American Expressのマネジメント・コンサルタント部門をサポートするプロジェクト・シートより。部門のサービス概要を示すチャート。

USA 2003
CD, D: Graham Hanson   DF, S: Graham Hanson Design   CL: American Express

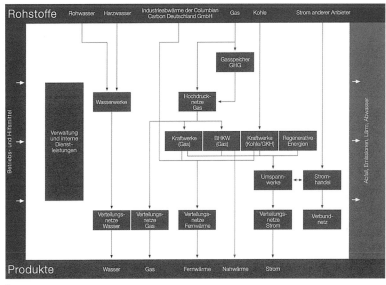

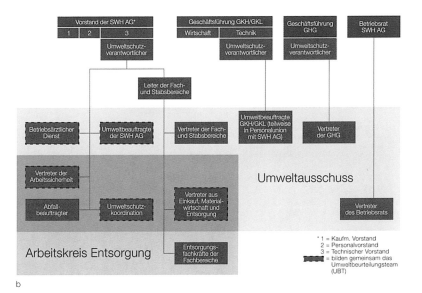

Diagrams showing the material flow of a power company. (a)
Diagrams explaining relationships between environmental groups and companies. (b)
Chart explaining the training concept and flow of IS-U(Industry Solutions for Utilities). (c)

電力会社の物流を示すチャート。 (a)
環境保護団体と企業の関係を説明するチャート。 (b)
IS-U（電気・ガスなどの公益企業向けの業務別料金システム・ソリューション）の研修コンセプトや流れを説明したチャート。 (c)

Germany 2003
CL, S: Stadtwerke Hannover AG

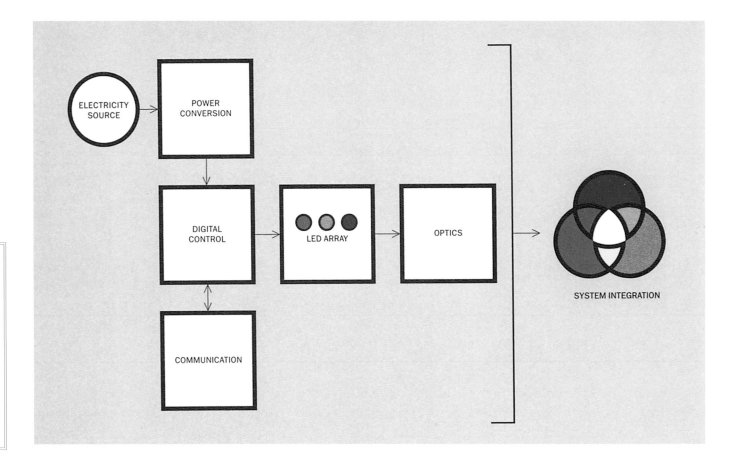

Charts explains the key technologies that are foundations of lighting systems.

照明システムの基盤である主要なテクノロジーを説明するチャート。

USA 2001

CD, AD, D: Dave Mason   AD, D: Pamela Lee   D: Nancy Willett   P: Victor John Penner   DF, S: Samata Mason   CL: TIR Systems Ltd.

(6) The layered network architecture
We are building flexible and cost-efficient
networks that make it easier for operators to
handle new services at lower cost

(8) Always best connected
We are leading the way into the new world of user-focused networks
by unifying personal, local and wide area mobile technology

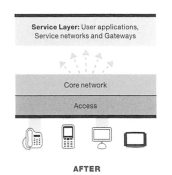

BEFORE   AFTER

● **Personal Area Network**
Wireless connections between laptops,
phones and pda's using bluetooth.

Local Area Network
Access to high capacity networks in locations
such as airports and offices through WLAN/WiFi

○ **Wide Area Network**
Access to voice and data services using
global mobile systems

Diagram explaining the layered network architecture.

階層型ネットワーク構築を説明する図。

UK 2004

CD, AD: Gilmar Wendt   CD: David Stocks   D, I: John-Paul Sykes   P: Peter Hoelstad   CW: Tim Rich / Mats Thoren   DF, S: SAS   CL: Ericsson

1. Maatschappelijk gedreven investeerder in (woning) vastgoed

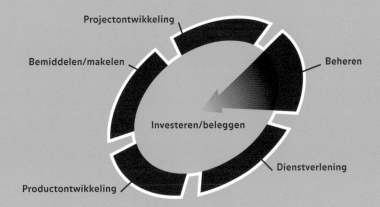

Projectontwikkeling

Bemiddelen/makelen

Beheren

Investeren/beleggen

Dienstverlening

Productontwikkeling

2. Componenten van (direct) rendement

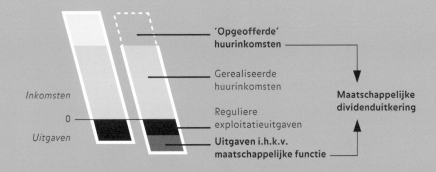

Inkomsten

0

Uitgaven

'Opgeofferde' huurinkomsten

Gerealiseerde huurinkomsten

Maatschappelijke dividenduitkering

Reguliere exploitatieuitgaven

Uitgaven i.h.k.v. maatschappelijke functie

3. 'Revolving fund': rendements-distributie

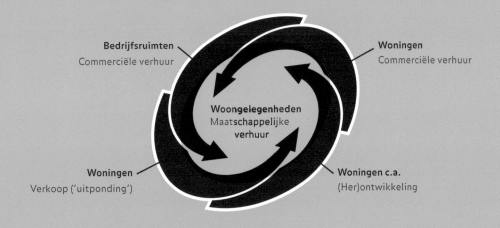

Bedrijfsruimten
Commerciële verhuur

Woningen
Commerciële verhuur

Woongelegenheden
Maatschappelijke verhuur

Woningen
Verkoop ('uitponding')

Woningen c.a.
(Her)ontwikkeling

Diagrams explaining investments, efficiency, and revolving fund of a real estate company.

不動産会社の投資、効率性、回転資金に関するダイアグラム。

Netherlands   2001
CD, D: Jaco Emmen   DF, S: TelDesign   CL: AEDEX

Technical Initiatives

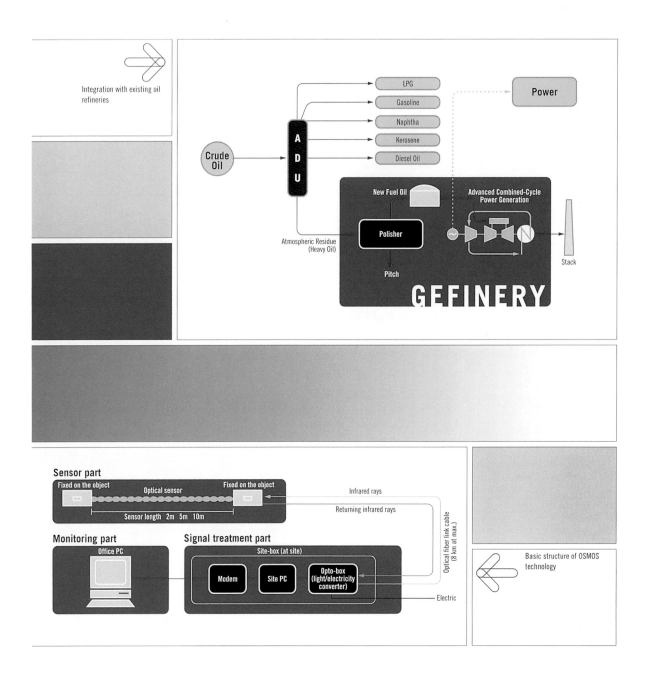

Integration with existing oil refineries

Crude Oil

A D U

LPG
Gasoline
Naphtha
Kerosene
Diesel Oil

Power

New Fuel Oil

Advanced Combined-Cycle Power Generation

Polisher

Atmospheric Residue (Heavy Oil)

Pitch

Stack

GEFINERY

Sensor part

Fixed on the object   Optical sensor   Fixed on the object

Sensor length 2m 5m 10m

Infrared rays

Returning infrared rays

Monitoring part

Office PC

Signal treatment part

Site-box (at site)

Modem   Site PC   Opto-box (light/electricity converter)

Optical fiber link cable (8 km at max.)

Electric

Basic structure of OSMOS technology

14

a

Biorek process flow chart showing the refining and combined cycle power generation of heavy crude oil and the basic composition of OSMOS. (a, d)
A chart showing the applicability and synthesis of dimethyl ether in addition to the position of an online marketing company. (b, c)

重質油の精製・複合発電、オスモスの基本構成、Biorekプロセスフローのチャート。(a, d)
ジメチルエーテルの適用分野と合成フロー、並びに電子商取引市場運営会社の位置付けを表すチャート。(b, c)

Japan   2000 (a, d) **/ 2001** (b, c)
D: Mayumi Noguchi (a, d) / Shinji Suzuki (b, c)   CL: JGC Corporation   S: The IR Corporation

APPLICATIONS OF DME

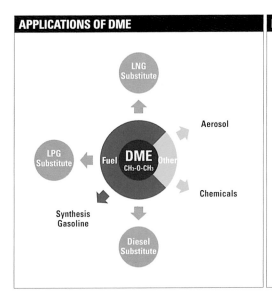

LNG Substitute

Aerosol

LPG Substitute — Fuel — **DME** CH₃-O-CH₃ — Other

Chemicals

Synthesis Gasoline

Diesel Substitute

BLOCK DIAGRAM OF DME

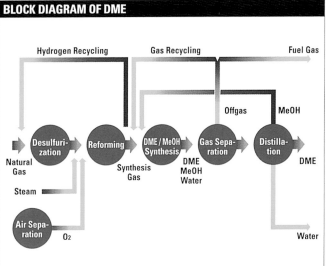

Hydrogen Recycling   Gas Recycling   Fuel Gas

Offgas   MeOH

Desulfuri-zation → Reforming → DME / MeOH Synthesis → Gas Sepa-ration → Distilla-tion

Natural Gas

Steam

Synthesis Gas

DME MeOH Water

DME

Air Sepa-ration   O₂

Water

b

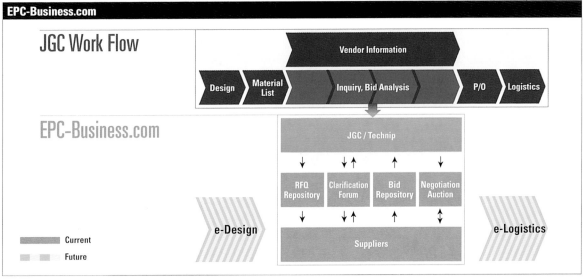

EPC-Business.com

JGC Work Flow

Vendor Information

Design | Material List | Inquiry, Bid Analysis | P/O | Logistics

EPC-Business.com

JGC / Technip

RFQ Repository | Clarification Forum | Bid Repository | Negotiation Auction

e-Design

Suppliers

e-Logistics

Current
Future

c

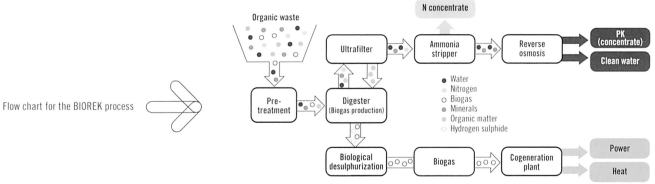

Flow chart for the BIOREK process

Organic waste

N concentrate

Ultrafilter → Ammonia stripper → Reverse osmosis → PK (concentrate) / Clean water

Pre-treatment → Digester (Biogas production)

- Water
- Nitrogen
- Biogas
- Minerals
- Organic matter
- Hydrogen sulphide

Biological desulphurization → Biogas → Cogeneration plant → Power / Heat

d

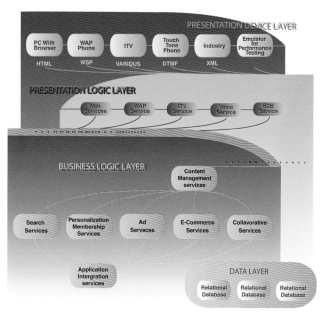

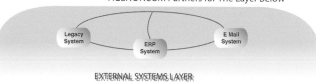

AGENCY.COM Handles the Layers Above

AGENCY.COM Partners for The Layer Below

EXTERNAL SYSTEMS LAYER

a

AGENCY.COM Handles The Layers Above

AGENCY.COM Partners For The Layer Below

b

Diagram explaining the various layers that the agency handles, and those that the agency partners handle. (a)
Diagram illustrating the routes of communication and services between working levels of management. (b)

広告代理店やそのパートナーが扱っている様々なビジネス層を説明するチャート。(a)
マネジメントの作業レベル間のコミュニケーションやサービスのルートを説明するチャート。(b)

USA 2001
CD, AD, D, I: Mike Quon   D: Anna Leonard / Ole Haentzschel   DF, S: Mike Quon / designation Inc.   CL: Agency.com

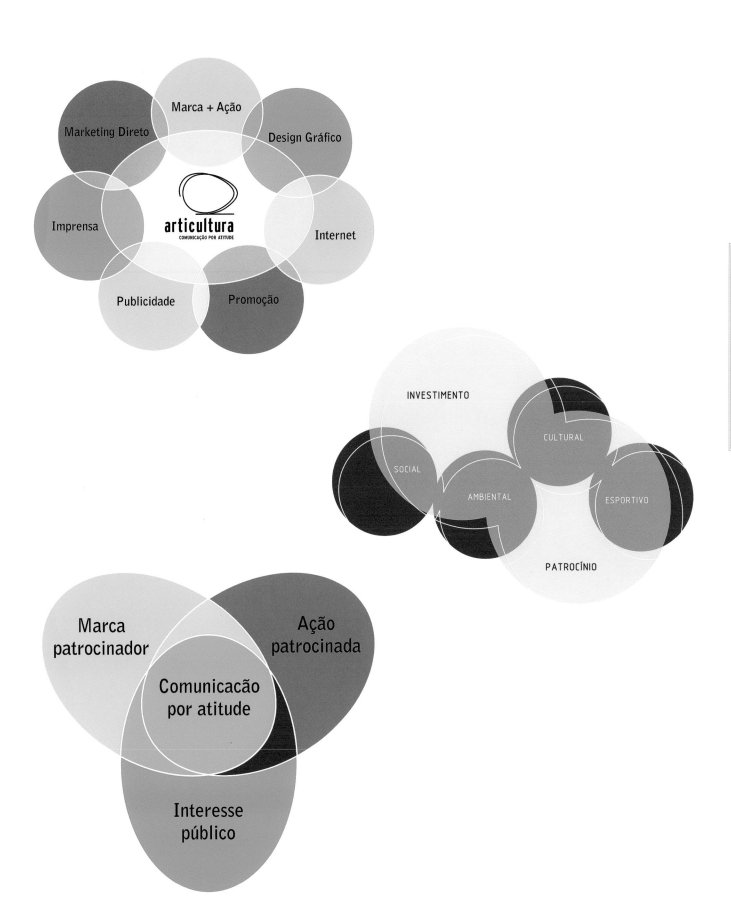

These diagrams highlight the concept of "communication by attitude," as an intersection of cultural events, sports sponsorship, social responsibility actions, and etc.

文化イベント、スポーツ・スポンサーシップ、社会的責任行動などを包括する、「態度によるコミュニケーション」というコンセプトを表すダイアグラム。

Brazil   2003
AD: Rico Lins   D: Marina Siqueira / Marina Oruê   DF, S: Rico Lins + Studio   CL: Articultura Comunicação Por Atitude

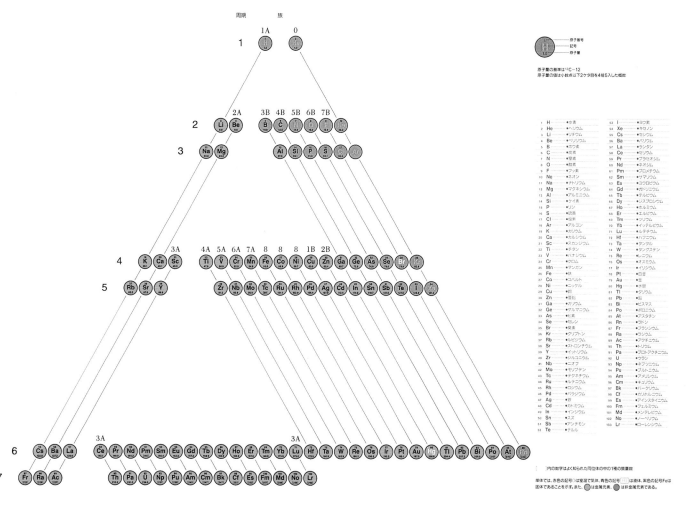

A periodic table of the elements expressed with triangles.

元素の周期表を三角形で表現。

Japan 2000
CD, AD, D, S: Tetsuya Ota   CL: Sanseido Publishing Co.,Ltd.

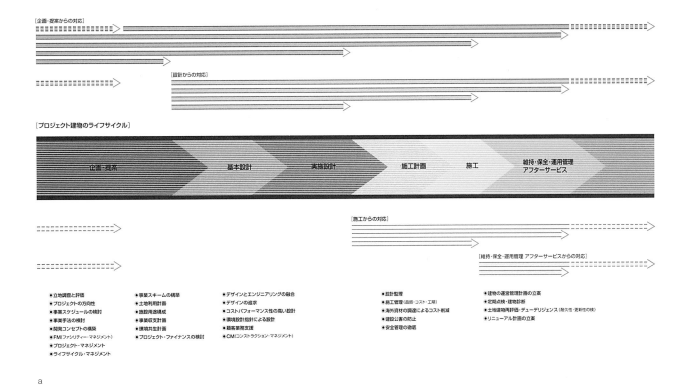

[企画・提案からの対応]

[設計からの対応]

[プロジェクト建物のライフサイクル]

企画・提案　　　基本設計　　　実施設計　　　施工計画　　　施工　　　維持・保全・運用管理 アフターサービス

[施工からの対応]

[維持・保全・運用管理 アフターサービスからの対応]

● 立地調査と評価
● プロジェクトの方向性
● 事業スケジュールの検討
● 事業手法の検討
● 開発コンセプトの構築
● FM（ファシリティ・マネジメント）
● プロジェクト・マネジメント
● ライフサイクル・マネジメント

● 事業スキームの構築
● 土地利用計画
● 施設用途構成
● 事業収支計画
● 環境共生計画
● プロジェクト・ファイナンスの検討

● デザインとエンジニアリングの融合
● デザインの追求
● コストパフォーマンス性の高い設計
● 環境設計指針による設計
● 顧客業務支援
● CM（コンストラクション・マネジメント）

● 設計監理
● 施工管理（品質・コスト・工程）
● 海外資材の調達によるコスト削減
● 建設公害の防止
● 安全管理の徹底

● 建物の運営管理計画の立案
● 定期点検・建物診断
● 土地建物再評価・デューデリジェンス（耐久性・更新性の検討）
● リニューアル計画の立案

a

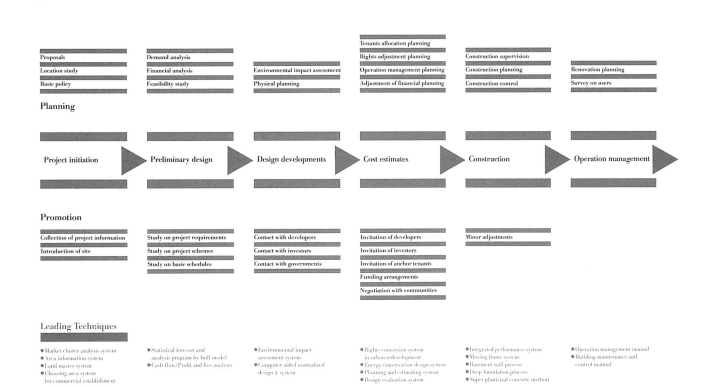

Tenants allocation planning			
Proposals	Demand analysis		Rights adjustment planning	Construction supervision
Location study	Financial analysis	Environmental impact assessment	Operation management planning	Construction planning	Renovation planning
Basic policy	Feasibility study	Physical planning	Adjustment of financial planning	Construction control	Survey on users

Planning

Project initiation　　Preliminary design　　Design developments　　Cost estimates　　Construction　　Operation management

Promotion

Collection of project information	Study on project requirements	Contact with developers	Invitation of developers	Minor adjustments
Introduction of site	Study on project schemes	Contact with investors	Invitation of investors	
	Study on basic schedules	Contact with governments	Invitation of anchor tenants	
			Funding arrangements	
			Negotiation with communities	

Leading Techniques

● Market cluster analysis system
● Area information system
● Land master system
● Choosing area system for commercial establishment

● Statistical forecast and analysis program by huff model
● Cash flow/Profit and loss analysis

● Environmental impact assessment system
● Computer aided normalized design & system

● Rights conversion system in urban redevelopment
● Energy conservation design system
● Planning and estimating system
● Design evaluation system

● Integrated performance system
● Moving frame system
● Basement wall process
● Deep foundation process
● Super plasticical concrete method

● Operation management manual
● Building maintenance and control manual

b

Lifecycle of a building expressed as single flow. (a)
Visualization of workflow using bars, typography and color only. (b)

プロジェクト建物のライフサイクルを一つのフローとして表現。 (a)
仕事の流れをバーとタイポグラフィと色のみで表現。 (b)

Japan　1999
CD, AD, D, S: Tetsuya Ota　CL: Takenaka Corporation

近未来へのビジョン。

ビジネスチャンスとして。
2000年3月、電気事業法の改正により、
お客さまが電力の購入先を自由に選ぶことができる
「電力小売りの部分自由化」がスタートしました。
現在は、対象となるお客さまを、大規模なビルや
工場などの大口需給者に限定する部分的な自由化ですが、
将来的にはさらなる自由化が検討されています。
従来の常識からは考えられない
売買のしくみができる可能性があり、
今後ますます、熾烈な競争市場となることは必至です。
沖縄電力では、経営の効率化を推進する一方、
これを大きなビジネスチャンスと捉え、
新しいプランに乗り出しました。

総合産業企業をめざして。
今回の改正では兼業規制が廃止され、電気事業者の
事業多角化が可能となりました。沖縄電力は、
電気事業以外の新規事業を積極的に拡大していく方針です。
情報処理や情報提供サービスおよびIT関連事業、ホテルや
マリンレジャー施設などの経営に関する観光関連事業、
エネルギー利用と環境の調査・コンサルティング事業など、
その他さまざまな事業展開を図っていきます。
新規事業の展開にあたっては、株主や地域社会から
コンセンサスを得られる事業であり、かつ直接、間接的に
電気事業と県内産業の発達に寄与するとともに、
お客さまへのサービスの充実・拡大をもたらす
事業でなくてはならないと考えています。
現在は、IT関連事業と観光関連事業の計画が進行中です。
将来的には、電力事業を全事業の6〜7割で保持し、
多角化事業を3〜4割まで拡大する方向で進めています。
沖縄電力がめざしているのは、電気という
エネルギーを軸とした総合産業企業なのです。

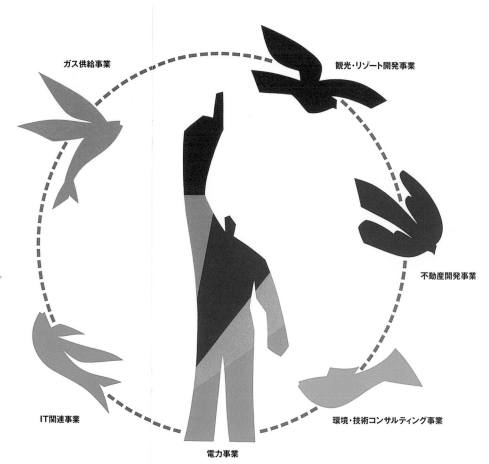

ガス供給事業　観光・リゾート開発事業　不動産開発事業　環境・技術コンサルティング事業　電力事業　IT関連事業

4　　　　　5

a

Capability charts expressing a vision of the near future. (a)
Illustration explaining the flow of electricity. (b)
Chart system explaining educational training. (c)

近未来のビジョンを表す機能チャート。 (a)
電気の流れをイラストレーションで解説。 (b)
教育研修を解説するチャート。 (c)

Japan　2003
CD, AD, D, S: Tetsuya Ota　I: Zenji Funabashi (a)　CL: Okinawa Electric Power Company

お客さまと電気をつなぐ、無限のパワーたち。

いつでもどこでもお客さまの家庭や職場などに電力を供給できるよう、沖縄電力の様々なセクションは日夜働き続けています。燃料の調達から、定期的なメンテナンス、万一のトラブルへの備え、より環境にやさしい新エネルギーの開発、窓口でのサービスなども、多種多様な業務のほんの一部です。
私たちは、安全で効率的かつ安定的に電力をお届けするために、互いに協力をおしまず、そして刺激しあって、ひとりひとりの個性と無限に広がる可能性を磨きつつ高めていきたいと考えています。
そして、より豊かな「ふるさと沖縄」を創るため、みんなの「おきでんパワー」をいかんなく発揮していきます。

電力輸送の動脈
自然災害で片方の送電がストップしても、もう一方から供給することで停電を未然に防ぐよう二つの輸送ルートを確保し、送電線のループ化を図っています。

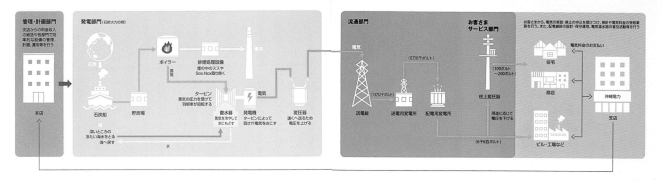

管理・計画部門
支店からの料金収入の総括や各部門で効率的な設備の管理、計画、運用等を行う
本店

発電部門（石炭火力の例）
ボイラー
排煙処理設備 煙の中のススやSox.Noxを取り除く
煙突
蒸気
石炭
石炭船
貯炭場
深いところの冷たい海水をとる 海へ戻す
タービン 蒸気の圧力を受けて羽根車が回転する
復水器 蒸気を冷やして水にもどす
発電機 タービンによって回され電気をおこす
電気
変圧器 遠くへ送るため電圧を上げる
水

流通部門
電気
送電線
(13万2千ボルト) 送電用変電所
(6万6千ボルト)
配電用変電所

お客さまサービス部門
柱上変圧器 (100ボルト～200ボルト) 用途に応じて電圧を下げる
(6千6百ボルト)

住宅
商店
ビル・工場など

お客さまから、電気の新設・廃止の申込を受けつけ、検針や電気料金の受取業務を行う。また、配電線路の設計・保守運用、電気水道の普及活動等を行う
電気料金のお支払い
沖縄電力
支店

石炭運搬船
外国から輸入されてきた石炭は、採炭機によって陸揚げされ、ベルトコンベヤや屋内貯炭場、石炭バンカへと運ばれ、最後に微粉炭機で粉末にされ、ボイラーに吹き込まれて燃やされます。

蒸気タービン発電機
ボイラーでつくられた高温、高圧の蒸気はタービンを回転させ、同軸の発電機をまわして電気を発生させます。

給電指令所
発電所の熱効率の向上と発電から配電に至る電力系統の最適経済負荷配分による効率的な運用に努めています。

6

7

b

階層別研修
管理職研修
新任特管職研修
新任係長研修
新任主任研修
新任主務II研修
新入社員研修

部門別研修
各種資格取得研修
技術系研修
事務系研修

特別教育
その他研修
語学研修・パソコン教室
通信教育・講演会
その他研修
派遣研修
県内外派遣研修
海外留学研修
海外派遣研修
社外セミナー
年代別研修（人生設計研修）

c

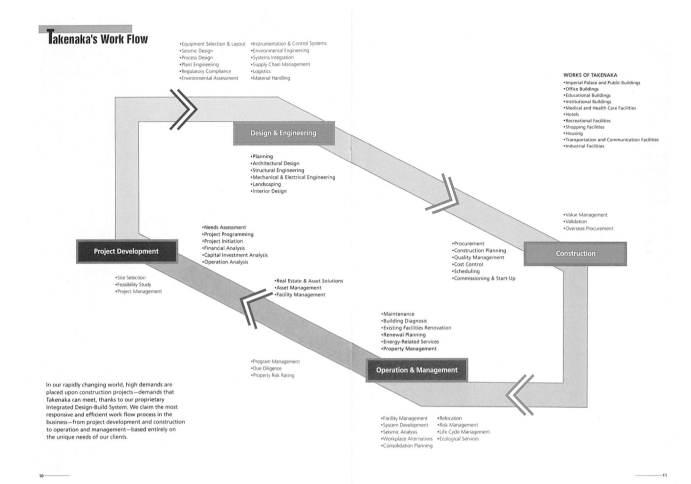

Takenaka's Work Flow

•Equipment Selection & Layout
•Seismic Design
•Process Design
•Plant Engineering
•Regulatory Compliance
•Environmental Assessment

•Instrumentation & Control Systems
•Environmental Engineering
•Systems Integration
•Supply Chain Management
•Logistics
•Material Handling

WORKS OF TAKENAKA
•Imperial Palace and Public Buildings
•Office Buildings
•Educational Buildings
•Institutional Buildings
•Medical and Health Care Facilities
•Hotels
•Recreational Facilities
•Shopping Facilities
•Housing
•Transportation and Communication Facilities
•Industrial Facilities

Design & Engineering

•Planning
•Architectural Design
•Structural Engineering
•Mechanical & Electrical Engineering
•Landscaping
•Interior Design

•Value Management
•Validation
•Overseas Procurement

Project Development

•Needs Assessment
•Project Programming
•Project Initiation
•Financial Analysis
•Capital Investment Analysis
•Operation Analysis

•Procurement
•Construction Planning
•Quality Management
•Cost Control
•Scheduling
•Commissioning & Start-Up

Construction

•Site Selection
•Feasibility Study
•Project Management

•Real Estate & Asset Solutions
•Asset Management
•Facility Management

•Maintenance
•Building Diagnosis
•Existing Facilities Renovation
•Renewal Planning
•Energy-Related Services
•Property Management

•Program Management
•Due Diligence
•Property Risk Rating

Operation & Management

In our rapidly changing world, high demands are placed upon construction projects—demands that Takenaka can meet, thanks to our proprietary Integrated Design-Build System. We claim the most responsive and efficient work flow process in the business—from project development and construction to operation and management—based entirely on the unique needs of our clients.

•Facility Management
•System Development
•Seismic Analysis
•Workplace Alternatives
•Consolidation Planning

•Relocation
•Risk Management
•Life Cycle Management
•Ecological Services

10 — ————— 11

a

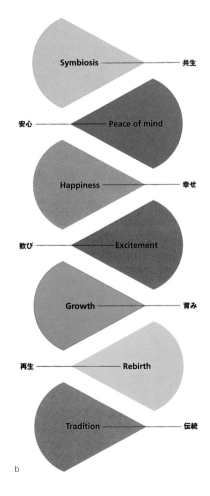

Symbiosis ——— 共生

安心 ——— Peace of mind

Happiness ——— 幸せ

歓び ——— Excitement

Growth ——— 育み

再生 ——— Rebirth

Tradition ——— 伝統

b

Flow chart expressing work process. (a)
Section chart representing an organization. (b)

仕事の流れを表すフローチャート。 (a)
組織を表す区分図。 (b)

Japan 2003
CD, AD, D, S: Tetsuya Ota   CL: Takenaka Corporation

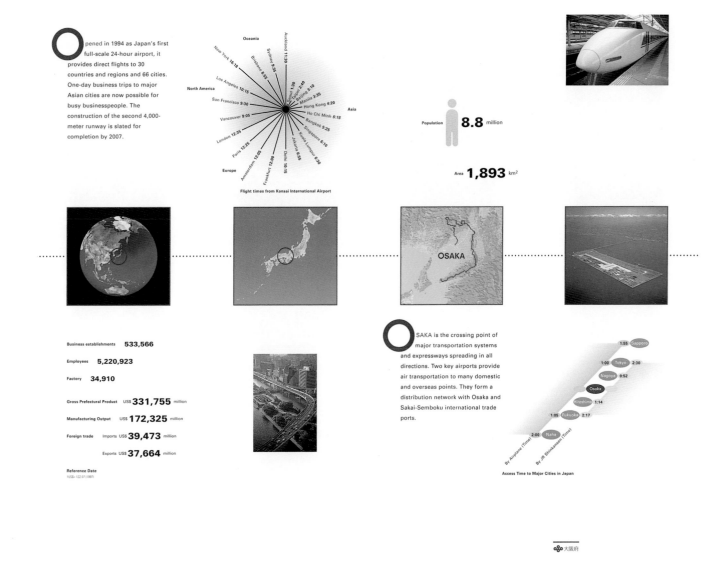

Opened in 1994 as Japan's first full-scale 24-hour airport, it provides direct flights to 30 countries and regions and 66 cities. One-day business trips to major Asian cities are now possible for busy businesspeople. The construction of the second 4,000-meter runway is slated for completion by 2007.

Flight times from Kansai International Airport

Oceania
Auckland 11:30
Sydney 9:35
Brisbane 8:55
New York 16:18
Los Angeles 10:15
North America
San Francisco 9:30
Vancouver 9:05
London 12:35
Paris 12:25
Europe
Amsterdam 12:05
Frankfurt 12:00
Delhi 10:15
Jakarta 6:55
Kuala Lumpur 6:30
Singapore 6:10
Bangkok 5:25
Ho Chi Minh 5:15
Hong Kong 4:20
Manila 3:35
Beijing 3:10
Taipei 2:40
Seoul 1:30
Asia

Population **8.8** million

Area **1,893** km²

Business establishments **533,566**

Employees **5,220,923**

Factory **34,910**

Gross Prefectural Product US$ **331,755** million

Manufacturing Output US$ **172,325** million

Foreign trade Imports US$ **39,473** million

Exports US$ **37,664** million

Reference Date
1US$= 122.07 (1997)

OSAKA is the crossing point of major transportation systems and expressways spreading in all directions. Two key airports provide air transportation to many domestic and overseas points. They form a distribution network with Osaka and Sakai-Semboku international trade ports.

Access Time to Major Cities in Japan

Sapporo 1:55
Tokyo 1:00 / 2:30
Nagoya 0:52
Osaka
Hiroshima 1:14
Fukuoka 1:05 / 2:17
Naha 2:00
By Airplane (Time)
By JR Shinkansen (Time)

大阪府

Osaka, a strategic base for international business, is an ideal metropolis for corporate activities.

●SAKA

Diagrams used in a pamphlet to attract foreign business to Osaka showing the population and area of the city,
flight times from Osaka to overseas destinations and travel times to other Japanese cities.

大阪への海外企業誘致のためのパンフレットに使用されたダイアグラム。大阪の人口と平面積、大阪から各国へのフライト時間、日本国内各都市への所要時間などを示している。

Japan 2000
AD: Shinnoske Sugisaki   D: Chiaki Okuno / Reika Kusaka   DF, S: Shinnosuke Inc.   CL: Osaka Prefecture

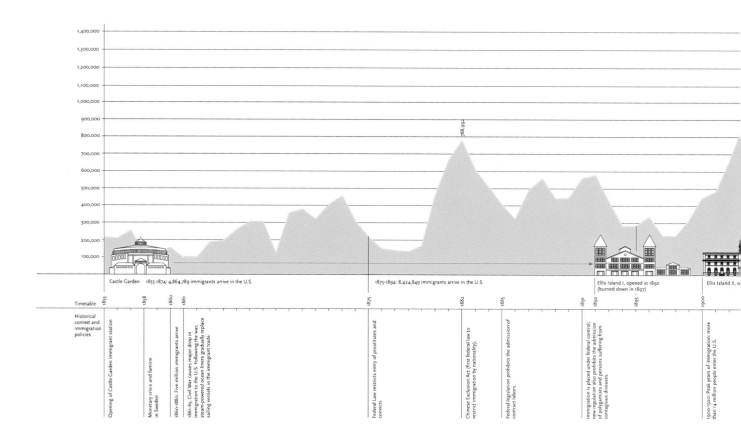

Graphic representation plotting the historical development of immigration to the U.S. (1855-1954) with peaks and troughs following political movements.

アメリカへの移民の歴史（1855年〜1954年）を、政局の動向に伴う人数の増減とともに示したグラフィック。

Germany 2002
D, I: Lisa Nieschlag   DF, S: Nieschlag + Wentrup

A chronological table of the sovereigns of the Netherlands.

歴代のオランダ君主を紹介する年表。

Netherlands 2004
CD: Paul Vermijs   D: Toon Tesser   DF, S: TelDesign   CL: Ministry Of Foreign Affairs

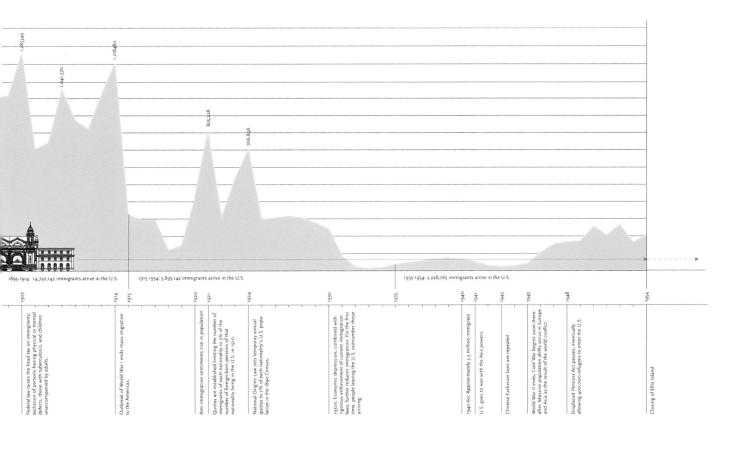

1,285,349

1,041,570

1,218,480

805,228

706,896

1895-1914: 14,750,142 immigrants arrive in the U.S.　1915-1934: 5,895,142 immigrants arrive in the U.S.　1935-1954: 2,228,065 immigrants arrive in the U.S.

1907 | Federal law raises the head tax on immigrants; exclusion of persons having physical or mental defects, those with tuberculosis, and children unaccompanied by adults.

1914 | Outbreak of World War I ends mass migration to the Americas.

1915

1920 | Anti-immigration sentiments rise in population.

1921 | Quotas are established limiting the number of immigrants of each nationality to 3% of the number of foreign-born persons of that nationality living in the U.S. in 1910.

1924 | National Origins Law sets temporary annual quotas to 2% of each nationality's U.S. population in the 1890 Census.

1930 | 1930s: Economic depression, combined with rigorous enforcement of current immigration laws, further reduces immigration. For the first time, people leaving the U.S. outnumber those arriving.

1935

1940 | 1940-60: Approximately 3.5 million immigrate

1941 | U.S. goes to war with the Axis powers.

1943 | Chinese Exclusion laws are repealed.

1945 | World War II ends. Cold War begins soon thereafter. Massive population shifts occur in Europe and Asia as the result of the world conflict.

1948 | Displaced Persons Act passes, eventually allowing 400,000 refugees to enter the U.S.

1954 | Closing of Ellis Island

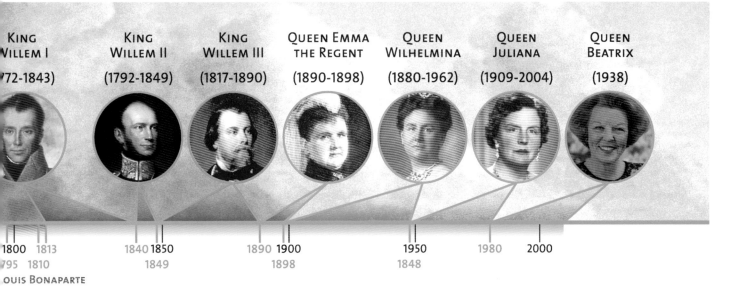

KING WILLEM I	KING WILLEM II	KING WILLEM III	QUEEN EMMA THE REGENT	QUEEN WILHELMINA	QUEEN JULIANA	QUEEN BEATRIX
(1772-1843)	(1792-1849)	(1817-1890)	(1890-1898)	(1880-1962)	(1909-2004)	(1938)

1800　1813　1840　1850　1890　1900　1950　1980　2000

1795　1810　1849　1898　1848

LOUIS BONAPARTE

Reuse

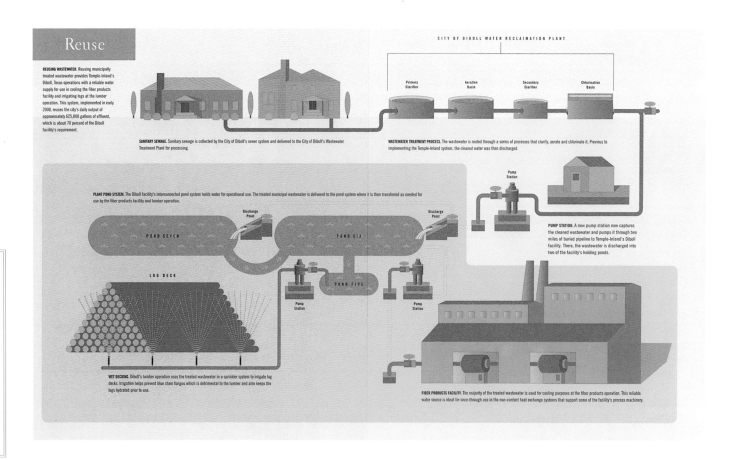

CITY OF DIBOLL WATER RECLAIMATION PLANT

Primary Clarifier · Aeration Basin · Secondary Clarifier · Chlorination Basin

REUSING WASTEWATER. Reusing municipally treated wastewater provides Temple-Inland's Diboll, Texas operations with a reliable water supply for use in cooling the fiber products facility and irrigating logs at the lumber operation. This system, implemented in early 2000, reuses the city's daily output of approximately 625,000 gallons of effluent, which is about 70 percent of the Diboll facility's requirement.

SANITARY SEWAGE. Sanitary sewage is collected by the City of Diboll's sewer system and delivered to the City of Diboll's Wastewater Treatment Plant for processing.

WASTEWATER TREATMENT PROCESS. The wastewater is routed through a series of processes that clarify, aerate and chlorinate it. Previous to implementing the Temple-Inland system, the cleaned water was then discharged.

PLANT POND SYSTEM. The Diboll facility's interconnected pond system holds water for operational use. The treated municipal wastewater is delivered to the pond system where it is then transferred as needed for use by the fiber products facility and lumber operation.

Discharge Point · POND SEVEN · POND SIX · POND FIVE · LOG DECK · Pump Station · Pump Station · Discharge Point · Pump Station

PUMP STATION. A new pump station now captures the cleaned wastewater and pumps it through two miles of buried pipeline to Temple-Inland's Diboll facility. There, the wastewater is discharged into two of the facility's holding ponds.

WET DECKING. Diboll's lumber operation uses the treated wastewater in a sprinkler system to irrigate log decks. Irrigation helps prevent blue stain fungus which is detrimental to the lumber and also keeps the logs hydrated prior to use.

FIBER PRODUCTS FACILITY. The majority of the treated wastewater is used for cooling purposes at the fiber products operation. This reliable water source is ideal for once-through use in the non-contact heat exchange systems that support some of the facility's process machinery.

Recycle

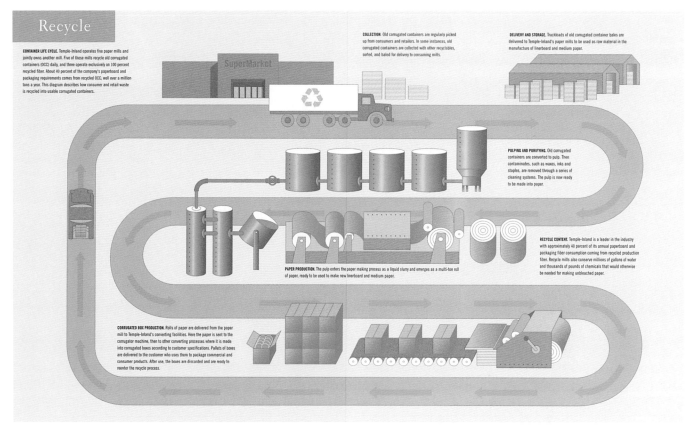

CONTAINER LIFE CYCLE. Temple-Inland operates five paper mills and jointly owns another mill. Five of these mills recycle old corrugated containers (OCC) daily, and three operate exclusively on 100 percent recycled fiber. About 40 percent of the company's paperboard and packaging requirements comes from recycled OCC; well over a million tons a year. This diagram describes how consumer and retail waste is recycled into usable corrugated containers.

COLLECTION. Old corrugated containers are regularly picked up from consumers and retailers. In some instances, old corrugated containers are collected with other recyclables, sorted, and baled for delivery to consuming mills.

DELIVERY AND STORAGE. Truckloads of old corrugated container bales are delivered to Temple-Inland's paper mills to be used as raw material in the manufacture of linerboard and medium paper.

PULPING AND PURIFYING. Old corrugated containers are converted to pulp. Then contaminates, such as waxes, inks and staples, are removed through a series of cleaning systems. The pulp is now ready to be made into paper.

PAPER PRODUCTION. The pulp enters the paper making process as a liquid slurry and emerges as a multi-ton roll of paper, ready to be used to make new linerboard and medium paper.

RECYCLE CONTENT. Temple-Inland is a leader in the industry with approximately 40 percent of its annual paperboard and packaging fiber consumption coming from recycled production fiber. Recycle mills also conserve millions of gallons of water and thousands of pounds of chemicals that would otherwise be needed for making unbleached paper.

CORRUGATED BOX PRODUCTION. Rolls of paper are delivered from the paper mill to Temple-Inland's converting facilities. Here the paper is sent to the corrugator machine, then to other converting processes where it is made into corrugated boxes according to customer specifications. Pallets of boxes are delivered to the customer who uses them to package commercial and consumer products. After use, the boxes are discarded and are ready to reenter the recycle process.

A step-by-step introduction to Temple-Inland's enviromentally friendly philosophy and process.

Temple-Inland社の環境に配慮した理念とプロセスを順を追って紹介する図。

USA 2000
AD, D, I, CW: Rex Peteet   D, I: Carrie Echo / Kristianne Kossler   P: Jay Brittain   CW: Carla Kienast   DF, S: Sibley Peteet   CL: Temple-Inland

Reclaim

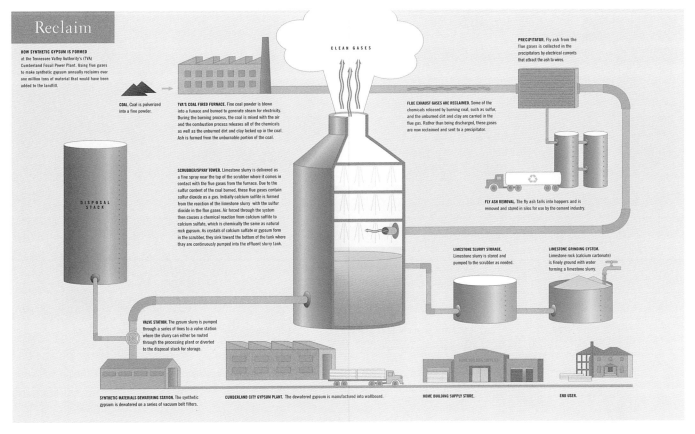

CLEAN GASES

HOW SYNTHETIC GYPSUM IS FORMED at the Tennessee Valley Authority's (TVA) Cumberland Fossil Power Plant. Using flue gases to make synthetic gypsum annually reclaims over one million tons of material that would have been added to the landfill.

COAL. Coal is pulverized into a fine powder.

TVA'S COAL FIRED FURNACE. Fine coal powder is blown into a funace and burned to generate steam for electricity. During the burning process, the coal is mixed with the air and the combustion process releases all of the chemicals as well as the unburned dirt and clay locked up in the coal. Ash is formed from the unburnable portion of the coal.

PRECIPITATOR. Fly ash from the flue gases is collected in the precipitators by electrical currents that attract the ash to wires.

FLUE EXHAUST GASES ARE RECLAIMED. Some of the chemicals released by burning coal, such as sulfur, and the unburned dirt and clay are carried in the flue gas. Rather than being discharged, these gases are now reclaimed and sent to a precipitator.

SCRUBBER/SPRAY TOWER. Limestone slurry is delivered as a fine spray near the top of the scrubber where it comes in contact with the flue gases from the furnace. Due to the sulfur content of the coal burned, these flue gases contain sulfur dioxide as a gas. Initially calcium sulfite is formed from the reaction of the limestone slurry with the sulfur dioxide in the flue gases. Air forced through the system then causes a chemical reaction from calcium sulfite to calcium sulfate, which is chemically the same as natural rock gypsum. As crystals of calcium sulfate or gypsum form in the scrubber, they sink toward the bottom of the tank where thay are continuously pumped into the effluent slurry tank.

FLY ASH REMOVAL. The fly ash falls into hoppers and is removed and stored in silos for use by the cement industry.

DISPOSAL STACK

LIMESTONE SLURRY STORAGE. Limestone slurry is stored and pumped to the scrubber as needed.

LIMESTONE GRINDING SYSTEM. Limestone rock (calcium carbonate) is finely ground with water forming a limestone slurry.

VALVE STATION. The gysum slurry is pumped through a series of lines to a valve station where the slurry can either be routed through the processing plant or diverted to the disposal stack for storage.

SYNTHETIC MATERIALS DEWATERING STATION. The synthetic gypsum is dewatered on a series of vacuum belt filters.

CUMBERLAND CITY GYPSUM PLANT. The dewatered gypsum is manufactured into wallboard.

HOME BUILDING SUPPLY STORE.

END USER.

Renew

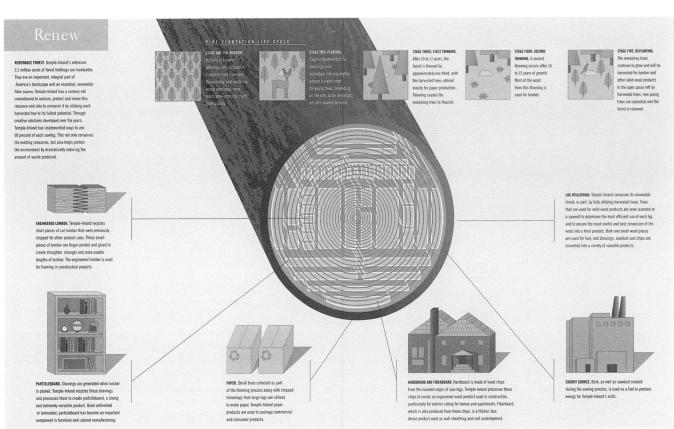

PINE PLANTATION LIFE CYCLE

STAGE ONE: THE NURSERY. Millions of superior seedlings are nurtured in Temple-Inland's nursery. By assisting and nurturing young seedlings, trees reach semi-maturity much more quickly.

STAGE TWO: PLANTING. Careful treatment of the seedlings and individual site preparation ensure a viable start for young trees. Depending on the site, some seedlings are still planted by hand.

STAGE THREE: FIRST THINNING. After 10 to 12 years, the forest is thinned by approximately one-third, with the harvested trees utilized mainly for paper production. Thinning causes the remaining trees to flourish.

STAGE FOUR: SECOND THINNING. A second thinning occurs after 18 to 22 years of growth. Most of the wood from this thinning is used for lumber.

STAGE FIVE: REPLANTING. The remaining trees continue to grow and will be harvested for lumber and other solid wood products. In the open space left by harvested trees, new young trees are replanted and the forest is renewed.

RENEWABLE FOREST. Temple-Inland's extensive 2.2 million acres of forest holdings are invaluable. They are an important, integral part of America's landscape and an essential, renewable fiber source. Temple-Inland has a century-old commitment to nurture, protect and renew this resource and also to conserve it by utilizing each harvested tree to its fullest potential. Through creative solutions developed over the years, Temple-Inland has implemented ways to use 98 percent of each sawlog. This not only conserves the existing resources, but also helps protect the environment by dramatically reducing the amount of waste produced.

ENGINEERED LUMBER. Temple-Inland recycles short pieces of cut lumber that were previously chipped for other product uses. These small pieces of lumber are finger-jointed and glued to create straighter, stronger and more usable lengths of lumber. The engineered lumber is used for framing in construction projects.

LOG UTILIZATION. Temple-Inland conserves its renewable forest, in part, by fully utilizing harvested trees. Trees that are used for solid wood products are laser scanned at a sawmill to determine the most efficient use of each log and to ensure the most useful and best conversion of the wood into a final product. Bark and small wood pieces are used for fuel; and shavings, sawdust and chips are converted into a variety of valuable products.

PARTICLEBOARD. Shavings are generated when lumber is planed. Temple-Inland recycles these shavings and processes them to create particleboard, a strong and extremely versatile product. Used unfinished or laminated, particleboard has become an important component in furniture and cabinet manufacturing.

PAPER. Small trees collected as part of the thinning process along with chipped trimmings from large logs are utilized to make paper. Temple-Inland paper products are used to package commercial and consumer products.

HARDBOARD AND FIBERBOARD. Hardboard is made of wood chips from the rounded edges of saw logs. Temple-Inland processes these chips to create an engineered wood product used in construction, particularly for exterior siding for homes and apartments. Fiberboard, which is also produced from these chips, is a thicker, less dense product used as wall sheathing and roof underlayment.

ENERGY SOURCE. Bark, as well as sawdust created during the sawing process, is used as a fuel to produce energy for Temple-Inland's mills.

Productive Presentation

Our primary operation is food, which consists of divisions for flour milling, vegetable oils, cornstarch and corn sweeteners, household foods and frozen foods. The food operations involve producing and selling a wide range of products for commercial and household use. The products, made from grains such as wheat, soybeans and corn, are a part of people's diet in a variety of forms.

We also makes good use of the by-products generated in the processing of these grains by producing and selling mixed animal feed. The animal feed operation also includes producing and selling eggs.

Other operations include warehousing business for grains and real-estate leasing business for effective use of real estates.

BUSINESS DEVELOPMENT

Showa Sangyo Group   Others

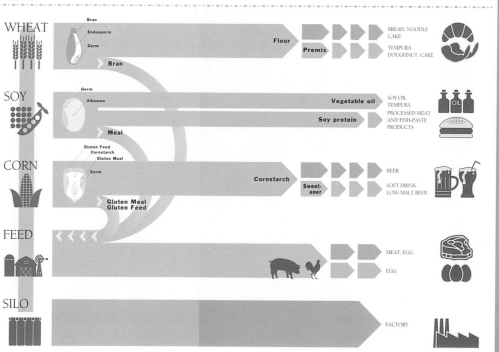

WHEAT

Bran
Endosperm
Germ

Bran

Flour → BREAD, NOODLE CAKE
Premix → TEMPURA DOUGHNUT, CAKE

SOY

Germ
Albumen

Meal

Vegetable oil
Soy protein

SOY OIL
TEMPURA
PROCESSED MEAT AND FISH-PASTE PRODUCTS

CORN

Gluten Feed
Cornstarch
Gluten Meal
Germ

Gluten Meal
Gluten Feed

Cornstarch → BEER
Sweet-ener → SOFT DRINK LOW-MALT BEER

FEED

MEAT, EGG
EGG

SILO

FACTORY

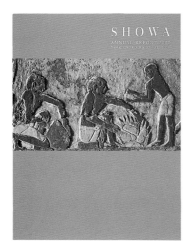

Easy to understand charting of the process from whole grains to products.

穀物から最終的なプロダクツに至るまでのプロセスを分かりやすくチャート化。

Japan 2002

DF: Interlux, Inc.   CL: Showa Sangyo Co., Ltd.   S: Nomura Investor Relations Co., Ltd.

Market strategy Ericsson is a business-to-business telecommunications supplier. We sell systems, services and technology to operators and service providers in 140 countries. We also create revenue through our licensed solutions and intellectual property rights. And we sell handsets to operators and retailers through Sony Ericsson.

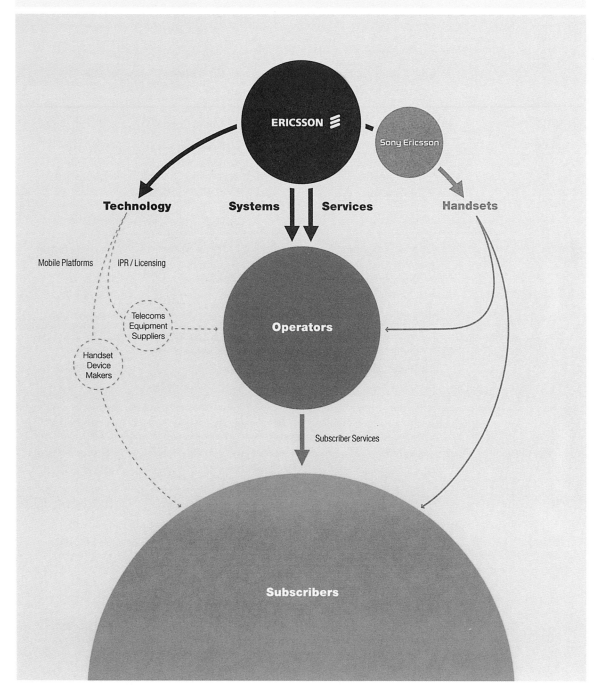

10　Ericsson 2002　Our Strategy

Diagrams Illustrating Ericsson's market strategy and customer service.
Ericsson社のマーケット戦略や顧客サービスを表すダイアグラム。

UK　2002
CD, AD, D, I: Gilmar Wendt　CD: David Stocks　P: Stefan Almers / Alexander farnsworth / Lee Mawdsley
CW: Tim Rich / Leonard Rau　DF, S: SAS　CL: Ericsson

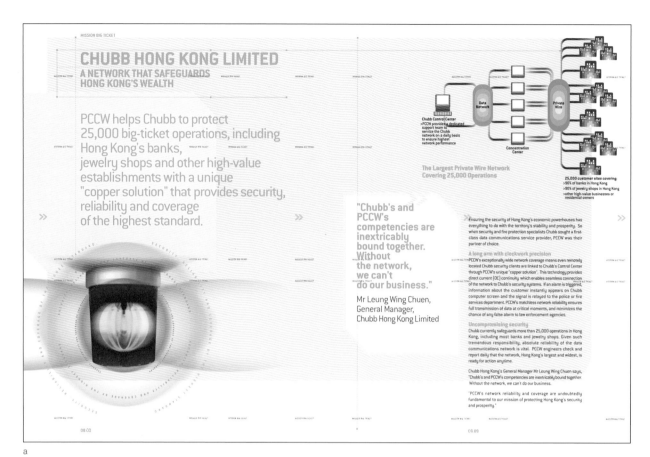

a

MISSION BIG TICKET

CHUBB HONG KONG LIMITED
A NETWORK THAT SAFEGUARDS HONG KONG'S WEALTH

PCCW helps Chubb to protect
25,000 big-ticket operations, including
Hong Kong's banks,
jewelry shops and other high-value
establishments with a unique
"copper solution" that provides security,
reliability and coverage
of the highest standard.

"Chubb's and
PCCW's
competencies are
inextricably
bound together.
Without
the network,
we can't
do our business."

Mr Leung Wing Chuen,
General Manager,
Chubb Hong Kong Limited

Ensuring the security of Hong Kong's economic powerhouses has everything to do with the territory's stability and prosperity. So when security and fire protection specialists Chubb sought a first-class data communications service provider, PCCW was their partner of choice.

A long arm with clockwork precision
PCCW's exceptionally wide network coverage means even remotely located Chubb security clients are linked to Chubb's Control Center through PCCW's unique "copper solution". This technology provides direct current (DC) continuity which enables seamless connection of the network to Chubb's security systems. If an alarm is triggered, information about the customer instantly appears on Chubb computer screen and the signal is relayed to the police or fire services department. PCCW's matchless network reliability ensures full transmission of data at critical moments, and minimizes the chance of any false alarm to law enforcement agencies.

Uncompromising security
Chubb currently safeguards more than 25,000 operations in Hong Kong, including most banks and jewelry shops. Given such tremendous responsibility, absolute reliability of the data communications network is vital. PCCW engineers check and report daily that the network, Hong Kong's largest and widest, is ready for action anytime.

Chubb Hong Kong's General Manager Mr Leung Wing Chuen says, "Chubb's and PCCW's competencies are inextricably bound together. Without the network, we can't do our business.

"PCCW's network reliability and coverage are undoubtedly fundamental to our mission of protecting Hong Kong's security and prosperity."

The Largest Private Wire Network
Covering 25,000 Operations

25,000 customer sites covering:
>90% of banks in Hong Kong
>90% of jewelry shops in Hong Kong
>other high-value businesses or residential owners

b

MISSION EMPATHY

MULTI-TIER POWER SUPPLY
SOLVING PROBLEMS BEFORE THEY'RE EVEN NOTICED

Going above and beyond the call of duty
to ensure that customer operations experience
no downtime, PCCW as a network service
provider proactively sent a diesel-
powered generator to a key
building after detecting an
electrical power failure.
In fact, PCCW has in place a
comprehensive procedure
for dealing with all
kinds of power supply
failures to ensure
business
continuity.

One of PCCW's mobile diesel generators for emergency power

1st tier
City Electricity
Power

2nd tier
UPS

3rd tier
UPS Backup

4th tier
Diesel
Generator

5th tier
Oil tank for
2 days' usage

Agreement
with oil company
for emergency
supply within
2 hours

Battery
Plant-
3 hours power
extension

PCCW Data Network

Multi-tier Power Supply to support the operation of PCCW Data Network

When PCCW's Network Management Center remotely detected a power failure at the North Point government building, the company realized that urgent action was necessary to protect network operations. Sustained power failure could not only lead to a network and communications breakdown, including data loss, but also potentially impact community services.

Responding quickly to crisis
Wasting no time, PCCW sent a diesel generator to keep the communication network operational — so promptly and smoothly, in fact, that neither network users nor the community were ever aware of the crisis, despite the fact that the power failure lasted for some 32 hours.

Proudly doing whatever it takes
Emergency situations like this highlight PCCW's commitment to service excellence. To protect business continuity in times of crisis, we have ensured that all PCCW exchanges are equipped with Uninterrupted Power Supply (UPS) and emergency batteries for short-term power failures — as well as generator backup for longer-term situations. It's just one of the ways in which we are working hard to make sure that customers stay connected through bad times and good.

Illustrations indicate seamless network connections to security systems. (a)
Illustrations showing a comprehensive procedure for dealing with power supply failures to ensure network connections. (b)

セキュリティ・システムへの途切れのないネットワーク接続を示す図。(a)
電力供給が遮断されてもネットワーク接続を保証する包括的な手順を説明する図。(b)

China 2004
CD: Eric Chan   AD, D: Francis Lee   DF, S: Eric Chan Design Co., Ltd.   CL: PCCW

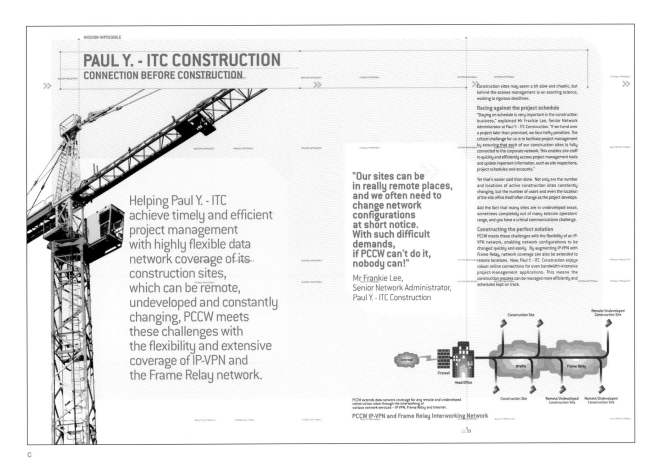

PAUL Y. - ITC CONSTRUCTION
CONNECTION BEFORE CONSTRUCTION

Helping Paul Y. - ITC achieve timely and efficient project management with highly flexible data network coverage of its construction sites, which can be remote, undeveloped and constantly changing, PCCW meets these challenges with the flexibility and extensive coverage of IP-VPN and the Frame Relay network.

"Our sites can be in really remote places, and we often need to change network configurations at short notice. With such difficult demands, if PCCW can't do it, nobody can!"

Mr Frankie Lee,
Senior Network Administrator,
Paul Y. - ITC Construction

Construction sites may seem a bit slow and chaotic, but behind-the-scenes management is an exacting science, working to rigorous deadlines.

Racing against the project schedule
"Staying on schedule is very important in the construction business," explained Mr Frankie Lee, Senior Network Administrator at Paul Y. - ITC Construction. "If we hand over a project later than promised, we face hefty penalties. The critical challenge for us is to facilitate project management by ensuring that each of our construction sites is fully connected to the corporate network. This enables site staff to quickly and efficiently access project management tools and update important information, such as site inspections, project schedules and accounts."

Yet that's easier said than done. Not only are the number and locations of active construction sites constantly changing, but the number of users and even the location of the site office itself often change as the project develops.

Add the fact that many sites are in undeveloped areas, sometimes completely out of many telecom operators' range, and you have a critical communications challenge.

Constructing the perfect solution
PCCW meets these challenges with the flexibility of an IP-VPN network, enabling network configurations to be changed quickly and easily. By augmenting IP-VPN with Frame Relay, network coverage can also be extended to remote locations. Now, Paul Y. - ITC Construction enjoys robust online connections for even bandwidth-intensive project-management applications. This means the construction process can be managed more efficiently and schedules kept on track.

PCCW extends data network coverage for any remote and undeveloped construction sites through the interworking of various network services – IP-VPN, Frame Relay and Internet.

PCCW IP-VPN and Frame Relay Interworking Network

32 33

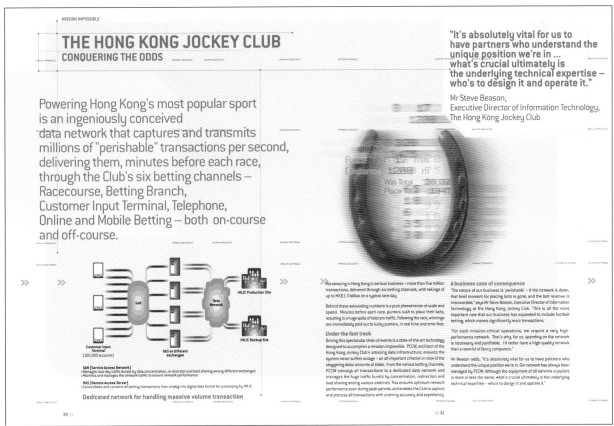

THE HONG KONG JOCKEY CLUB
CONQUERING THE ODDS

Powering Hong Kong's most popular sport is an ingeniously conceived data network that captures and transmits millions of "perishable" transactions per second, delivering them, minutes before each race, through the Club's six betting channels – Racecourse, Betting Branch, Customer Input Terminal, Telephone, Online and Mobile Betting – both on-course and off-course.

"It's absolutely vital for us to have partners who understand the unique position we're in ... what's crucial ultimately is the underlying technical expertise – who's to design it and operate it."

Mr Steve Beason,
Executive Director of Information Technology,
The Hong Kong Jockey Club

Horseracing in Hong Kong is serious business – more than five million transactions, delivered through six betting channels, with takings of up to HK$1.3 billion on a typical race day.

Behind these astounding numbers is a pure phenomenon of scale and speed. Minutes before each race, punters rush to place their bets, resulting in a huge spike of telecom traffic. Following the race, winnings are immediately paid out to lucky punters, in real time and error-free.

Under the fast track
Driving this spectacular chain of events is a state-of-the-art technology designed to accomplish a mission impossible. PCCW, architect of the Hong Kong Jockey Club's amazing data infrastructure, ensures the system never suffers outage – an all-important criterion in view of the staggering dollar amounts at stake. From the various betting channels, PCCW conveys all transactions to a dedicated data network and manages the huge traffic bursts by concentration, redirection and load sharing among various switches. This ensures optimum network performance even during peak periods, and enables the Club to capture and process all transactions with unerring accuracy and expediency.

A business case of consequence
"The nature of our business is 'perishable' – if the network is down, that brief moment for placing bets is gone, and the lost revenue is irrecoverable," says Mr Steve Beason, Executive Director of Information Technology at the Hong Kong Jockey Club. "This is all the more important now that our business has expanded to include football betting, which means significantly more transactions.

"For such mission-critical operations, we require a very high-performance network. That's why, for us, spending on the network is necessary and justifiable. I'd rather have a high-quality network than a roomful of fancy computers."

Mr Beason adds, "It's absolutely vital for us to have partners who understand the unique position we're in. Our network has always been managed by PCCW. Although the equipment of all network suppliers is more or less the same, what's crucial ultimately is the underlying technical expertise – who's to design it and operate it."

SAN (Service Access Network)
- Manages race day traffic bursts by data concentration, re-direction and load sharing among different exchanges
- Monitors and manages the network traffic to ensure network performance

RAS (Remote Access Server)
- Consolidates and converts all betting transactions from analog into digital data format for processing by HKJC

Dedicated network for handling massive volume transaction

Customer Input Terminal (100,000 accounts)

RAS at different exchanges

HKJC Production Site

HKJC Backup Site

SAN

Data Network

30 31

Illustrations explain the construction company's computer network extended to remote locations. (c)
Horseracing is an important business transaction in Hong Kong. Illustrations showing the Hong Kong Jockey Club's data infrastructure. (d)

遠隔地にまでおよぶ建設会社のコンピュータ・ネットワークを説明する図。(c)
競馬は香港で重要なビジネスである。図は香港ジョッキー・クラブのデータ・インフラストラクチャを表している。(d)

図05 ｜ 自動車に使われている高張力鋼板・高強度部材

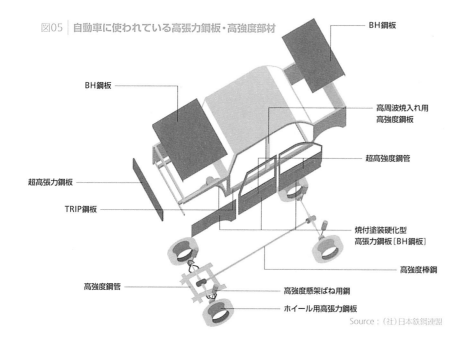

BH鋼板

BH鋼板

高周波焼入れ用
高強度鋼板

超高強度鋼管

超高張力鋼板

TRIP鋼板

焼付塗装硬化型
高張力鋼板［BH鋼板］

高強度棒鋼

高強度鋼管

高強度懸架ばね用鋼

ホイール用高張力鋼板

Source：（社）日本鉄鋼連盟

図06 ｜ 燃料電池の発電原理

Source :日本ガス協会

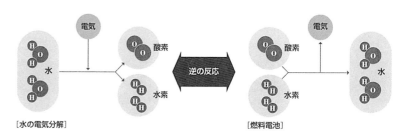

電気

水

酸素

水素

逆の反応

電気

酸素

水素

水

［水の電気分解］

［燃料電池］

図07 ｜ 廃プラスチック再資源化

プラスチックの主成分は石炭と同じ炭素と水素です。そのために石炭の替わりに廃プラスチックを使うことができます。これによって、廃プラスチックは燃料ガスとして活用されたり、新しいプラスチックの原料に生まれ変わります。また、工程の途中で発生する水素ガスは未来のエネルギーとして期待されています。

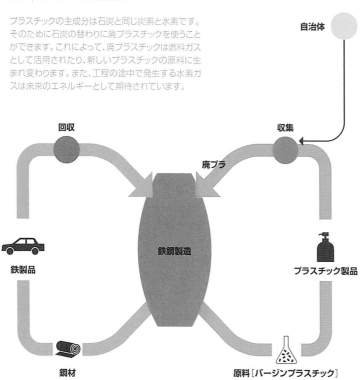

自治体

回収

収集

廃プラ

鉄鋼製造

鉄製品

プラスチック製品

鋼材

原料［バージンプラスチック］

From a pamphlet on global warming.
38 key words defined using easy-to-understand comments and illustrations.

地球温暖化に関するパンフレットより。
38のキーワードを分かりやすい解説と図で説明。

Japan 2004
CD: Reiji Oshima   AD: Kenzo Nakagawa
D: Satoshi Morikami / Infogram   I: Kumiko Nagasaki
CW: Yasuko Seki   DF, S: NDC Graphics Inc.
CL: The Japan Iron and Steel Federation

DocGenerator's automated process

1.

2.

3.

4.

5.

6.

7.

Illustrations showing the process of the web-based solution for automated document management.

自動書類管理のためのウェブ基盤のソリューション・プロセスを説明する図表。

USA 2004
CD: Mark Allen   AD: Nigel Walker   D: Erica Heitman   I: Elan Harris   CW: Tamera Adams   DF, S: That's Nice Llc   CL: Scrittura

Sony style PlayStation, introduced more than a decade ago, has become Sony's all-time bestseller. Airboard, a wireless TV, will roll out in the U.S. this year.

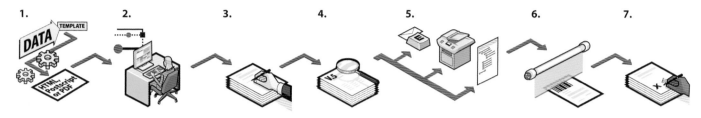

*Purchased for $2 billion. **Purchased for $5 billion. Sources: Bloomberg, Sony

Timeline of Sony's achievements.

ソニーの業績を示す年表。

USA 2004
AD: Carol Macrini   D, I, S: Eliot Bergman   CL: Bloomberg Markets Magazine

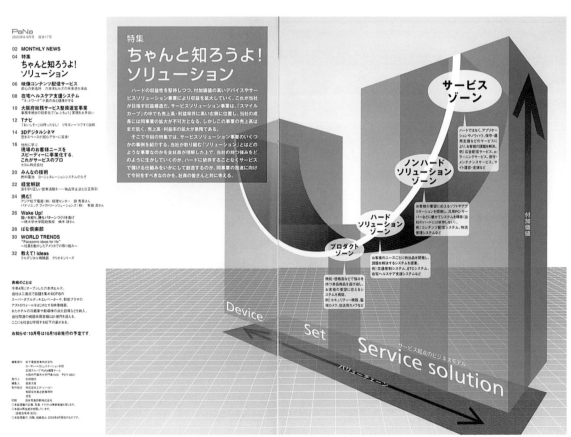

a

b

A chart showing foreign-operations deployment of Matsushita Electric Industrial Co., Ltd. (a)
A chart showing position of the service solution business. (b)

松下電器産業の海外事業展開を表すチャート。(a)
サービスソリューション事業の位置を表すチャート。(b)

Japan 2003
AD: Shinnoske Sugisaki   D: Jun Itadani / Shinsuke Suzuki   DF, S: Shinnoske Inc.   CL: Matsushita Electric Industrial Co., Ltd.

A diagram showing the drug discovery process of
BioNumerik Pharmaceuticals, Inc.

製薬会社、BioNumerik Pharmaceuticals社の創薬プロセスを表す図。

USA 2000
CD, AD, D: Wing Chan   I: Jared Schneidman (JSD)
DF, S: Wing Chan Design, Inc.   CL: BloNumgrik Pharmacauticats, Inc.

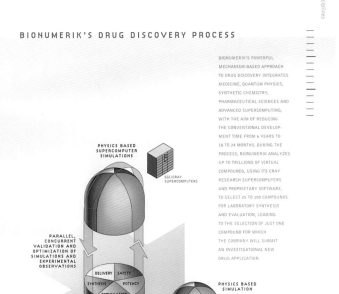

BIONUMERIK'S DRUG DISCOVERY PROCESS

Integrating disciplines

BIONUMERIK'S POWERFUL MECHANISM-BASED APPROACH TO DRUG DISCOVERY INTEGRATES MEDICINE, QUANTUM PHYSICS, SYNTHETIC CHEMISTRY, PHARMACEUTICAL SCIENCES AND ADVANCED SUPERCOMPUTING, WITH THE AIM OF REDUCING THE CONVENTIONAL DEVELOP-MENT TIME FROM 6 YEARS TO 18 TO 24 MONTHS. DURING THE PROCESS, BIONUMERIK ANALYZES UP TO TRILLIONS OF VIRTUAL COMPOUNDS, USING ITS CRAY RESEARCH SUPERCOMPUTERS AND PROPRIETARY SOFTWARE, TO SELECT 25 TO 100 COMPOUNDS FOR LABORATORY SYNTHESIS AND EVALUATION, LEADING TO THE SELECTION OF JUST ONE COMPOUND FOR WHICH THE COMPANY WILL SUBMIT AN INVESTIGATIONAL NEW DRUG APPLICATION.

PHYSICS BASED SUPERCOMPUTER SIMULATIONS

SGI/CRAY SUPERCOMPUTERS

PARALLEL, CONCURRENT VALIDATION AND OPTIMIZATION OF SIMULATIONS AND EXPERIMENTAL OBSERVATIONS

DELIVERY   SAFETY
SYNTHESIS   POTENCY
FORMULATION

LABORATORY VALIDATION

PHYSICS BASED SIMULATION

VALIDATION

EXPERIMENT

BIONUMERIK   5

お客さまの満足度向上と裾野拡大

日立ソフトウェア
エンジニアリング

日本IBM

SAPジャパン

マイクロソフト

日本ヒューレット・
パッカード

ビジネス領域の
拡大

信頼性・生産性の
向上

競争力の強化

a

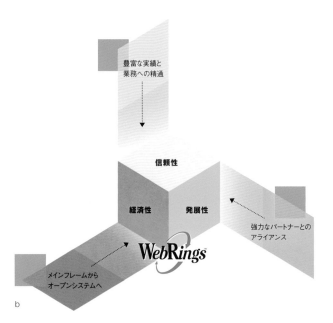

豊富な実績と
業務への精通

信頼性

経済性   発展性

WebRings

強力なパートナーとの
アライアンス

メインフレームから
オープンシステムへ

b

Projected effects of partnerships and alliances with INES. (a)
Three feautures of a software product reflecting the strengths of INES. (b)

アイネス社の提携先とアライアンスによって期待できる効果。(a)
アイネス社の強みが凝縮されたソフトウェア製品の3つの特長。(b)

Japan 2003
Producer: Akiyo Yamamoto   AD: Yukichi Asahara (Asahara Design Company)   D: Yuka suzuki (Asahara Design Company)
DF: Asahara Design Company   CL: INES Corporation   S: Alex-Net Corporation

‹Backup›

GRAPHIC SANDWICH I BY NIGEL HOLMES

Four Flavors of Fast

Cable, DSL, satellite, or wireless. Take your pick of broadband options.

 MAIN PROVIDERS

 MAXIMUM SPEED*
receive ➤ ⬅ send
longer arrow means greater speed

 DOWNLOAD TIME**
for a 25MB file
1 clock = 1 minute

 CONSUMER COST
to install monthly
longer bar means higher cost

 READY NOW?
% of the nation with service available

 SUBSCRIBERS
1 icon = 100,000 people

 BUT...
woes you might want to consider

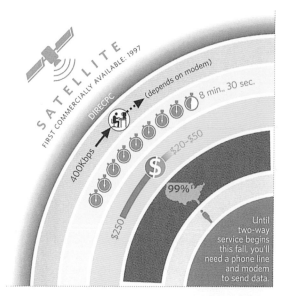

SATELLITE
FIRST COMMERCIALLY AVAILABLE: 1997
DIRECPC
(depends on modem)
400Kbps
8 min., 30 sec.
$20–$50
$250
99%
Until two-way service begins this fall, you'll need a phone line and modem to send data.

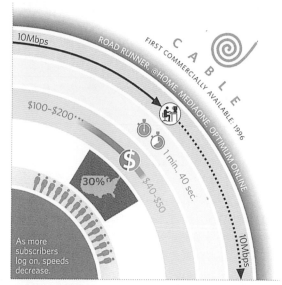

CABLE
FIRST COMMERCIALLY AVAILABLE: 1996
ROAD RUNNER, @HOME, MEDIAONE, OPTIMUM ONLINE
10Mbps
$100–$200**
1 min., 40 sec.
$40–$50
10Mbps
30%
As more subscribers log on, speeds decrease.

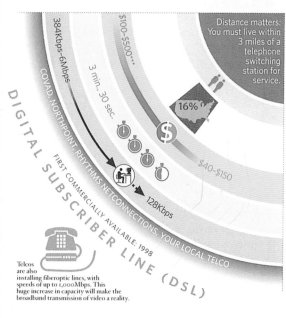

DIGITAL SUBSCRIBER LINE (DSL)
FIRST COMMERCIALLY AVAILABLE: 1998
COVAD, NORTHPOINT, RHYTHMS NETCONNECTIONS, YOUR LOCAL TELCO
384Kbps–6Mbps
$100–$500**
3 min., 30 sec.
$40–$150
128Kbps
16%
Distance matters: You must live within 3 miles of a telephone switching station for service.

Telcos are also installing fiberoptic lines, with speeds of up to 1,000Mbps. This huge increase in capacity will make the broadband transmission of video a reality.

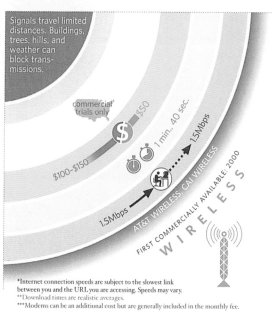

WIRELESS
FIRST COMMERCIALLY AVAILABLE: 2000
AT&T WIRELESS, CAI WIRELESS
1.5Mbps
$100–$150
1 min., 40 sec.
$50
1.5Mbps
commercial trials only
Signals travel limited distances. Buildings, trees, hills, and weather can block transmissions.

*Internet connection speeds are subject to the slowest link between you and the URL you are accessing. Speeds may vary.
**Download times are realistic averages.
***Modems can be an additional cost but are generally included in the monthly fee.

Source: Broadband Intelligence   Reporting by Kathleen Adams

Diagrams explaining 4 broad band options: cable, DSL, Satellite, and wireless.

ケーブル、DSL、衛星、ワイヤレスという、4つのブロードバンドの選択肢を説明する図。

USA   2000
CD: Susan Casey   AD: Susan Scandrett   D, I, CW, S: Nigel Holmes   DF: Explanation Graphics   CL: E-Company

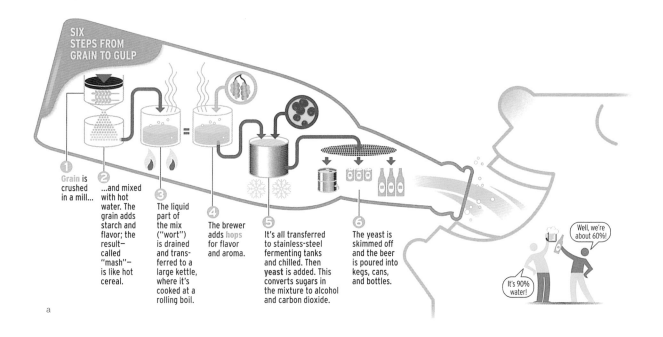

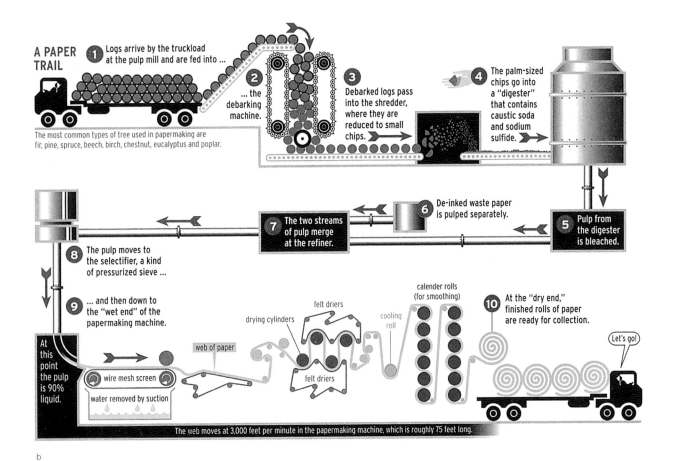

Diagram showing the process of beer making. (a)
The process of paper manufacturing. (b)

ビールの製造過程を図解。 (a)
紙ができるまでの過程を図解。 (b)

USA 2001
AD: Holly Holliday   D, I, S: Nigel Holmes   DF: Explanation Graphics   CL: Attaché Magazine

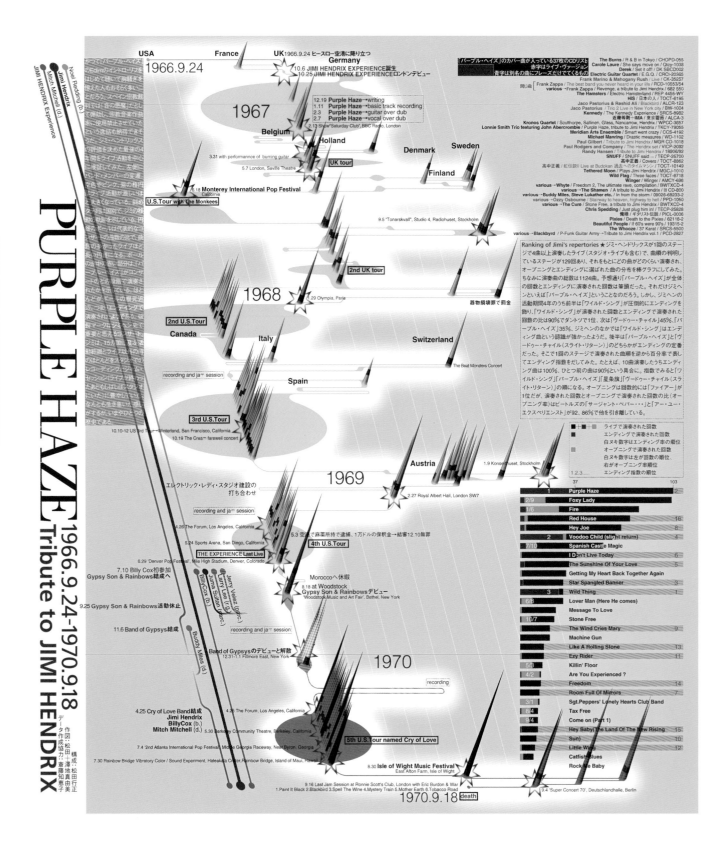

Jimi Hendrix concert history: a tour of Jimi Hendrix concerts centered on the position occupied by "Purple Haze."

ジミ・ヘンドリックス・ライブ史──「パープル・ヘイズ」の占める位置を軸としたジミヘン・コンサートめぐり。

Japan　2000

CD, AD, D, CW, S: Yukimasa Matsuda　I: Mayumi Sawachi　CL: INAX Publishing Co., Ltd.

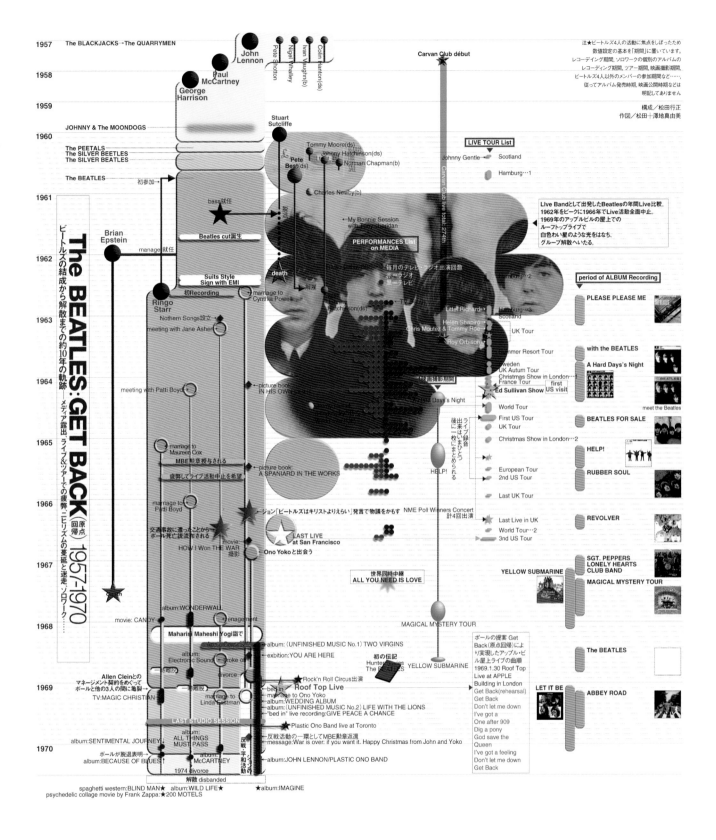

1957　The BLACKJACKS→The QUARRYMEN

John Lennon
Pete Shotton
Nigel Whalley
Ivan Vaughn(b)
Colin Hanton(ds)

Carvan Club début

1958　Paul McCartney

George Harrison

1959

構成／松田行正
作図／松田＋澤地真由美

JOHNNY & The MOONDOGS

Stuart Sutcliffe

1960

The PEETALS
The SILVER BEETLES
The SILVER BEETLES

Tommy Moore(ds)
Johnny Hatchinson(ds)
Norman Chapman(b)

The BEATLES　初参加

Pete Best(ds)

LIVE TOUR List
Johnny Gentle — Scotland
Hamburg…1

1961
bass就任

Charles Newby(b)

Live Bandとして出発したBeatlesの年間Live比較。
1962年をピークに1966年でLive活動全面中止。
1969年のアップルビルの屋上でのルーフトップライブで
白色わい星のような光をはなち、グループ解散へいたる。

Beatles cut誕生
—My Bonnie Session with Tony Sheridan

Brian Epstein

1962　The BEATLES: GET BACK
ビートルズの結成から解散までの約10年の軌跡──メディア露出、ライブ＆ツアーでの疲弊、ニヒリズムの蔓延と迷走、ソロワーク……

manage就任

Suits Style
Sign with EMI

PERFORMANCES List
on MEDIA
毎月のテレビ・ラジオ出演回数
赤─ラジオ
黒─テレビ

period of ALBUM Recording

PLEASE PLEASE ME

death　解雇

Hamburg…2

初Recording
marriage to Cynthia Powell

Ringo Starr

1963　Nothern Songs設立
meeting with Jane Asher

Littel Richard
Helen Shapiro
Chris Moutez & Tommy Roe
Roy Orbison

Hamburg…3
Scotland

UK Tour

with the BEATLES

A Hard Days's Night

1964　meeting with Patti Boyd

picture book:
IN HIS OWN

映画撮影期間

Summer Resort Tour
Sweden
UK Autum Tour
Christmas Show in London…1
France Tour

Ed Sullivan Show　first US visit

BEATLES

1965　marriage to Maureen Cox

MBE勲章授与される

疲弊してライブ活動中止を希望

picture book:
A SPANIARD IN THE WORKS

World Tour
First US Tour
UK Tour
Christmas Show in London…2

meet the Beatles

BEATLES FOR SALE

HELP!

HELP!

European Tour
2nd US Tour

RUBBER SOUL

1966　marriage to Patti Boyd

ション「ビートルズはキリストよりえらい」発言で物議をかもす

交通事故に遭ったことからポール死亡説流布される

LAST LIVE at San Francisco

movie: HOW I WON THE WAR 撮影

Ono Yokoと出会う

NME Poll Winners Concert 計4回出演

Last UK Tour

Last Live in UK
World Tour…2
3nd US Tour

REVOLVER

1967
世界同時中継
ALL YOU NEED IS LOVE

SGT. PEPPERS LONELY HEARTS CLUB BAND

YELLOW SUBMARINE

MAGICAL MYSTERY TOUR

album: WONDERWALL

movie: CANDY

MAGICAL MYSTERY TOUR

1968　Maharisi Maheshi Yogi詣で

album:
Electronic Sound

YOU ARE HERE

broke of

album: (UNFINISHED MUSIC No.1) TWO VIRGINS

exbition: YOU ARE HERE

初の伝記
Hunter Davies
The BEATLES

YELLOW SUBMARINE

The BEATLES

engagement

divorce

Allen Cleinとのマネージメント契約をめぐってポールと他の3人の間に亀裂→

1969　TV: MAGIC CHRISTIAN

marriage to Linda Eastman

bed in
Roof Top Live
marriage to Ono Yoko
album: WEDDING ALBUM
album: (UNFINISHED MUSIC No.2) LIFE WITH THE LIONS
"bed in" live recording: GIVE PEACE A CHANCE

Rock'n Roll Circus出演

ポールの提案 Get Back(原点回帰)により実現したアップル・ビル屋上ライブの曲順
1969.1.30 Roof Top Live at APPLE Building in London
Get Back(rehearsal)
Get Back
Don't let me down
I've got a
One after 909
Dig a pony
God save the Queen
I've got a feeling
Don't let me down
Get Back

LET IT BE

ABBEY ROAD

LAST STUDIO SESSION

Plastic Ono Band live at Toronto

反戦活動の一環としてMBE勲章返還
message: War is over. if you want it. Happy Christmas from John and Yoko

album: SENTIMENTAL JOURNEY

album:
ALL THINGS MUST PASS

1970　ポールが脱退表明
album: BECAUSE OF BLUES！

album: McCARTNEY

album: JOHN LENNON/PLASTIC ONO BAND

1974 divorce

解散 disbanded

spaghetti western: BLIND MAN★　album: WILD LIFE★　★album: IMAGINE
psychedelic collage movie by Frank Zappa: ★200 MOTELS

Beatles history: a roughly ten-year history of The Beatles' live concerts comparing number of concerts per year.

ビートルズ史──年間のライブ数比較を軸に展開するライブバンド・ビートルズの約10年の歴史。

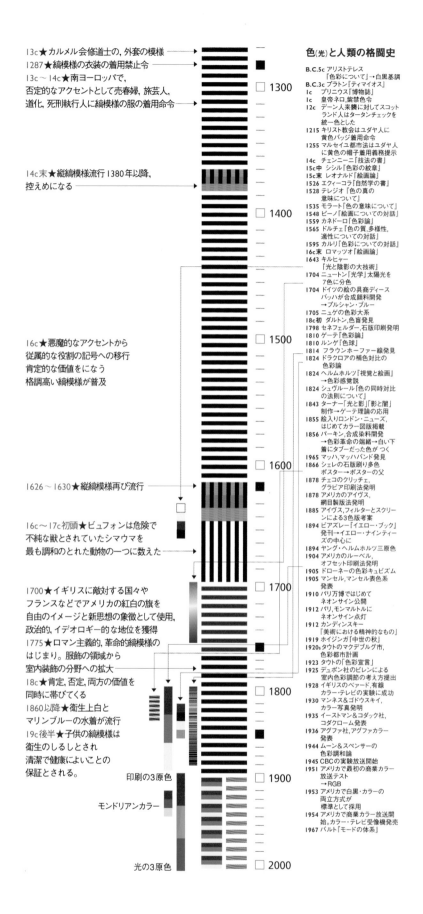

13c★カルメル会修道士の，外套の模様

1287★縞模様の衣装の着用禁止令

13c〜14c★南ヨーロッパで，
否定的なアクセントとして売春婦，旅芸人，
道化，死刑執行人に縞模様の服の着用命令

14c末★縦縞模様流行 1380年以降，
控えめになる

16c★悪魔的なアクセントから
従属的な役割の記号への移行
肯定的な価値をになう
格調高い縞模様が普及

1626〜1630★縦縞模様再び流行

16c〜17c初頃★ビュフォンは危険で
不純な獣とされていたシマウマを
最も調和のとれた動物の一つに数えた

1700★イギリスに敵対する国々や
フランスなどでアメリカの紅白の旗を
自由のイメージと新思想の象徴として使用，
政治的，イデオロギー的な地位を獲得

1775★ロマン主義的，革命的縞模様の
はじまり。服飾の領域から
室内装飾の分野への拡大

18c★肯定，否定，両方の価値を
同時に帯びてくる

1860以降★衛生上白と
マリンブルーの水着が流行

19c後半★子供の縞模様は
衛生のしるしとされ
清潔で健康によいことの
保証とされる。

印刷の3原色

モンドリアンカラー

光の3原色

1300
1400
1500
1600
1700
1800
1900
2000

色(光)と人類の格闘史

B.C.5c アリストテレス
　　　『色彩について』→白黒基調
B.C.3c プラトン『ティマイオス』
1c　　プリニウス『博物誌』
1c　　皇帝ネロ，紫禁色色
12c　 デーン人来襲に対してスコット
　　　ランド人はタータンチェックを
　　　統一色とした
1215　キリスト教会はユダヤ人に
　　　黄色バッジ着用命令
1255　マルセイユ都市法はユダヤ人
　　　に黄色の帽子着用義務提示
14c　 チェンニーニ『技法の書』
15c中 シシル『色彩の紋章』
15c末 レオナルド『絵画論』
1526　エクィーコラ『自然学の書』
1528　テレジオ『色の真の
　　　意味について』
1535　モラート『色の意味について』
1548　ピーノ『絵画についての対話』
1559　カネードロ『色彩論』
1565　ドルチェ『色の質，多様性，
　　　適性についての対話』
1595　カルリ『色彩についての対話』
16c末 ロマッツオ『絵画論』
1643　キルヒャー
　　　『光と陰影の大技術』
1704　ニュートン『光学』太陽光を
　　　7色に分色
1704　ドイツの絵の具商ディース
　　　バッハが合成顔料開発
　　　→プルシャン・ブルー
1705　ニュゲの色彩大系
18c初 ダルトン，色盲発見
1798　セネフェルダー，石版印刷発明
1810　ゲーテ『色彩論』
1810　ルンゲ『色球』
1814　フラウンホーファー線発見
1824　ドラクロアの補色対比の
　　　色彩論
1824　ヘルムホルツ『視覚と絵画』
　　　→色彩感覚説
1824　シュヴルール『色の同時対比
　　　の法則について』
1843　ターナー「光と影」「影と闇」
　　　制作→ゲーテ理論の応用
1855　絵入りロンドン・ニューズ，
　　　はじめてカラー図版掲載
1856　パーキン，合成染料開発
　　　→色彩革命の端緒→白い下
　　　着にタブーだった色がつく
1965　マッハ，マッハバンド発見
1866　シェレの石版刷り多色
　　　ポスター→ポスターの父
1878　チェコのクリッチェ，
　　　グラビア印刷法発明
1878　アメリカのアイヴス，
　　　網目製版法発明
1885　アイヴス，フィルターとスクリー
　　　ンによる3色版発明
1894　ビアズレー『イエロー・
　　　ブック』発刊→イエロー・ナインティー
　　　ズの中心に
1894　ヤング・ヘルムホルツ三原色
1904　アメリカのルーベル，
　　　オフセット印刷法発明
1905　ドローネーの色彩キュビズム
1905　マンセル，マンセル表色系
　　　発表
1910　パリ万博ではじめて
　　　ネオンサイン公開
1912　パリ，モンマルトルに
　　　ネオンサイン点灯
1912　カンディンスキー
　　　『美術における精神的なもの』
1919　ホイジンガ『中世の秋』
1920s タウトのマクデブルグ市，
　　　色彩都市計画
1923　タウトの「色彩宣言」
1925　デュポン社のビレンによる
　　　室内色彩調節の考え方提出
1928　イギリスのベアード，有線
　　　カラー・テレビの実験に成功
1930　マンネス＆ゴドウスキイ，
　　　カラー写真発明
1935　イーストマン＆コダック社，
　　　コダクローム発表
1936　アグファ社，アグファカラー
　　　発表
1944　ムーン＆スペンサーの
　　　色彩調和論
1945　CBCの実験放送開始
1951　アメリカで最初の商業カラー
　　　放送テスト
　　　→RGB
1953　アメリカで白黒・カラーの
　　　両立方式が
　　　標準として採用
1954　アメリカで商業カラー放送開
　　　始。カラー・テレビ受像機発売
1967　バルト『モードの体系』

The history of stripes, from their role as pattern of discrimination to their counteractive role as a symbol of revolution.

差別のための模様から，その反作用としての革命の模様という両極端の使われ方をしたストライプの歴史。

Japan　1999
CD, AD, D, CW, S: Yukimasa Matsuda　I: Mayumi Sawachi　CL: JT Biohistory Research Hall

優生思想史
The history of eugenics

構成・作図：**松田行正**
画像作成：**澤地真由美**

人をランクづける安易な方法は人種であり、知能を含めた障害の有無などである。遺伝子研究の歴史は、それらを加速させたが、現在のDNA論のなかにも差別の予兆がある。「淘汰」に対する「逆淘汰」といういびつな考え――頑健な者は戦争にいって死に、体の弱い者が結果的に生き残って子をなす――も生まれ、20世紀は、優生思想花盛りだった。イギリスで始まった優生学はアメリカで盛り上がり、ドイツがアメリカにならい、日本はドイツにならった。ナチスの優生的暴虐ばかりが語られるが、アメリカが（本人の承諾なしに行う）断種の歴史に果たした役割は大きい。今やインド・中国では普通に断種が行われているという。そこで各国の断種法の歴史を中心に優生思想の発展・変貌を概観してみた。

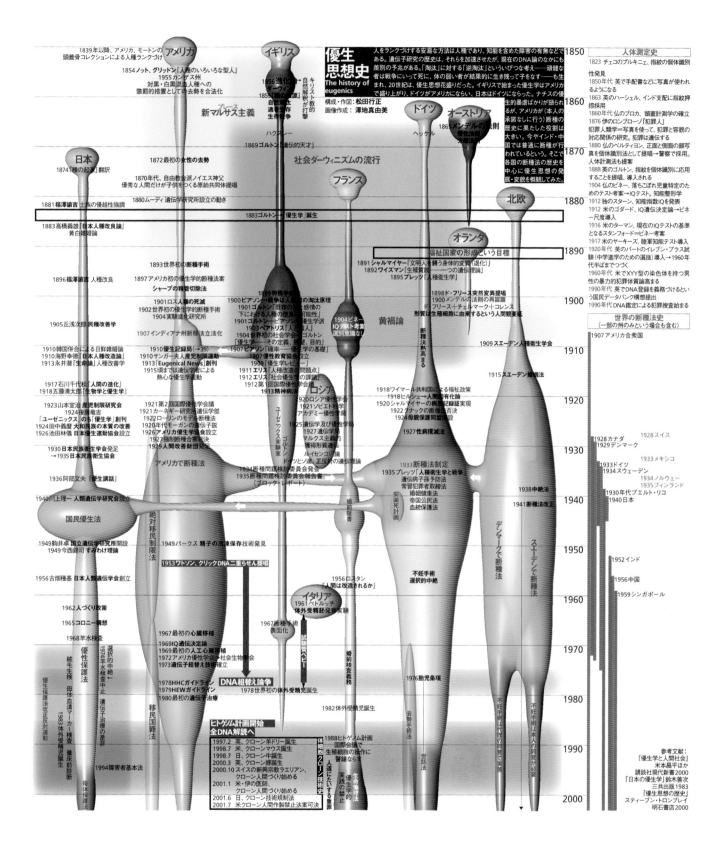

人体測定史
1823 チェコのプルキニェ、指紋の個体識別性発見
1850年代 英で手配書などに写真が使われるようになる
1863 英のハーシェル、インド支配に指紋押捺採用
1860年代 仏のブロカ、頭蓋計測学の確立
1876 伊のロンブローゾ「犯罪人」 犯罪人類学＝写真を使って、犯罪と容貌の対応関係の研究。犯罪は遺伝する
1880 仏のベルティヨン、正面と側面の顔写真を個体識別法として提唱→警察で採用。人体計測法も提案
1888 英のゴルトン、指紋を個体識別法に応用することを提唱、導入される
1904 仏のビネー、落ちこぼれ児童特定のためのテスト考案→IQテスト。知能整形学
1912 独のスターン、知能指数IQを発表
1912 米のゴダード、IQ遺伝決定論→ビネー尺度導入
1916 米のターマン、現在のIQテストの基準となるスタンフォード=ビネー考案
1917 米のヤーキーズ、陸軍知能テスト導入
1920年代 英のバートのイレブン・プラス試験（中学進学のための選抜）導入→1960年代半ばまでつづく
1960年代 米でXYY型の染色体を持つ男性の暴力的犯罪者質論高まる
1990年代 米でDNA登録を義務づけるという国民データバンク構想提出
1990年代 DNA鑑定による犯罪捜査始まる

世界の断種史
（一部の州による場合も含む）
1907 アメリカ合衆国
1928 カナダ
1928 スイス
1929 デンマーク
1933 ドイツ
1933 メキシコ
1934 スウェーデン
1934 ノルウェー
1935 フィンランド
1930年代 プエルト・リコ
1940 日本
1952 インド
1956 中国
1959 シンガポール

参考文献：
『優生学と人間社会』
米本昌平ほか
講談社現代新書2000
『日本の優生学』鈴木善次
三共出版1983
『優生思想の歴史』
スティーブン・トロンブレイ
明石書店2000

Tracing the history of eugenic thought, the most discriminatory ideology of the 20th century, which seeks identity through race and breed.

優生思想史――20世紀最大の差別思想は人種と血にアイデンティティを求めた優生思想。その断種の歴史を追う。

Japan　2001
CD, AD, D, CW, S: Yukimasa Matsuda　I: Mayumi Sawachi　CL: INAX Publishing Co., Ltd.

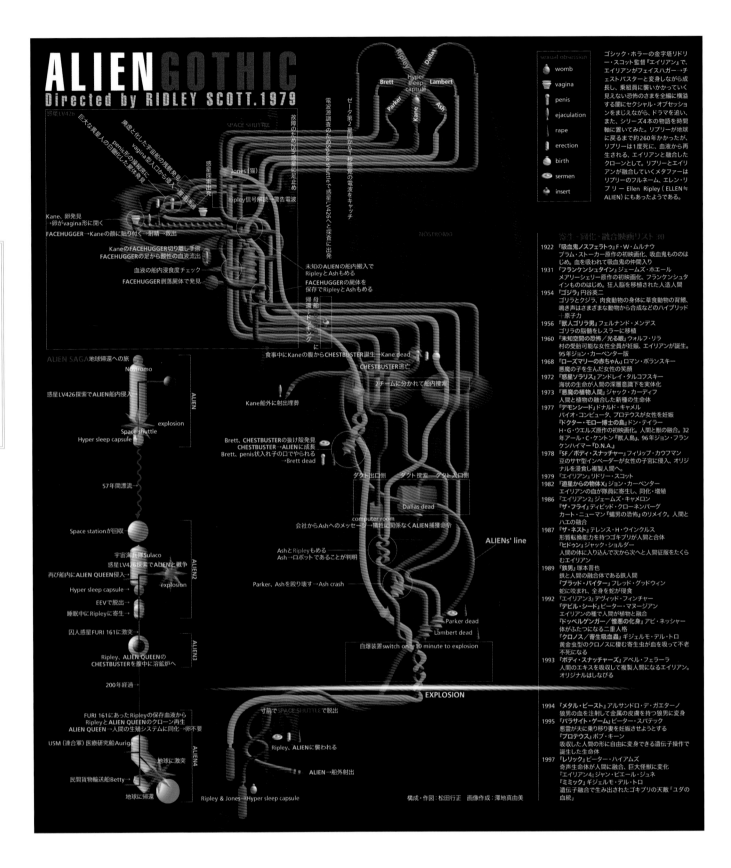

Tracing the lives and deaths of the characters appearing in Ridley Scott's "Alien" centering around Ripley and the aliens.

リドリー・スコット監督の映画『エイリアン』のリプリーとエイリアンを中心とした登場人物の生死の軌跡。

Japan 2002
CD, AD, D, CW, S: Yukimasa Matsuda I: Mayumi Sawachi CL: INAX Publishing Co., Ltd.

1832　ネッカー L.A.Necker の立方体

奥行き反転図形

1895 ティエリー A.Thiéry

ありえない立体図形

1916　デュシャン M.Duchamp
Apolinère enameled
網膜の絵をめざす

1920

bauhaus

surrealism

1930

3柱構造の誕

1934　レウテルシュヴェド
O.Reutersvärd
3柱構造の誕生で
ありえない立体に
たいする関心が高まる

1940　レウテルシュヴェド

1940

1936-1939
アルバース」Albers
→擬空間と呼ばれた奥行き反転図形群
『ストラクチュアの星座』

ヴァザルリ V.Vasarely　網目→構造透けて見えるもの

マグリット R.Magritte　不条理絵画

エッシャーの図形のヒントとなった図形群

1950

シュローダー Schröder の階段

レウテルシュヴェド

ペンローズ

レウテルシュヴェド1950

1955　エッシャー
M.C.Escher
ありえない立体4部作

1955『凹面と凸面』

1958『物見の塔』

1960『上昇と下降』

1961『滝』

1957　エッシャー
『立方体とマジックリボン』

1958　ペンローズの3柱構造
R.Penrose

1960

1964
レウテルシュヴェド
O.Reutersvärd
悪魔のフォーク

1970

エルンスト B.Ernst 1柱構造

1980 ファルカス T.Farcas

1980

1984 クルパ Z.Kulpa 2柱構造

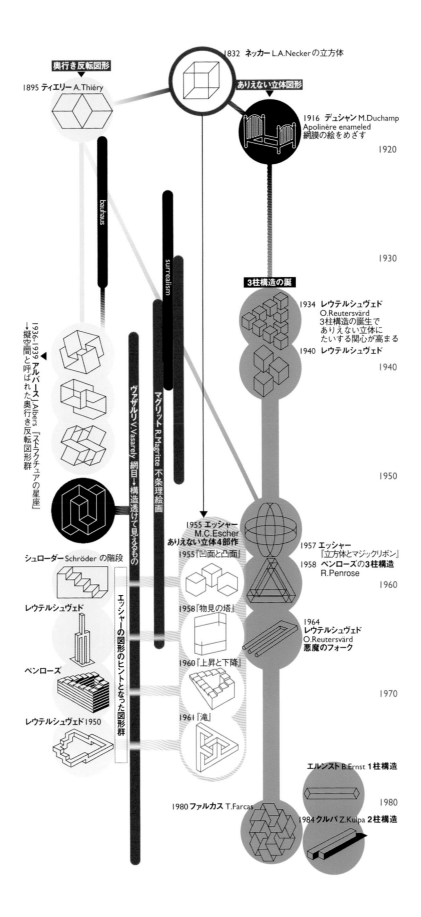

The history of two-dimensional expression of "preposterous 3-D form."

平面図形で表された「ありえない立体」の表現の歴史。

Japan　2000
CD, AD, D, CW, S: Yukimasa Matsuda　I: Mayumi Sawachi　CL: JT Biohistory Research Hall

ORIENTE-SE
UMA COPA EM TRÊS TEMPOS

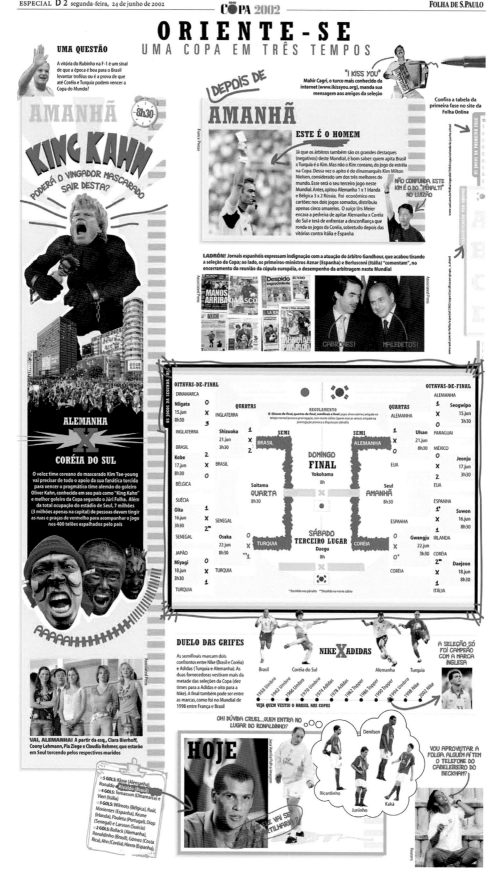

The task was to inform readers about the past, present and future of the world cup, as well as to entertain them.
The red marks and the handwritten letters assumed the role of the readers.

ワールドカップの過去、現在、未来について読者に伝えると同時に、読者を楽しませることが目的。赤いマークや手書きの文字は読者が書いたという想定。

Brazil 2002
CD, S: Eduardo Asta   CW: José Mariante / Luiz Rivoiro / Lúcio Ribeiro / Rodrigo Bertolotto   CL: Folha de São Paulo

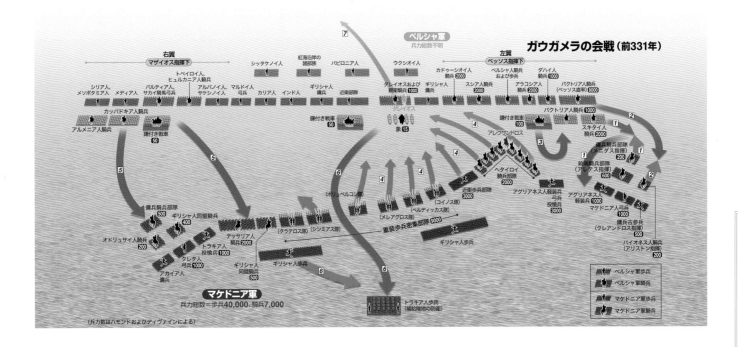

Diagram illustrating the Macedonian victory of over the Persian army in the Battle of Gaugamela.

ガウガメラの会戦におけるペルシャ軍とマケドニア軍の戦いの様子を図解した。

Japan   2003

CD: Hiroyuki Kimura   D: Sachiko Hagiwara   DF, S: Tube Graphics   CL: Japan Broadcast Publishing Co., Ltd.

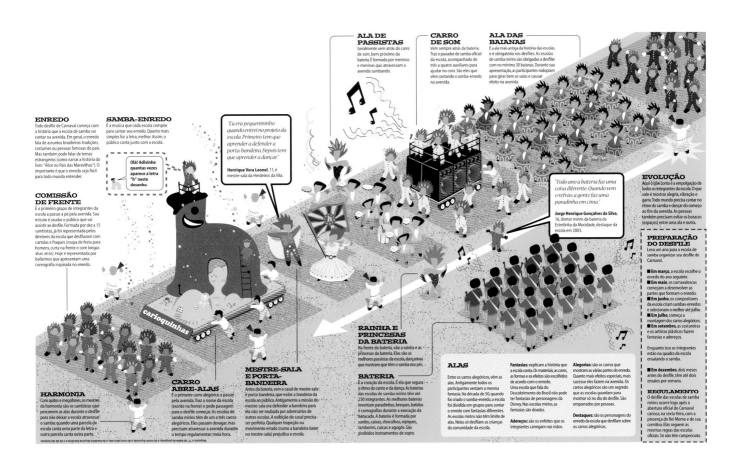

Illustration explains children how a parade of Samba's school is organized. The character "h" on the first car is the mascot of this children's supplement.

サンバのパレードがどのように編成されているのかを子どもに説明するためのイラスト。先頭の車に乗っている「h」の形をしたキャラクターは、この子ども向けの付録のマスコット。

Brazil   2001

CD, S: Eduardo Asta   CL: Folha de São Paulo

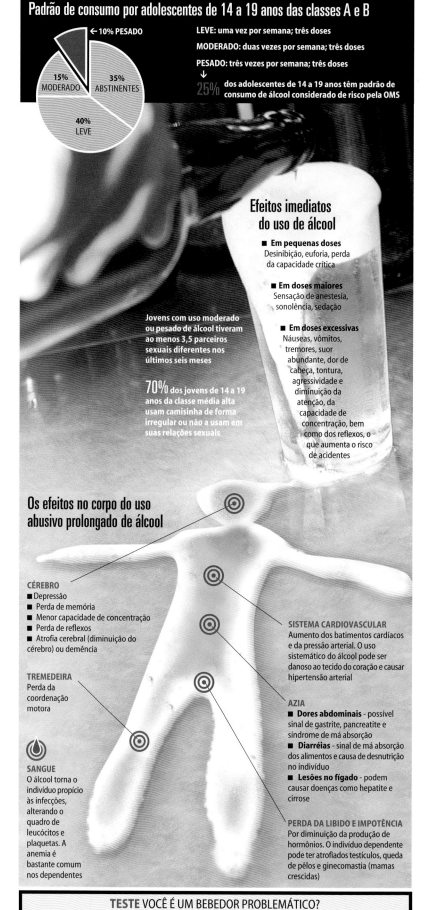

USO DE ÁLCOOL

Padrão de consumo por adolescentes de 14 a 19 anos das classes A e B

← 10% PESADO

15% MODERADO

35% ABSTINENTES

40% LEVE

LEVE: uma vez por semana; três doses

MODERADO: duas vezes por semana; três doses

PESADO: três vezes por semana; três doses

↓

25% dos adolescentes de 14 a 19 anos têm padrão de consumo de álcool considerado de risco pela OMS

Efeitos imediatos do uso de álcool

■ **Em pequenas doses**
Desinibição, euforia, perda da capacidade crítica

■ **Em doses maiores**
Sensação de anestesia, sonolência, sedação

■ **Em doses excessivas**
Náuseas, vômitos, tremores, suor abundante, dor de cabeça, tontura, agressividade e diminuição da atenção, da capacidade de concentração, bem como dos reflexos, o que aumenta o risco de acidentes

Jovens com uso moderado ou pesado de álcool tiveram ao menos 3,5 parceiros sexuais diferentes nos últimos seis meses

70% dos jovens de 14 a 19 anos da classe média alta usam camisinha de forma irregular ou não a usam em suas relações sexuais

Os efeitos no corpo do uso abusivo prolongado de álcool

CÉREBRO
■ Depressão
■ Perda de memória
■ Menor capacidade de concentração
■ Perda de reflexos
■ Atrofia cerebral (diminuição do cérebro) ou demência

TREMEDEIRA
Perda da coordenação motora

SANGUE
O álcool torna o indivíduo propício às infecções, alterando o quadro de leucócitos e plaquetas. A anemia é bastante comum nos dependentes

SISTEMA CARDIOVASCULAR
Aumento dos batimentos cardíacos e da pressão arterial. O uso sistemático do álcool pode ser danoso ao tecido do coração e causar hipertensão arterial

AZIA
■ **Dores abdominais** - possível sinal de gastrite, pancreatite e síndrome de má absorção
■ **Diarréias** - sinal de má absorção dos alimentos e causa de desnutrição no indivíduo
■ **Lesões no fígado** - podem causar doenças como hepatite e cirrose

PERDA DA LIBIDO E IMPOTÊNCIA
Por diminuição da produção de hormônios. O indivíduo dependente pode ter atrofiados testículos, queda de pêlos e ginecomastia (mamas crescidas)

TESTE VOCÊ É UM BEBEDOR PROBLEMÁTICO?

1 Você se sente culpado pela maneira com que costuma beber?
[ ] Sim   [ ] Não

2 Você costuma beber pela manhã para diminuir o nervosismo ou a ressaca?
[ ] Sim   [ ] Não

3 As pessoas o aborrecem porque criticam o seu modo de beber?
[ ] Sim   [ ] Não

4 Alguma vez sentiu que deveria diminuir a quantidade de bebida ou parar de beber?
[ ] Sim   [ ] Não

Resp: se você respondeu positivamente a duas ou mais perguntas, é um provável bebedor problemático e deve procurar auxílio de um especialista para uma avaliação mais profunda
Fonte: Proad (Programa de Orientação e Atendimento de Dependentes)

The graph brings information about the increasing number of teenagers addicted to alcohol and the consequences of the addiction on the body.

増加しつつあるアルコール中毒のティーンエイジャーの人数と、中毒が身体へ及ぼす影響に関する情報を伝える図。

Brazil   2001

CD, S: Eduardo Asta   I: Sandro Falsetti   CL: Folha de São Paulo

A calendar showing all summer events in Salvador, Brazil.

ブラジルのサルバドルで行われる夏のイベントを紹介するカレンダー。

Brazil   2003

D, S: Douglas Okasaki   P: Antônio Saturnino   CW: Roberto Albergaria   CL: A Tarde Newspaper

A chart explains the history of Christmas tree including the origin of its rite and its ornaments.

クリスマス・ツリーを飾る習慣やツリーの飾りなどに関する歴史を説明するチャート。

Germany 2000
CD, D: Jlka Eiche   DF, CL, S: Eiche, Oehjne Design

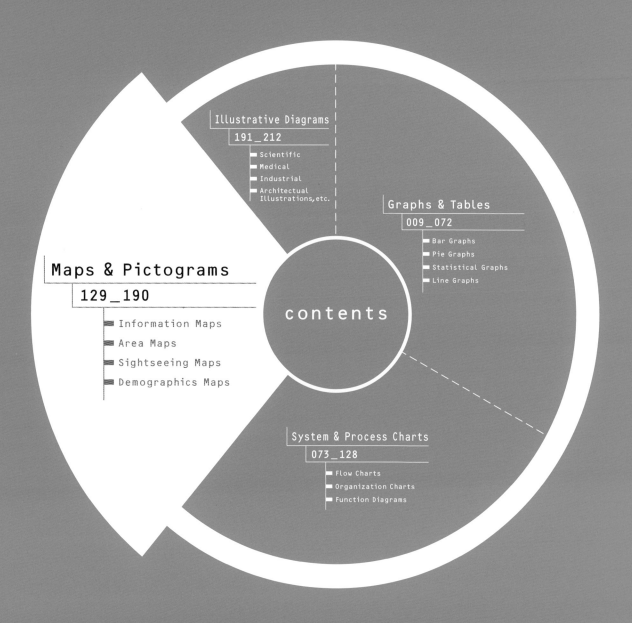

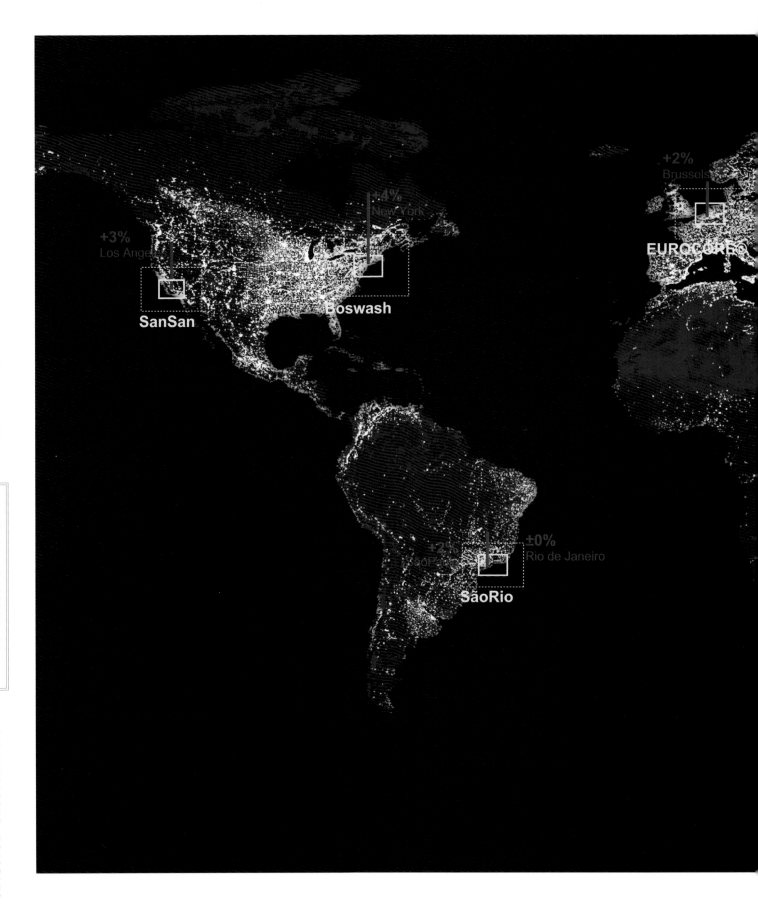

+4%
New York

+3%
Los Angeles

SanSan

Boswash

+2%
Brussels

EUROCORE

+2%
São Paulo

±0%
Rio de Janeiro

SãoRio

A map indicating the world's ten most populous urban cores with annual GDP growth and population density.

世界で最も人口の多い10大都心部を、年間のGDP成長率や人口密度とともに示したマップ。

Netherlands 2002-2003
Material, S: AMO

+12% Tianjin

+11% Beijing

+10% Shanghai

+7% Seoul

+9% Dhaka

+4% Calcutta

+5% Hong Kong

+1% Osaka **+2%** Tokyo

BTT

Sechon

YRD

Tokaido

Ganges Delta

PRD

+1%

annual GDP City growth

50

20

10

million inhabitants

Sources:
United Nations, World Urbanization Prospects 2001
http://www.worldroom.com/pages/cityguides.phtml
http://www.chreod.com/publications/2002022_9582919990908.pdf
http://www.stadtplanung-dr-jansen.de/europlan/europlan/01-12.pdf

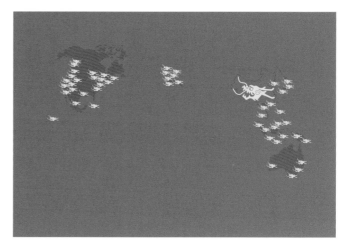

6,702 US military bases located in 41 countries.
41ヵ国に6,702の米軍基地が置かれている。

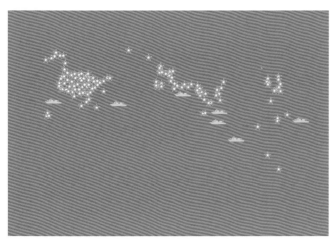

37 Chinatowns in 13 countries.
チャイナタウンは13ヵ国に37ある。

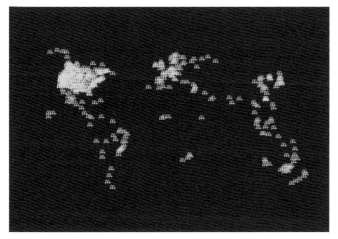

31,295 McDonalds outlets in 119 coutries.
マクドナルドは119ヵ国に31,295店舗ある。

♀ Astronaut
♀ Cosmonaut
♀ Taikonaut

306 astronauts, 124 cosmonauts, and 1 taikonauts in 41 countries.
41ヵ国に、米国の宇宙飛行士は306人、旧ソ連・ロシアの宇宙飛行士は124人、
中国の宇宙飛行士が1人いる。

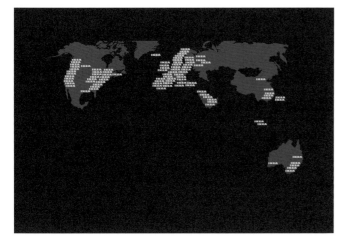

184 IKEA warehouses in 34 countries.
イケアは34ヵ国に184店舗ある。

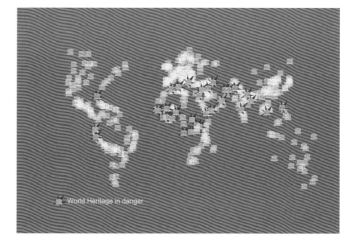

World Heritage in danger

730 World Heritage Sites in 129 countries.
世界遺産に指定された地域は129ヵ国に730カ所ある。

A series of maps illustrating the various forms of globalism.
様々なグローバリズムの形態を示したマップのシリーズ。

Netherlands 2002-2003
Material, S: AMO

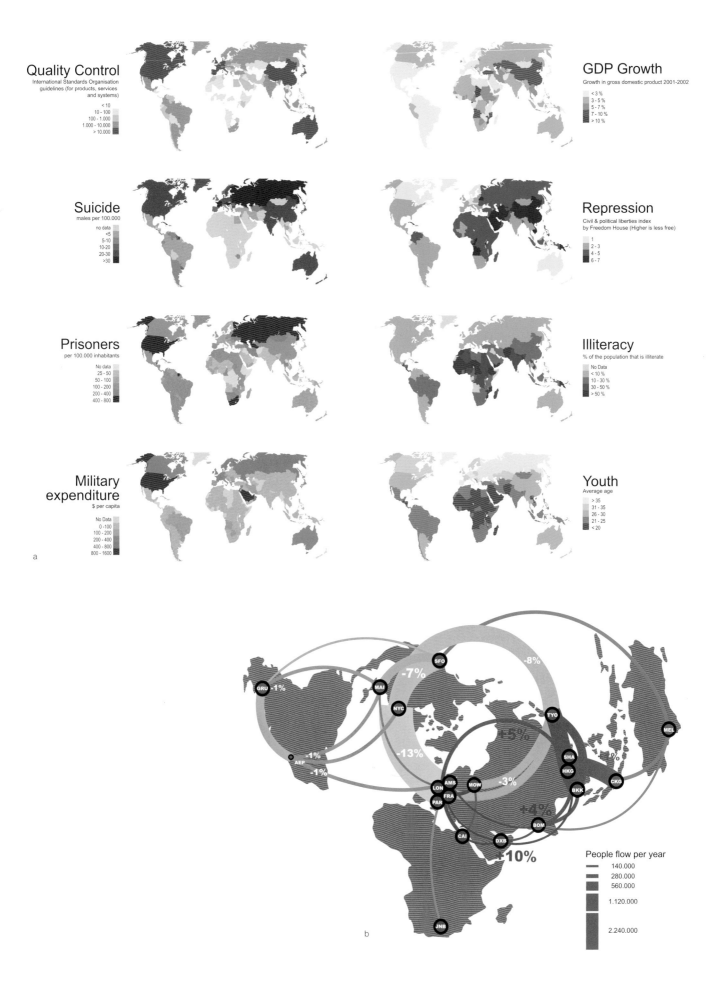

Quality Control

International Standards Organisation
guidelines (for products, services
and systems)

< 10
10 - 100
100 - 1.000
1.000 - 10.000
> 10.000

Suicide

males per 100.000

no data
<5
5-10
10-20
20-30
>30

Prisoners

per 100.000 inhabitants

No Data
25 - 50
50 - 100
100 - 200
200 - 400
400 - 800

Military expenditure

$ per capita

No Data
0 -100
100 - 200
200 - 400
400 - 800
800 - 1600

a

GDP Growth

Growth in gross domestic product 2001-2002

< 3 %
3 - 5 %
5 - 7 %
7 - 10 %
> 10 %

Repression

Civil & political liberties index
by Freedom House (Higher is less free)

1
2 - 3
4 - 5
6 - 7

Illiteracy

% of the population that is illiterate

No data
< 10 %
10 - 30 %
30 - 50 %
> 50 %

Youth

Average age

> 35
31 - 35
26 - 30
21 - 25
< 20

GRU -1%
SFO
-8%
-7%
MAI
NYC
TYO
MEL
-1%
AEP
-5%
-13%
SHA
HKG
-1%
LON AMS MOW -3%
PAR FRA
BKK
CKG
+4%
BOM
CAI DXB
+10%
JNB

People flow per year

140.000
280.000
560.000
1.120.000
2.240.000

b

Color-coded maps illustrating statistics of quality control, suicide, prisoners, military expenditure, GDP growth, repression, illiteracy, and youth. (a)
A map showing changes of passenger air traffic in the world. (b)

品質管理、自殺、囚人、軍事費、GDP成長率、弾圧、非識字率、若者の人口といった統計を示す、色分けされたマップ。 (a)
飛行機の航路別乗客数の増減を示すマップ。 (b)

133

M16
May 16 1998
Geneva WTO Meeting
~ 10.000 people

Geneva

N30
November 30 1999
Seattle WTO Meeting
~ 40.000 people

Seattle

A16
April 16 2000
IMF & World Bank
Meeting Washington DC
~ 50.000 people

Washington DC

J20
July 20-22 2001
G8 Summit,
Genoa, Italy
~ 280.000 people

Genoa

D20
December 20/21 2002
Global Day of Action
for Argentina
~ 500.000 people

Buenos Aires

F15

Global Action Day for Peace
February 15 2003
~ 14.000.000 people

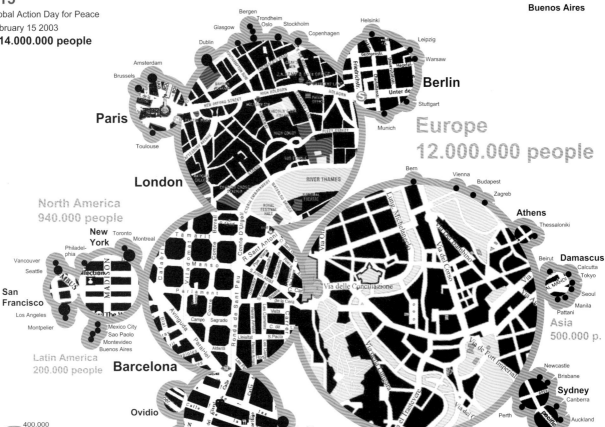

North America
940.000 people

Europe
12.000.000 people

Latin America
200.000 people

Asia
500.000 p.

Africa
30.000 people

Oceania
700.000 people

Paris

London

Berlin

Athens

Damascus

New York

San Francisco

Barcelona

Ovidio

Madrid

Rome

Sydney

Melbourne

400.000
200.000
<50.000 Activists

Showing an increasing number of left-wing activists: on May 16, 1988, 10,000 people demonstrated against WTO (M16),
and on February 15, 2003, several groups orchestrated F15, the first-ever global protest against war in Iraq.

増加する左派の活動家の人数を示す。1988年5月16日、WTOに反対するデモに1万人が参加した (M16)。2003年2月15日、いくつかの団体がF15を組織した。
これはイラク戦争に反対する初の世界規模のデモである。

Netherlands   2002-2003
Material, S: AMO

NORTH AMERICA

EUROPE

ASIA

AFRICA

LATIN AMERICA

AUSTRALIA

Douglas J. Feith
Under Secretary of
Defense for Policy

Richard Perle
Chairman Defence
Policy Board

James G. Roche
Secretary of the
Air Force

Lynne Cheney
Scholar

Dick Cheney
Vice President
USA

David Frum
Speech writer
of G. Bush

Newt Gingrich
ex House Speaker

Mitch Daniels
Director of the Office
of Management
and Budget

John Ashcroft
Attorney General

Canada

Richard Perle
Chairman Defence
Policy Board

Margaret Thatcher
ex Prime Minister
United Kingdom

Antonio Martino
Minister of
Defence Italy

Siim Kallas
Minister of Finance
Estonia

Vaclav Klaus
President of
Czech Republic

Iceland

Ireland

Netherlands   Germany   Denmark

Belg.

Sweden

United
Kingdom

Estonia

France

Lithuania

Belarus   Ukraine

Russia

Spain

Switzer-
land   Italy
Albania

Slov.
Czech

Israel

China

South Korea

Taiwan

India

Hong
Kong

Elaine Chao
Secretary
of Labor

Michael Gerson
Bush's chief
speechwriter

Portugal   Malta

Slova-
kia

Kosovo

Serbia

Hungary

Bulgaria

USA

Greece

Turkey

Ghana

Kenya

Phillipines

Nigeria

Bangladesh   Thailand

Australia

Mexico

South Africa

Lewis Libby
Cheney's Chief
of Staff

William Kristol
Bush Advisor

John Bolton
Under Secr. Arms Control
and Intern. Security

Paul Wolfowitz
Deputy Secretary
of Defense

Ronald Reagan
ex US President

Donald Rumsfeld
Secr. of Defense

Condoleezza Rice
Nat. Sec. Advisor

Haiti   Bahamas

Guate-
mala

El
Salvador
Costa
Rica
Panama

Jamaica

Dominican
Republic

Venezuela

Bolivia

Colombia

Brazil

Ecuador

Paraguay

Peru

New Zealand

John Howard
Prime Minister
Australia

Roger Douglas
ex Minister of Finance
New Zealand

Chile

Uruguay

Argentina

Augusto Pinochet
ex Dictator, Chili

10

1

Think Tanks

Diagrams explaining a network of right-wing think tanks. The neoconservatives are influencing governments in America, Europe, and Asia.

右派のシンクタンクのネットワークを解説するマップ。新保守派はアメリカ大陸、ヨーロッパ、アジアの政府に影響を及ぼしている。

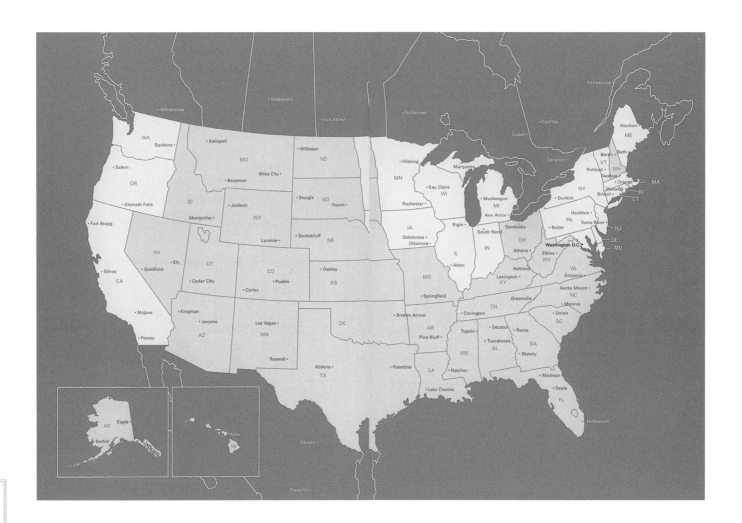

A series of maps from AIGA brochure including a guide showing landmarks in Washington D.C.

AIGAのブローシャーより。ワシントンD.C.のランドマークを示す案内図を含むマップのシリーズ。

USA   2001

CD, AD: Bill Cahan   AD, D: Michael Braley   AD, D, P: Sharrie Brooks   AD, D, P, I, CW: Bob Dinetz   AD, D, P, CW: Kevin Roberson   D, I, CW: Gary William

CW, CL: AIGA   DF, S: Cahan & Associates

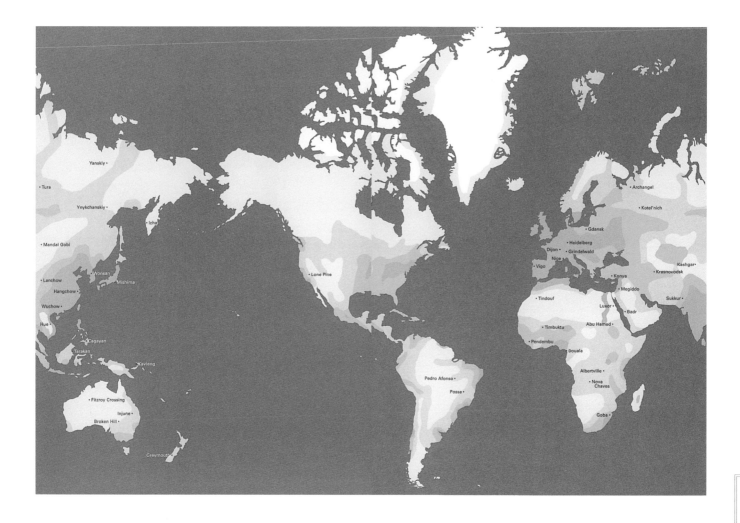

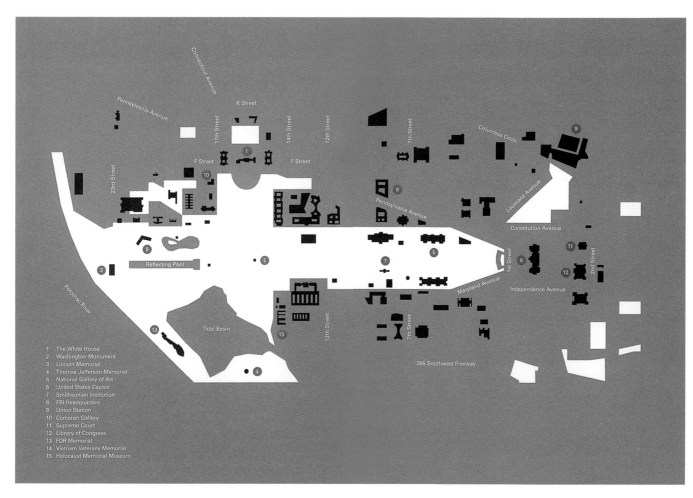

Improved customer service To create efficiencies and enhance our support for customers, we have reorganized the way we do business. Our measures include a rationalization of our companies in 140 countries into 31 market units, each responsible for providing world-class expertise to operators in that area.

We have the same global capability we had before, but it is now delivered through a more efficient and effective network. Our new organization has enabled us to create efficiencies, removing duplication and cutting costs in areas such as offices, human resources and administration. Our market units also enhance the support we can give to our customers. The local expertise we have built up over many years remains in place, and we are continuing to help our customers develop their activities in new areas.

Europe

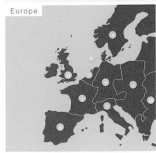

○ Market Unit

World

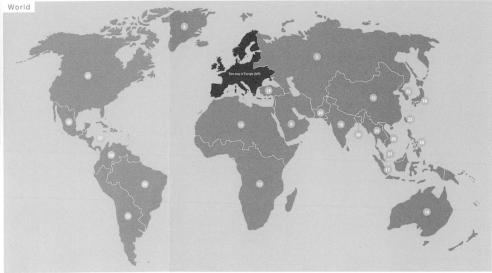

Market Units

Europe, Middle East & Africa

1. **Benelux**
Belgium, Netherlands and Luxemburg

2. **Central Europe**
Bosnia-Herzegovina, Croatia, Czech Republic, Hungary, Poland, Republika Srpska (Serbia), Slovakia and Slovenia

3. **Eastern Europe & Central Asia**
Belarus, Georgia, Kazakhstan, Russia and Ukraine

4. **France**

5. **Germany, Austria, Switzerland & Liechtenstein (DACH)**
Austria, Germany, Liechtenstein and Switzerland

6. **Iberia**
Portugal and Spain

7. **Italy**

8. **Middle East**
Bahrain, Iran, Jordan, Kuwait, Lebanon, Oman, Qatar, Saudi Arabia, Syria and United Arab Emirates

9. **Nordic & Baltic (NOBA)**
Denmark, Estonia, Finland, Iceland, Latvia, Lithuania, Norway and Sweden

10. **Northern Africa**
Algeria, Egypt, Eritrea, Ethiopia, Gambia, Kenya, Libya, Morocco, Sudan and Tunisia

11. **North West Europe**
Ireland and UK

12. **South East Europe**
Bulgaria, Cyprus, Greece, Moldova, and Romania

13. **Southern Africa**
Angola, Botswana, Ghana, Nigeria, South Africa and Zambia

Asia/Pacific

14. **Australia & New Zealand**
Australia, New Zealand and Pacific Islands

15. **China**

16. **India & Sri Lanka**

17. **Indonesia**

18. **Israel & Turkey**

19. **Japan**

20. **Malaysia, Bangladesh, Pakistan and the Philippines**
Bangladesh, Malaysia, Pakistan, Philippines

21. **Singapore**

22. **South Korea**

23. **Taiwan**

24. **Thailand**

25. **Vietnam**

Americas

26. **Brazil**

27. **Central America**
Costa Rica, Cuba, El Salvador, Guatemala, Honduras, Jamaica, Nicaragua, Panama

28. **Latin America – North**
Colombia, Dominican Republic, Netherlands Antilles, Puerto Rico, Trinidad & Tobago and Venezuela

29. **Latin America – South**
Argentina, Bolivia, Chile, Paraguay, Peru and Uruguay

30. **Mexico**

31. **North America**
Canada and US

18 Ericsson 2002 Our Market

Our Market Ericsson 2002 19

Ericsson 2002

**2002 was tough.
Our customers bought less equipment, competition increased, the roll-out of 3G was slow, and the market was hard to predict. Some observers see no end to these difficulties.**

We take a very different view.

ERICSSON ≡

A map illustrating Ericsson's customer services. Their measures include a rationalization of companies in 140 countries into 31 market units, each responsible for providing world-class expertise to operators in that area.

Ericsson社の顧客サービス拠点を表すマップ。企業の合理化を図るため、140カ国にある企業を31の市場ごとに分割し、各地域で国際的レベルの専門知識をオペレーターに提供している。

UK 2002
CD, AD, D, I: Gilmar Wendt   CD: David Stocks   P: Stefan Almers / Alexander Farnsworth / Lee Mawdsley   CW: Tim Rich / Leonard Rau   DF, S: SAS   CL: Ericsson

PROGRESS THROUGH COPPER

KM EUROPA METAL AG
PRODUCTION AND
DISTRIBUTION LOCATIONS

➡

At production and distribution locations in Germany, France, Italy, Spain, United Kingdom and China, the KME Group manufactures products for national and international markets. The KME distribution network ensures a local presence in relevant markets around the world.

LEGEND

● Headquarter | Distribution Location
▲ Distribution Location

PRODUCTION AND DISTRIBUTION LOCATION OF:

◉ ›Brass Rods‹ – Division
◉ ›Tube Systems‹ – Division
● ›Rolled Products‹ – Division
◉ ›Special Products‹ – Division
◉ ›Research and Development Center‹

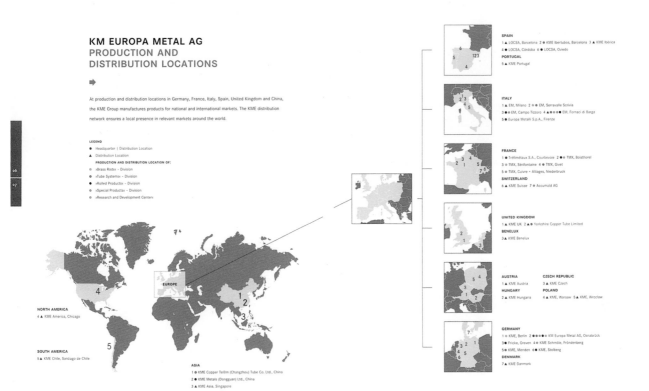

EUROPE

NORTH AMERICA
4 ▲ KME America, Chicago

SOUTH AMERICA
5 ▲ KME Chile, Santiago de Chile

ASIA
1 ● KME Copper Tellm (Changzhou) Tube Co. Ltd., China
2 ● KME Metals (Dongguan) Ltd., China
3 ▲ KME Asia, Singapore

SPAIN
1 ▲ LOCSA, Barcelona 2 ◉ ● KME Ibertubos, Barcelona 3 ▲ KME Ibérica
4 ● LOCSA, Córdoba 6 ● LOCSA, Oviedo
PORTUGAL
5 ▲ KME Portugal

ITALY
1 ▲ EM, Milano 2 ◉ ● EM, Serravalle Scrivia
3 ● ● EM, Campo Tizzoro 4 ▲ ● ◉ ● EM, Fornaci di Barga
5 ● Europa Metalli S.p.A., Firenze

FRANCE
1 ● Tréfimétaux S.A., Courbevoie 2 ◉ ● TMX, Boisthorel
3 ● TMX, Sérifontaine 4 ● TMX, Givet
5 ● TMX, Cuivre + Alliages, Niederbruck
SWITZERLAND
6 ▲ KME Suisse 7 ◉ Accumold AG

UNITED KINGDOM
1 ▲ KME UK 2 ▲ ● Yorkshire Copper Tube Limited
BENELUX
3 ▲ KME Benelux

AUSTRIA   CZECH REPUBLIC
1 ▲ KME Austria   3 ▲ KME Czech
HUNGARY   POLAND
2 ▲ KME Hungaria   4 ▲ KME, Warsaw 5 ▲ KME, Wrocław

GERMANY
1 ● KME, Berlin 2 ◉ ● ◉ ● KM Europa Metal AG, Osnabrück
3 ● Fricke, Greven 4 ● KME Schmöle, Fröndenberg
5 ● KME, Menden 6 ● KME, Stolberg
DENMARK
7 ▲ KME Danmark

KME

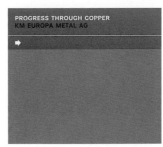

PROGRESS THROUGH COPPER
KM EUROPA METAL AG

➡

SM Group

From a corporate brochure of KME Group, a world's largest manufacturers of copper and copper alloy products. Maps showing their production and distribution locations.
世界最大の銅や銅合金製品のメーカーであるKMEグループの会社案内より。同社の製造や販売部門の場所を示すマップ。

Germany   2003
AD, D: Bernd Vollmöller   CW: Franziska Schlingmann   DF, S: Simon & Goetz Design   CL: KM Europa Metal AG

De File Top-Tien
Files worden door Verkeer en
Waterstaat berekend aan de hand
van drie aspecten: het aantal files, de
lengte in kilometers en de duur in
minuten. De filezwaarte van een file is
de lengte vermenigvuldigd met de
duur van een file. Op die manier telt
bijvoorbeeld een file van 5 kilometer
die 20 minuten duurt even zwaar
mee als een file van 2,5 kilometer die
40 minuten duurt (beide files hebben
een filezwaarte van 100 kilometer).
Er is sprake van een file wanneer er
langzamer gereden wordt dan 50
kilometer per uur en de lengte langer
is dan twee kilometer.
(Uit: *Management Team* 08.03.)

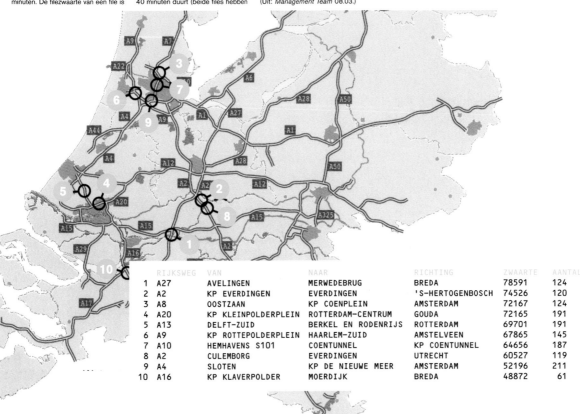

	RIJKSWEG	VAN	NAAR	RICHTING	ZWAARTE	AANTAL
1	A27	AVELINGEN	MERWEDEBRUG	BREDA	78591	124
2	A2	KP EVERDINGEN	EVERDINGEN	'S-HERTOGENBOSCH	74526	120
3	A8	OOSTZAAN	KP COENPLEIN	AMSTERDAM	72167	124
4	A20	KP KLEINPOLDERPLEIN	ROTTERDAM-CENTRUM	GOUDA	72165	191
5	A13	DELFT-ZUID	BERKEL EN RODENRIJS	ROTTERDAM	69701	191
6	A9	KP ROTTEPOLDERPLEIN	HAARLEM-ZUID	AMSTELVEEN	67865	145
7	A10	HEMHAVENS S101	COENTUNNEL	KP COENTUNNEL	64656	187
8	A2	CULEMBORG	EVERDINGEN	UTRECHT	60527	119
9	A4	SLOTEN	KP DE NIEUWE MEER	AMSTERDAM	52196	211
10	A16	KP KLAVERPOLDER	MOERDIJK	BREDA	48872	61

Map showing the top ten traffic jams in the Netherlands.

オランダ国内の交通渋滞のベストテンを示すマップ。

Netherlands 2003
CD, AD: André Toet   CD: Jan Sevenster   D: Bas Meulendijks   CW: Paul Van Koningsbruggen   DF, S: Samenwerkende Ontwerpers   CL: Grafische Cultuurstichting

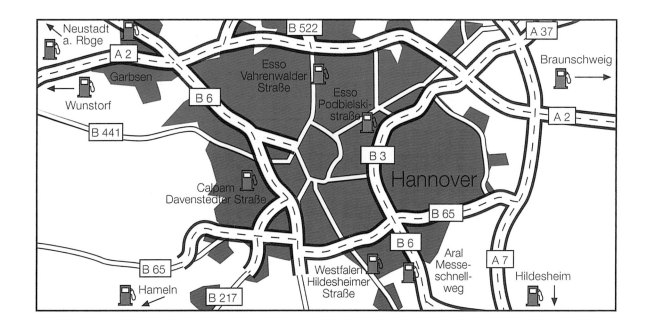

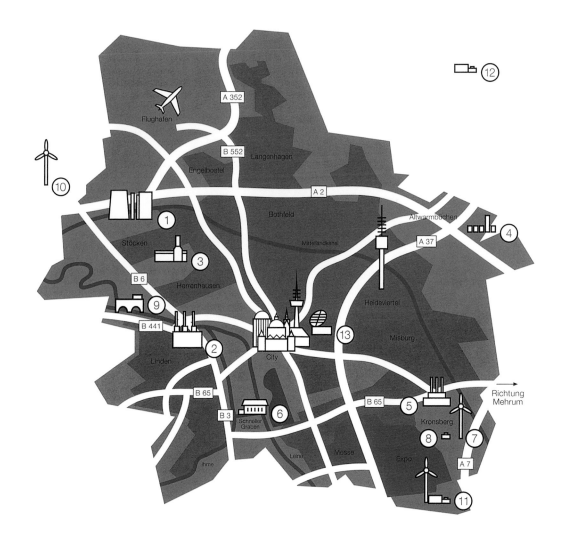

From a corporate brochure of a power company. Maps showing the locations of power plants, manufacturing plants, gas stations, and so on.

電力会社の会社案内より。発電所や製造工場、ガソリンスタンドなどの位置を示すマップ。

Germany 2003
CL, S: Stadtwerke Hannover AG

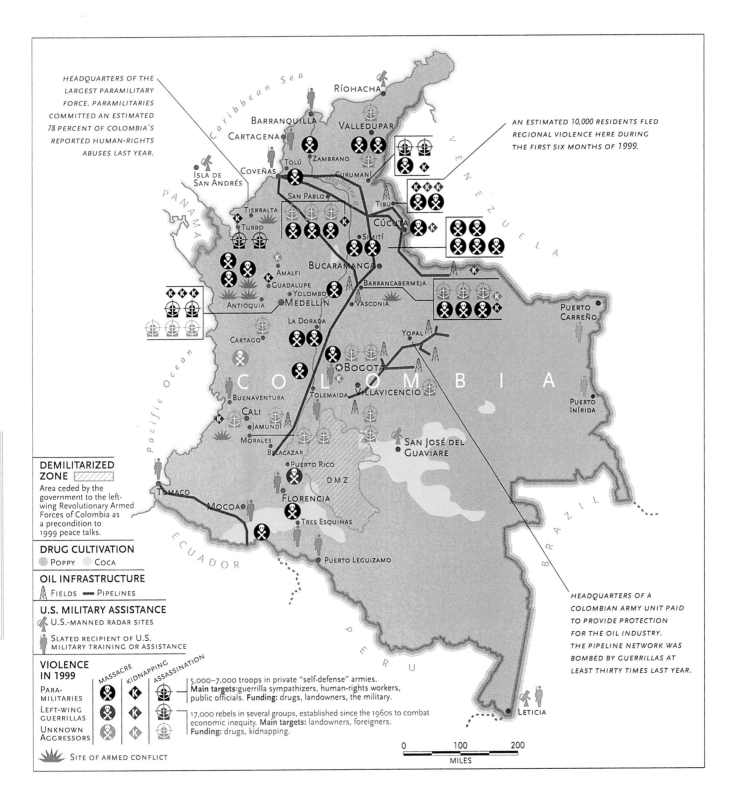

HEADQUARTERS OF THE LARGEST PARAMILITARY FORCE. PARAMILITARIES COMMITTED AN ESTIMATED 78 PERCENT OF COLOMBIA'S REPORTED HUMAN-RIGHTS ABUSES LAST YEAR.

AN ESTIMATED 10,000 RESIDENTS FLED REGIONAL VIOLENCE HERE DURING THE FIRST SIX MONTHS OF 1999.

HEADQUARTERS OF A COLOMBIAN ARMY UNIT PAID TO PROVIDE PROTECTION FOR THE OIL INDUSTRY. THE PIPELINE NETWORK WAS BOMBED BY GUERRILLAS AT LEAST THIRTY TIMES LAST YEAR.

DEMILITARIZED ZONE [////]
Area ceded by the government to the left-wing Revolutionary Armed Forces of Colombia as a precondition to 1999 peace talks.

DRUG CULTIVATION
Poppy   Coca

OIL INFRASTRUCTURE
Fields   Pipelines

U.S. MILITARY ASSISTANCE
U.S.-MANNED RADAR SITES
SLATED RECIPIENT OF U.S. MILITARY TRAINING OR ASSISTANCE

VIOLENCE IN 1999
	MASSACRE	KIDNAPPING	ASSASSINATION
PARA-MILITARIES			
LEFT-WING GUERRILLAS			
UNKNOWN AGGRESSORS			

5,000–7,000 troops in private "self-defense" armies. **Main targets:** guerrilla sympathizers, human-rights workers, public officials. **Funding:** drugs, landowners, the military.

17,000 rebels in several groups, established since the 1960s to combat economic inequity. **Main targets:** landowners, foreigners, **Funding:** drugs, kidnapping.

SITE OF ARMED CONFLICT

0   100   200
MILES

A map of Colombia showing drug-related activity.

麻薬関連の活動を示すコロンビアのマップ。

USA   2000
AD: Angela Riechers   D, I, S: Nigel Holmes   DF: Explanation Graphics   CL: Harper's

WHICH CAME FIRST, THE CHICKEN OR THE TOWN?

Some people liked animals so much, they named their whole town after them. Here are some beastly examples.

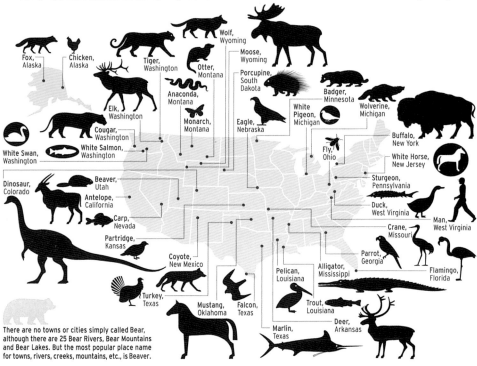

Fox, Alaska
Chicken, Alaska
Tiger, Washington
Wolf, Wyoming
Moose, Wyoming
Otter, Montana
Porcupine, South Dakota
Badger, Minnesota
Elk, Washington
Anaconda, Montana
White Pigeon, Michigan
Wolverine, Michigan
Cougar, Washington
Monarch, Montana
Eagle, Nebraska
Buffalo, New York
White Swan, Washington
White Salmon, Washington
Fly, Ohio
White Horse, New Jersey
Dinosaur, Colorado
Beaver, Utah
Sturgeon, Pennsylvania
Antelope, California
Duck, West Virginia
Man, West Virginia
Carp, Nevada
Crane, Missouri
Partridge, Kansas
Parrot, Georgia
Coyote, New Mexico
Alligator, Mississippi
Flamingo, Florida
Pelican, Louisiana
Turkey, Texas
Trout, Louisiana
Mustang, Oklahoma
Falcon, Texas
Deer, Arkansas
Marlin, Texas

There are no towns or cities simply called Bear, although there are 25 Bear Rivers, Bear Mountains and Bear Lakes. But the most popular place name for towns, rivers, creeks, mountains, etc., is Beaver.

a

HEY! WHAT PLANET ARE YOU FROM?

These days you can hop in your car and drive to the next planet. Oh, OK, it *is* just the next town, but we bet you never thought the United States had so many places named for otherworldly locales. We sure didn't.

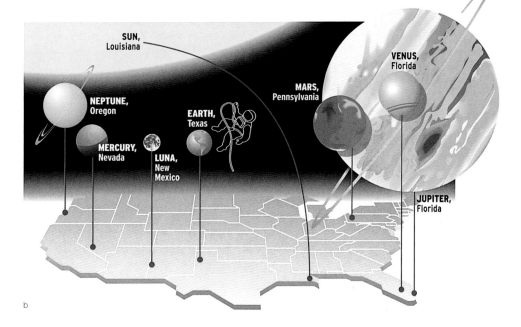

SUN, Louisiana
NEPTUNE, Oregon
VENUS, Florida
MARS, Pennsylvania
EARTH, Texas
MERCURY, Nevada
LUNA, New Mexico
JUPITER, Florida

b

A map of America with cities that are named after animals. (a)
A map of America with cities that are named after planets. (b)

動物にちなんで名付けられたアメリカの町を示すマップ。 (a)
惑星にちなんで名付けられたアメリカの町を示すマップ。 (b)

USA   2000 (a) / 2001 (b)
AD: Kevin De Miranda   D, I, S: Nigel Holmes   DF: Explanation Graphics   CL: Navigator Magazine

BEYOND COLUMBINE

Despite the outcry over the multiple killings at schools in Kentucky, Arkansas, Oregon, and Colorado in the last two years, these incidents represent less than half of all violent school deaths during that period. Although the annual number of fatalities—on campus, at off-campus school events, and in transit to and from school—has dropped since the early Nineties, the portion involving guns has remained fairly steady. At the same time, the incidence of suicide has increased by a third. Girls, who once accounted for 5 percent of murder victims, now account for 27 percent. In the 1992–93 school year, nearly one in two of all school deaths took place in California, Texas, or New York; last year one in six did.

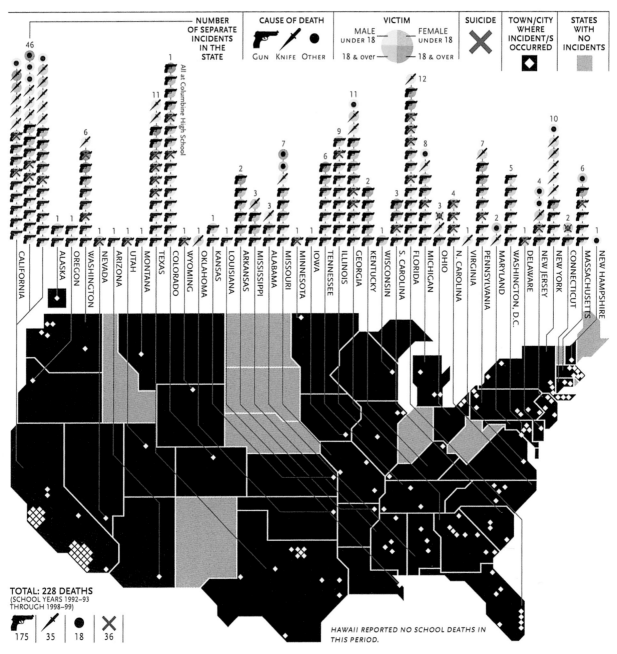

TOTAL: 228 DEATHS
(SCHOOL YEARS 1992–93
THROUGH 1998–99)

175 | 35 | 18 | 36

HAWAII REPORTED NO SCHOOL DEATHS IN THIS PERIOD.

Map by Nigel Holmes, based on information from the National School Safety Center

A map of America showing killings at schools around the country.

アメリカ国内の学校で起きた殺人についての様々なデータを示すマップ。

USA 1999
AD: Angela Riechers   D, I, S: Nigel Holmes   DF: Explanation Graphics   CL: Harper's

A SLICE OF AMERICA (OR FIVE)

The continental United States is a diverse place. One interesting perspective is to slice it horizontally and highlight some of the flora and elevations. Sort of makes you wish you hadn't skipped geography class, doesn't it?

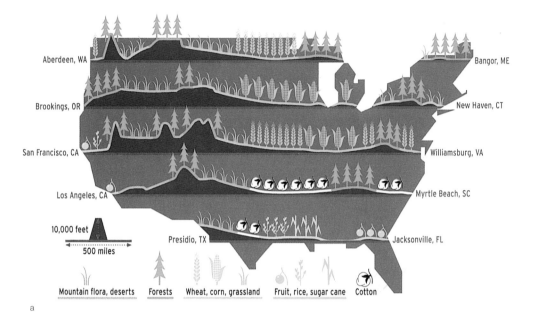

Aberdeen, WA

Bangor, ME

Brookings, OR

New Haven, CT

San Francisco, CA

Williamsburg, VA

Los Angeles, CA

Myrtle Beach, SC

10,000 feet

Presidio, TX

Jacksonville, FL

500 miles

Mountain flora, deserts | Forests | Wheat, corn, grassland | Fruit, rice, sugar cane | Cotton

a

FOODLAND

It's hard to imagine living in Sandwich, Massachusetts, without feeling hungry a lot. What if you lived in Mango, Florida, or Peanut, California, or (slurp) Napoleon, North Dakota? The USA is stuffed with towns that have mouth-watering names.

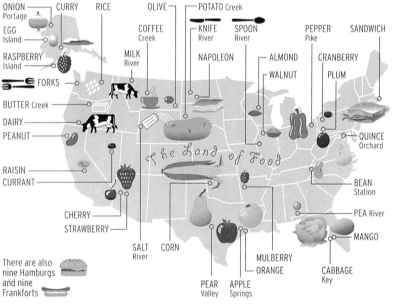

ONION Portage — CURRY — RICE — OLIVE — POTATO Creek — PEPPER Pike — SANDWICH
EGG Island — COFFEE Creek — KNIFE River — SPOON River — CRANBERRY
RASPBERRY Island — MILK River — NAPOLEON — ALMOND — PLUM
FORKS — WALNUT
BUTTER Creek
DAIRY — QUINCE Orchard
PEANUT
RAISIN — BEAN Station
CURRANT — PEA River
— MANGO
CHERRY — SALT River — CORN — MULBERRY — CABBAGE Key
STRAWBERRY — ORANGE

There are also nine Hamburgs and nine Frankforts

PEAR Valley APPLE Springs

The Land of Food

SOURCE: NATIONAL GEOGRAPHIC ATLAS

b

A map of America showing slices of across the nation with elevations and flora. (a)
A map of America with cities named after food items. (b)

アメリカ全土の標高と植物層を示す断面図。 (a)
食物の名前にちなんで名付けられたアメリカの町を示すマップ。 (b)

USA 2002 (a) / 1999 (b)
AD: Kevin De Miranda   D, I, S: Nigel Holmes   DF: Explanation Graphics   CL: Navigator Magazine

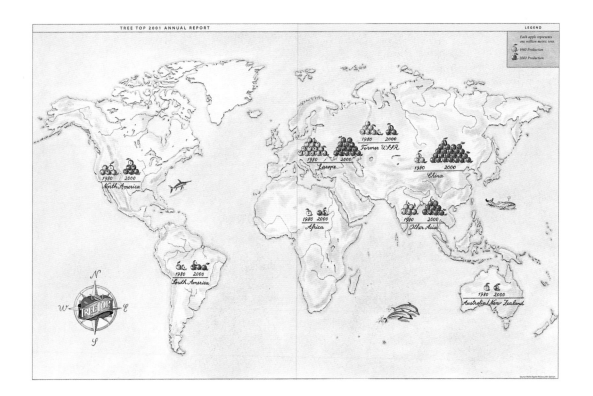

A map illustrating the production of apples both in 1980 and 2000.

1980年および2000年のリンゴの生産量を示すマップ。

USA 2001
AD, D: Katha Dalton D: Jana Nishi / Michael Brugman I: Rodica Prato CW: Evelyne Rozner
DF, S: Hornall Anderson Design Works, Inc. CL: Tree Top

A world map formed by 'cells' inside a petri dish illustrates the growing importance of genomics in animal health and breeding programmes globally.

ペトリ皿の中の細胞が形づくる世界地図は、動物の健康や世界的な繁殖プログラムにおけるゲノミクスの重要性を表している。

UK 2001
CD: Tor Pettersen AD: David Brown D, CW: Jim Allsopp DF, S: Tor Pettersen & Partners CL: Sygen International

Dat Bavaria ontzettend populair is in Brabant,
dat wist u waarschijnlijk wel. Maar dat deze familie-
brouwerij uit Lieshout net zo succesvol wil worden
in de rest van Nederland, dat wist u waarschijnlijk
nog niet. Samen met een team van Brabantse
ambassadeurs, starten we vandaag een belangrijke
missie: Bavaria gaat Nederland veroveren. Het bier
is namelijk veel te lekker om voor ons zelf te houden.
We rekenen op uw medewerking!

Zo Nederland,
nu eerst een Bavaria.

Graphic showing the success of Dutch beer named Bavaria.

オランダ国内におけるBavariaというオランダ・ビールの成功を示すマップ。

Neterlands   2004
CD, AD: Erik Kessels   D: Design Politie   DF, S: Kesselskramer   CL: Bavaria

6217 B.C.

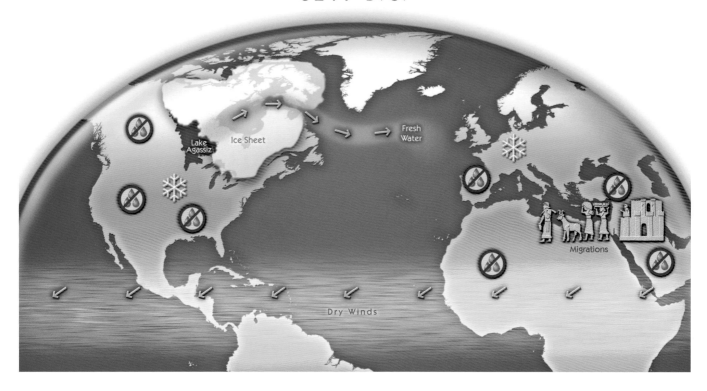

Illustration showing the impact of a global warming event in 6217 B.C. on climate, wind direction, and human migration.

紀元前6217年の地球規模の温暖化が気候や風向き、人間の移動などに与えた影響を示すイラスト。

USA 2004
CD: Blaize Mekinna   AD: Blaize Mekinna   D, I: Tracy Sabin   DF, S: Sabingrafik, Incorporated   CL: Scripps Institute of Oceanography

Map showing the distance between Shanghai and its neighboring cities, with die-cutting and silver stamping spots printed on double-folded tracing paper. From an information brochure of Expo 2010.

上海と周辺都市との距離を示すマップ。
型抜きを使用し、トレーシングペーパーに印刷した
銀の箔押しの点が見えるようにした。
2010年のエキスポのインフォメーション・ブローシャーより。

China 2002
CD, AD, D: Hon Bing-Wah   DF, S: HS Art & Design
CL: EXPO 2010 Shanghai Bidding China Office

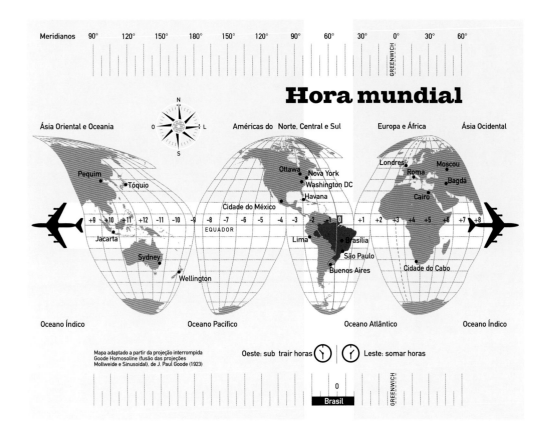

A map designed for Brazilian travellers. The task was to create a time zone chart with Brazil in the center.

ブラジル人の旅行者のためにデザインされたマップ。ブラジルを中央に配置した標準時間図を作成することが目的。

Brazil   2003
AD: Vincenzo Scarpelini   D, S: Eduardo Asta   CL: Infraero

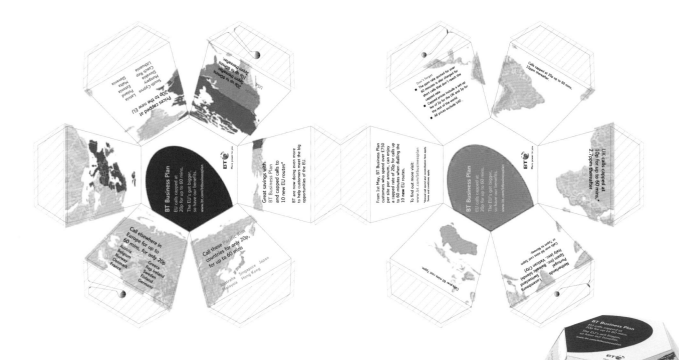

A three-dimensional piece of collateral illustrating telephone rate for around the world.

世界各国への国際電話料金を示した立体的な販促グッズ。

UK   2004
CD: Geoff Aldridge   D: Sarah Mckewan   DF, S: Communication by Design   CL: BT

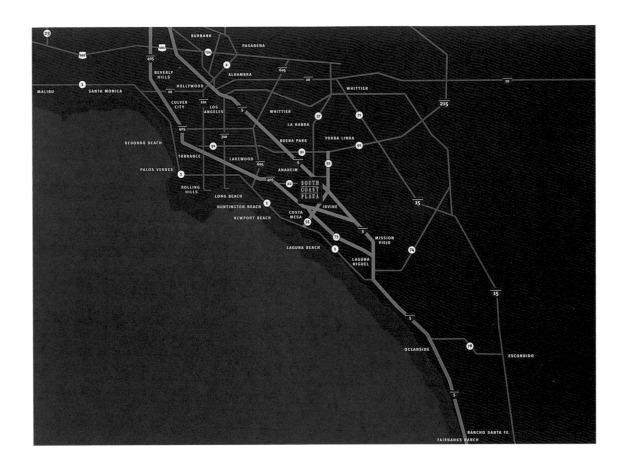

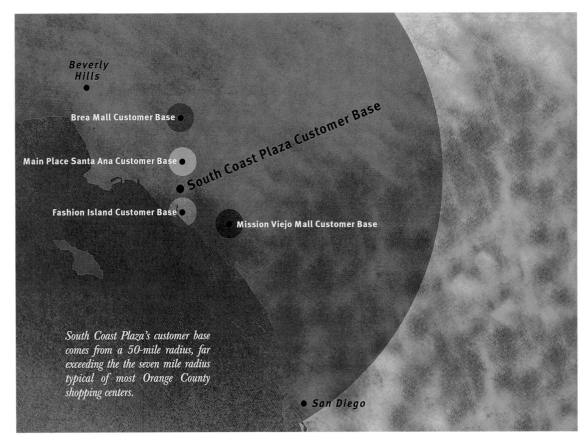

South Coast Plaza's customer base comes from a 50-mile radius, far exceeding the the seven mile radius typical of most Orange County shopping centers.

Maps of South Coast Plaza, a newly developed shopping center.

新しく開発されたショッピング・センター、South Coast Plazaのマップ。

USA 2003
AD: Mike Salisbury   DF, S: Mike Salisbury LLC.   CL: South Coast Plaza

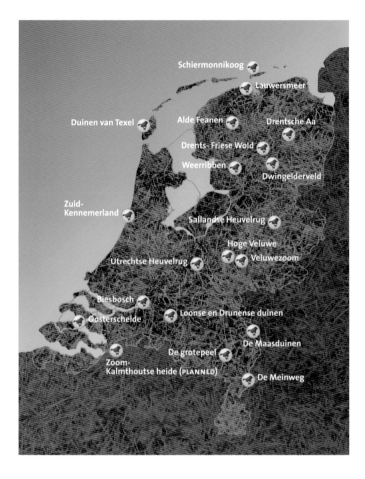

Schiermonnikoog
Lauwersmeer
Duinen van Texel
Alde Feanen
Drentsche Aa
Drents- Friese Wold
Weerribben
Dwingelderveld
Zuid-Kennemerland
Sallandse Heuvelrug
Hoge Veluwe
Veluwezoom
Utrechtse Heuvelrug
Biesbosch
Loonse en Drunense duinen
Oosterschelde
De Maasduinen
De grotepeel
Zoom-Kalmthoutse heide (PLANNED)
De Meinweg

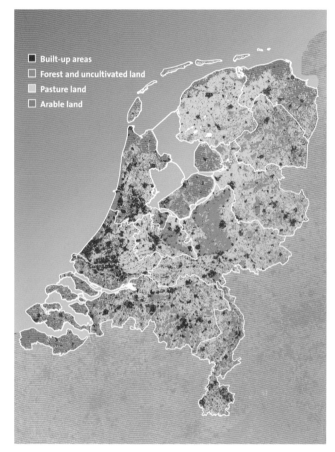

■ Built-up areas
□ Forest and uncultivated land
▨ Pasture land
□ Arable land

Map from a book on the Netherlands providing various data.

オランダを紹介する本から抜粋された、様々なデータを示すマップ。

Netherlands 2004
CD: Paul Vermijs   D: Toon Tesser   DF, S: TelDesign   CL: Ministry of Foreign Affairs

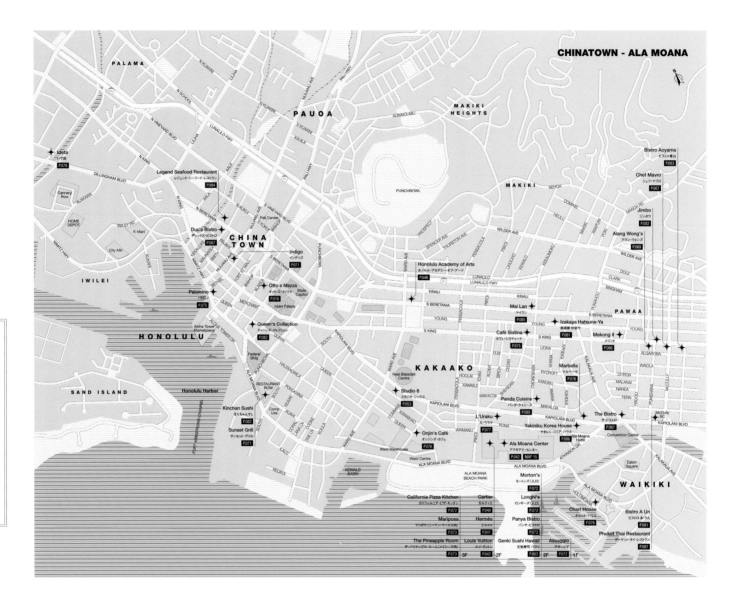

A guide map of Oahu from the magazine "Priority Hawaii."

雑誌『プライオリティー・ハワイ』より。オアフ島のガイドマップ。

Japan 2004
AD: Takahito Noguchi   D: Takahiro Imai   I: Tokuma   DF: Dynamite Brothers Syndicate Co., Ltd.   CL: Access Publishing Co., Ltd.   S: Bowlgraphics

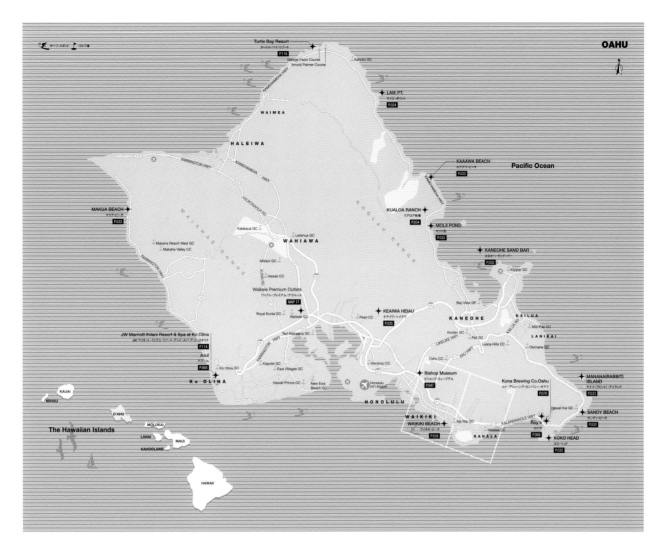

OAHU

The Hawaiian Islands

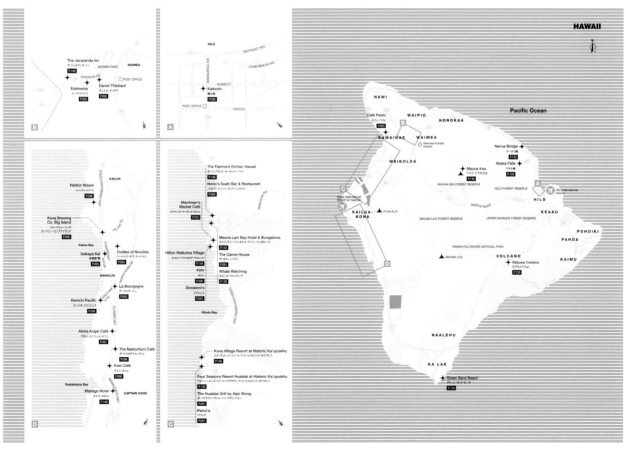

HAWAII

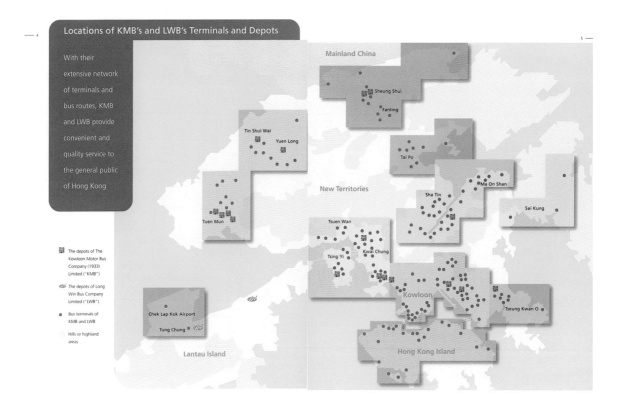

A map showing the locations of terminals and depots of the Kowloon Mortor Bus Company and Long Win Bus Company.

バス会社、Kowloon Motor Bus CompanyおよびLong Win Bus Companyのターミナルと発着場の場所を示すマップ。

Hong Kong   2000
CD, AD, D: Freeman Lau Sin Hong   AD, D: Eddy Yu   DF, S: Kan & Lau Design Consultants   CL: the Kowloon Motor Bus Holdings Ltd.

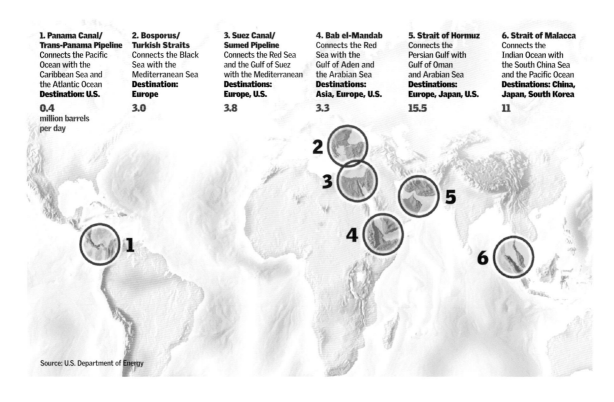

Map illustrating oil-distribution choke points.

石油の流通における重要な航路を表すマップ。

USA   2004
AD: Carol Macrini   D, I, S: Eliot Bergman   CL: Bloomberg Markets Magazine

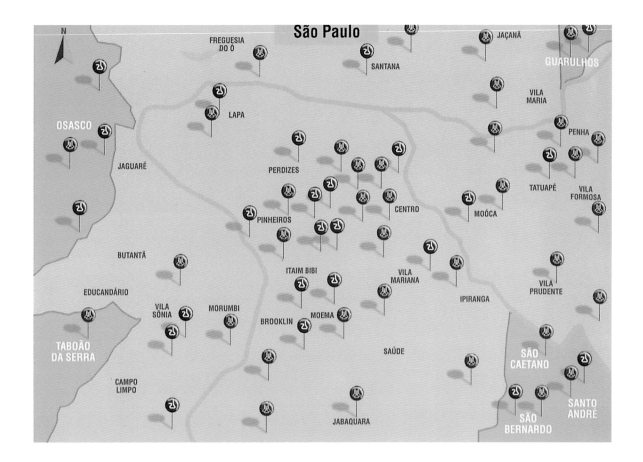

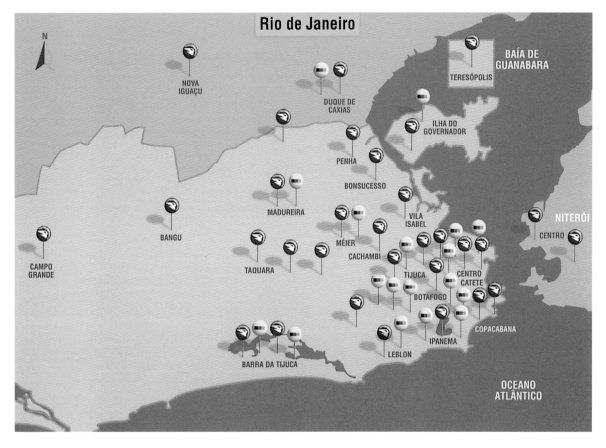

Maps indicating the locations of clinical laboratories in 3 states in Brazil.

ブラジルの3つの州にある臨床検査室の場所を示すマップ。

Brazil　2003
CD: Ronaldo da Silva Rego　AD: Celia Emy Ushizawa　D: Hamilton B. Furtado　P: Daniel Dayan / Eduardo Barcellos / Lucio Cunha / Roberto Rosa
I: Gil de Godoy　CW: Sylvia Muller　DF, S: Graphic Designers S. C. Ltda　CL: Diagnosticos da America S/A

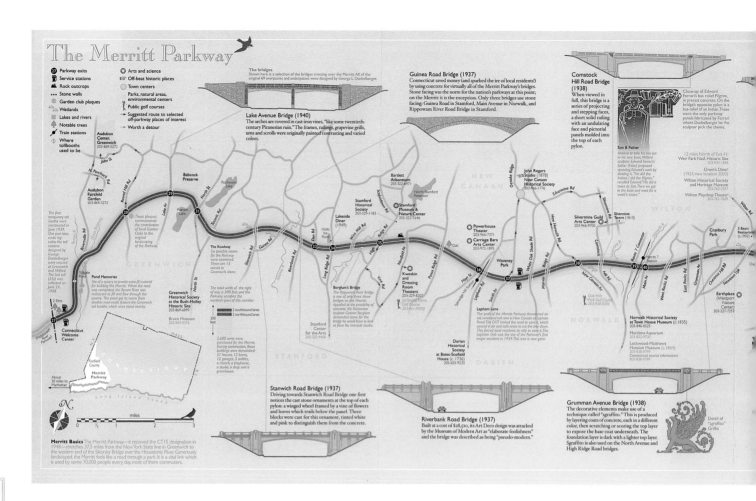

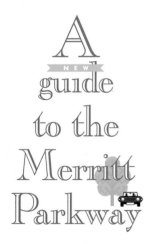

FAMOUS BRIDGES

MAN-MADE & NATURAL FEATURES

PLACES NEARBY
THAT ARE WORTH A VISIT

Merritt Parkway Conservancy
© 2004

A map of a road in Connecticut in USA showing bridges, points of interest, and history.

橋や名所、歴史を紹介する、アメリカのコネチカット州のロードマップ。

USA 2004

CD, AD, D, I, S: Nigel Holmes   CW: Peter Szabo   DF: Explanation Graphics   CL: Merritt Parkway Conservancy

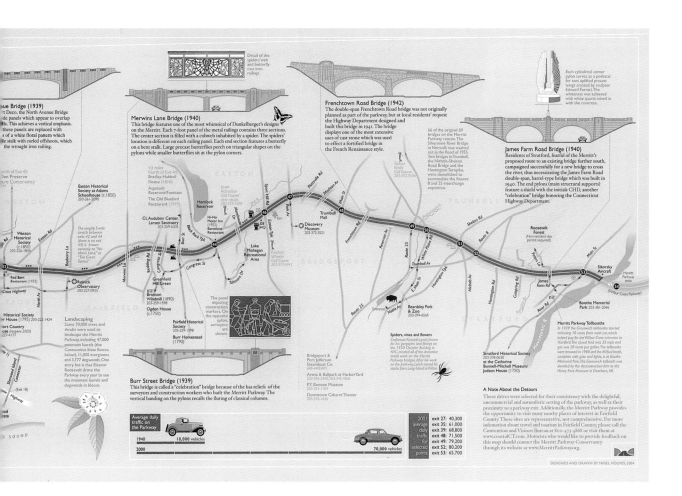

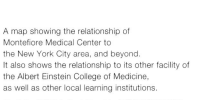

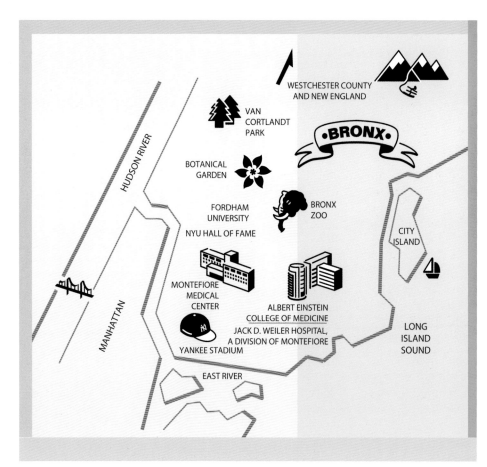

A map showing the relationship of
Montefiore Medical Center to
the New York City area, and beyond.
It also shows the relationship to its other facility of
the Albert Einstein College of Medicine,
as well as other local learning institutions.

Montefiore医療センターとニューヨーク周辺の位置関係を
示したマップ。また、薬科大学やそのほかの教育施設などの
位置も紹介している。

USA　1999
CD, AD: Diane Bennett　CD, AD, D, I: Mike Quon
DF, S: Mike Quon / Designation Inc.
CL: Montefiore Medical Center

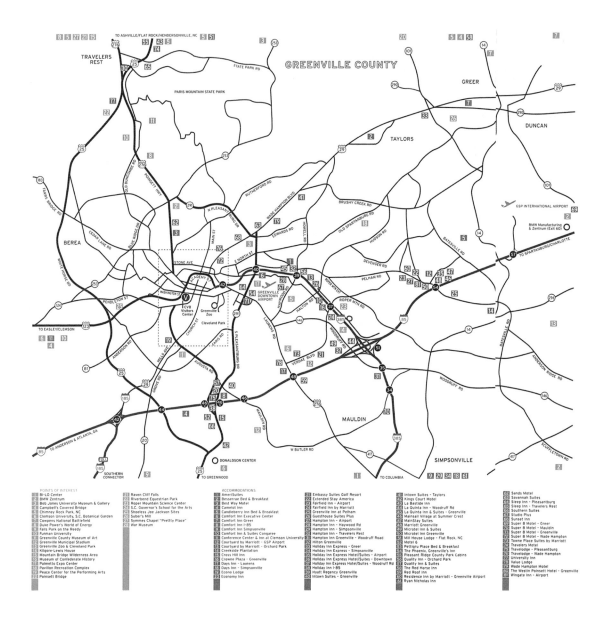

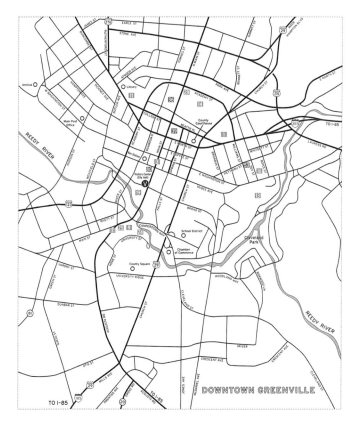

POINTS OF INTEREST

1 Bi-LO Center
2 BMW Zentrum
3 Bob Jones University Museum & Gallery
4 Campbell's Covered Bridge
5 Chimney Rock Park, NC
6 Clemson University, S.C. Botanical Garden
7 Cowpens National Battlefield
8 Duke Power's World of Energy
9 Falls Park on the Reedy
10 Furman University
11 Greenville County Museum of Art
12 Greenville Municipal Stadium
13 Greenville Zoo & Cleveland Park
14 Kilgore-Lewis House
15 Mountain Bridge Wilderness Area
16 Museum of Confederate History
17 Palmetto Expo Center
18 Pavilion Recreation Complex
19 Peace Center for the Performing Arts
20 Poinsett Bridge

21 Raven Cliff Falls
22 Riverbend Equestrian Park
23 Roper Mountain Science Center
24 S.C. Governor's School for the Arts
25 Shoeless Joe Jackson Sites
26 Suber's Mill
27 Symmes Chapel "Pretty Place"
28 War Museum

ACCOMMODATIONS

1 AmeriSuites
2 Besserrae Bed & Breakfast
3 Best Way Motel
4 Camelot Inn
5 Candleberry Inn Bed & Breakfast
6 Comfort Inn Executive Center
7 Comfort Inn Greer
8 Comfort Inn - I-85
9 Comfort Inn - I-85
10 Comfort Inn Simpsonville
11 Comfort Inn & Suites Congaree
12 Conference Center & Inn at Clemson University
13 Courtyard by Marriott - GSP Airport
14 Courtyard by Marriott - Orchard Park
15 Creekside Plantation
16 Cross Hill Inn
17 Crowne Plaza - Greenville
18 Days Inn - Laurens
19 Days Inn - Simpsonville
20 Econo Lodge
21 Economy Inn

22 Embassy Suites Golf Resort
23 Extended Stay America
24 Fairfield Inn - Airport
25 Fairfield Inn by Marriott
26 Greenville Inn at Pelham
27 Guesthouse Suites Plus
28 Hampton Inn - Airport
29 Hampton Inn - Haywood Rd
30 Hampton Inn - Simpsonville
31 Hampton Inn - Travelers Rest
32 Hampton Inn Greenville - Woodruff Road
33 Hilton Greenville
34 Holiday Inn Express - Greer
35 Holiday Inn Express - Simpsonville
36 Holiday Inn Express Hotel/Suites - Airport
37 Holiday Inn Express Hotel/Suites - Downtown
38 Holiday Inn Express Hotel/Suites - Woodruff Rd
39 Holiday Inn I-85
40 Hyatt Regency Greenville
41 Intown Suites - Greenville

42 Intown Suites - Taylors
43 Kings Court Motel
44 La Bastide Inn
45 La Quinta Inn - Woodruff Rd
46 La Quinta Inn & Suites - Greenville
47 Mainsail Village at Summer Crest
48 MainStay Suites
49 Marriott Greenville
50 Microtel Inn & Suites
51 Microtel Inn Greenville
52 Mill House Lodge - Flat Rock, NC
53 Motel 6
54 Pettigru Place Bed & Breakfast
55 The Phoenix, Greenville's Inn
56 Pleasant Ridge County Park Cabins
57 Quality Inn - Orchard Park
58 Quality Inn & Suites
59 The Red Horse Inn
60 Red Roof Inn
61 Residence Inn by Marriott - Greenville Airport
62 Ryan Nicholas Inn

62 Sands Motel
63 Savannah Suites
64 Sleep Inn - Pleasantburg
65 Sleep Inn - Travelers Rest
66 Southern Suites
67 Studio Plus
68 Sunset Inn
69 Super 8 Motel - Greer
70 Super 8 Motel - Mauldin
71 Super 8 Motel - Greenville
72 Super 8 Motel - Wade Hampton
73 Towne Place Suites by Marriott
74 Travelers Motel
75 Travelodge - Pleasantburg
76 Travelodge - Wade Hampton
77 University Inn
78 Value Lodge
79 Wade Hampton Motel
80 The Westin Poinsett Hotel - Greenville
81 Wingate Inn - Airport

Maps for visitors to Greenville, South Carolina.

サウスカロライナ州グリーンビルを訪れる人々のためのマップ。

Canada 2004
CD, AD: Frank Viva D, I: Todd Temporale P: Frances Juriansz
CW: Doug Dolan DF, S: Viva Dolan Communications & Design Inc.
CL: Greenville Convention & Visitors Bureay

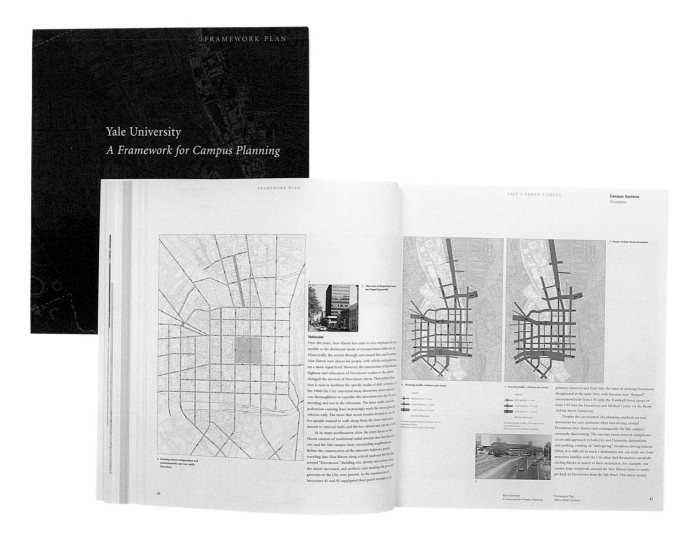

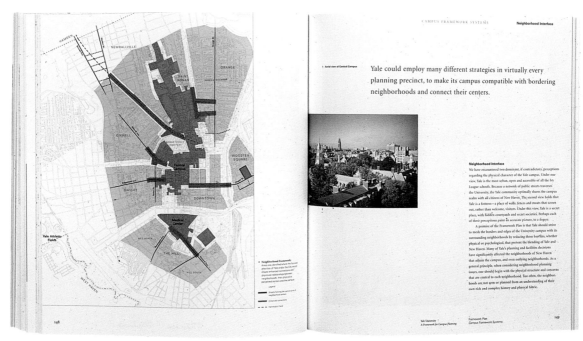

Maps and diagrams from design guidelines that provides a comprehensive plan for the future growth of the Yale University campus.
Not only did the University seek to develop its campus, but also the University's physical and aesthetic relationship to the city of New Haven.

イェール大学キャンパス拡張基本計画のデザイン・ガイドラインから抜粋したマップやダイアグラム。大学はキャンパスの拡大だけではなく、ニューヘブン市との物理的・美的な関係を模索していた。

USA 2003
D: L. Richard Poulin / Amy Kwon   DF, S: Poulin + Morris Inc.   CL: Yale University

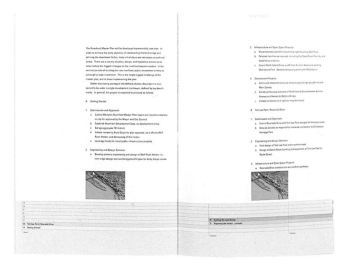

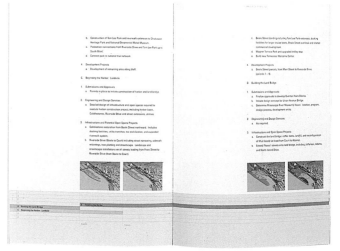

From the master plan for Memphis' riverfront incorporating over twelve miles of Mississippi River frontage with a system of connected parks leading to a new commercial harbor at the foot of downtown. Maps illustrating the site, and other diagrams showing technical data, planning and architectural criteria.

ダウンタウンにある新しい商業港へと公園が続く、メンフィスのリバーフロントのためのマスタープランより。現場を紹介するマップや、建築プランなどを示す図。

USA   2003
D: L. Richard Poulin / Rosemary Markowski   DF, S: Poulin + Morris Inc.   CL: Memphis Riverfront Redevelopment

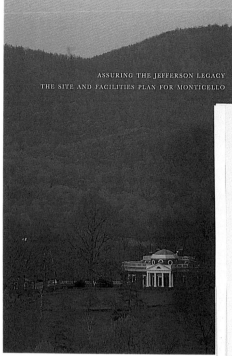

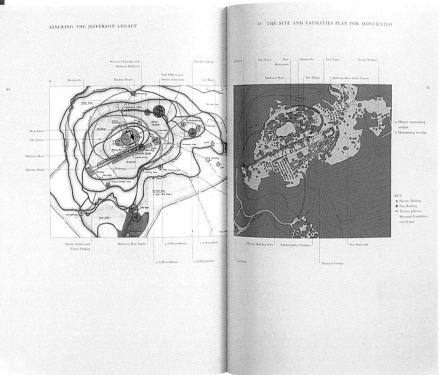

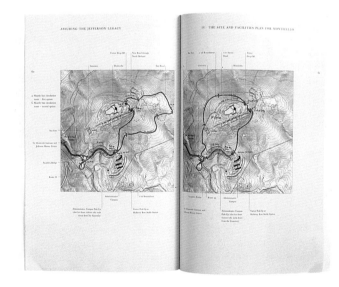

A series of maps illustrating the site and facilities plan for Monticello.
It establishes an appropriate and achievable framework for the foundation's mission goals over the next ten years.

モンティチェッロのためのサイトプランおよび施設案を紹介するマップ。今後10年間におよぶ財団の目標の適切かつ達成可能な枠組を構築している。

USA 2003
D: L. Richard Poulin / Amy Kwon   DF, S: Poulin + Morris Inc.   CL: The Thomas Jefferson Memorial Foundation

The Next Step

THE UNIVERSITY OF NORTH CAROLINA AT CHARLOTTE MASTER PLAN

From the publication that outlines the University's master plan guidelines for the development of their campus over the next twenty years. Drawings illustrating the potential for an improved and expanded campus.

今後20年間にわたる大学キャンパスの開発マスタープラン・ガイドラインを紹介する本から抜粋。図版は拡大・改良されたキャンパスの可能性を表現している。

USA 2003
D: L. Richard Poulin / Brian Brindisi   DF, S: Poulin + Morris Inc.   CL: University of North Carolina

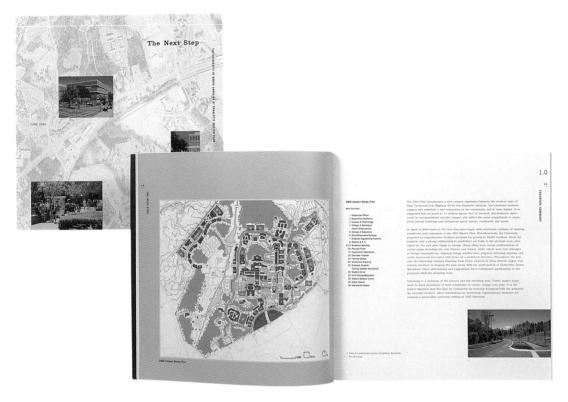

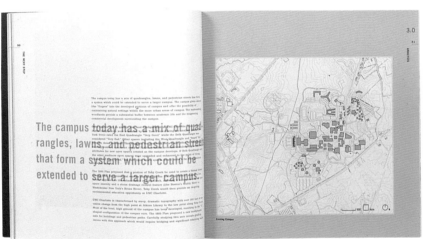

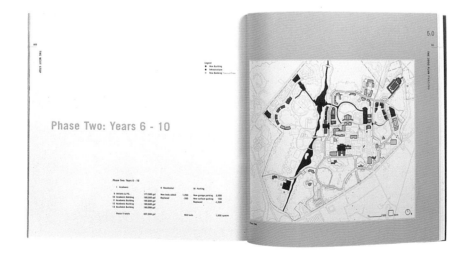

A series of illustrations from the University's master plan guidelines.

大学のマスタープラン・ガイドラインから抜粋した一連の図版。

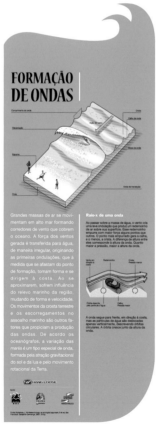

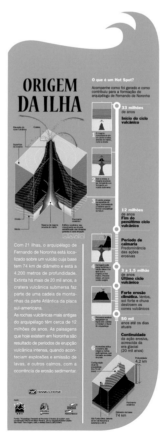

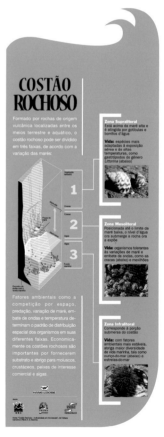

From a signage system developed for the important ecological sanctuaries.
Providing information on geography, biology, and wave of the island and the rules to protect its nature.

重要な環境保護区のために作成されたサイン・システムより。島の地理や生態系、波に関する情報や、自然保護のルールを紹介。

Brazil 2003
CD, S: Eduardo Asta   I: Daniel Lopes (Noronha Ondas. Ai)   CW: Janaina Gava   CL: Surf CO

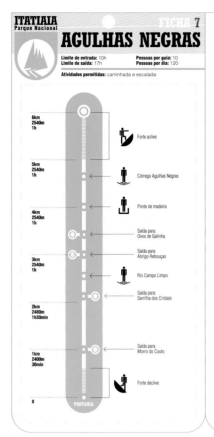

A prototype of signage system and informational diagrams designed for Itatiaia Natural Park.
There are two tasks envolved to protect visitors from dangerous situations and to protect the park from the visitors.

イタチアイア国立公園のためにデザインされた、サインのシステムとダイアグラムのプロトタイプ。危険なシチュエーションから観光客を守ること、観光客から公園を守ること、という2つの課題のもとに制作された。

Brazil 2001
CD, S: Eduardo Asta CL: PNI Office / Ibama-RJ

Maps Illustrated in the style of 1920-30 railway posters showing commuter rail lines from London.
1920〜30年代の鉄道ポスターを思わせるマップ。ロンドンからの通勤鉄道路線を示す。

UK 2004
Graphic Editor, I, S: Phillip Green   CL: The Sunday Telegraph

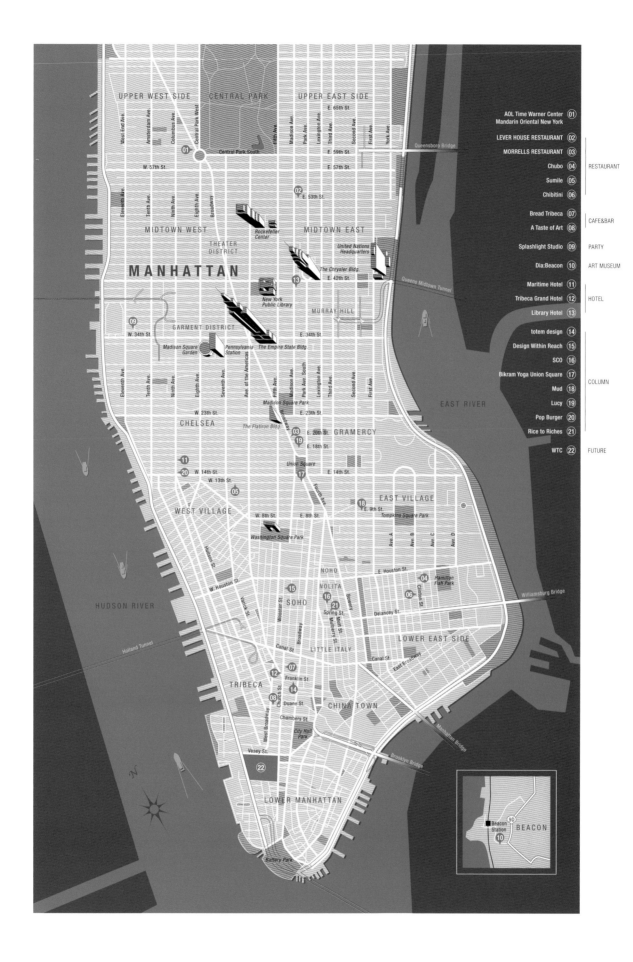

A map from a feature article on New York in the magazine "Tokyo Calendar."

雑誌『東京カレンダー』より。ニューヨークの特集内で使用したマップ。

Japan   2003

AD: Mayuko Horikawa   I: Tokuma   DF: Dynamite Brothers Syndicate Co., Ltd.   CL: Access Publishing Co., Ltd.   S: Bowlgraphics

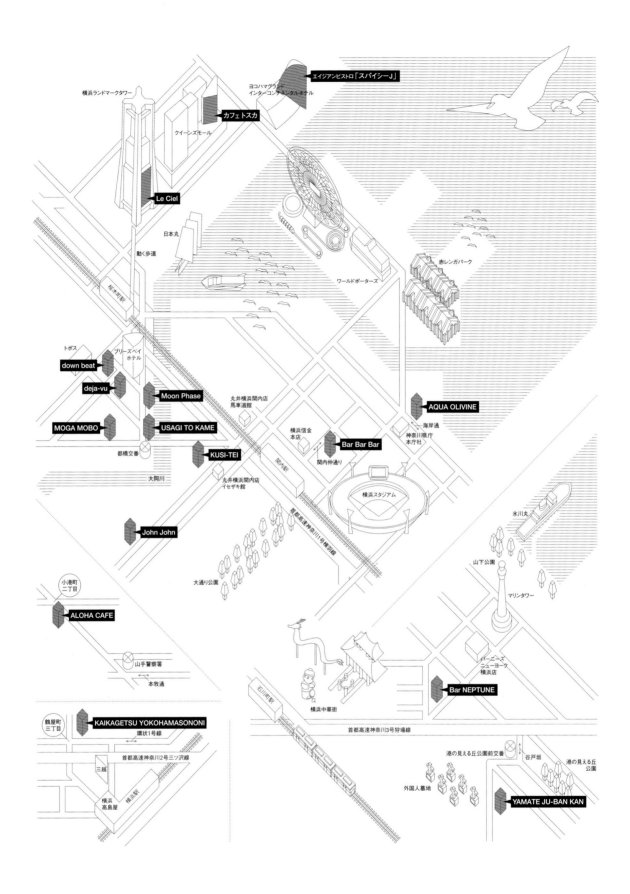

横浜ランドマークタワー

エイジアンビストロ「スパイシーJ」

ヨコハマグランド
インターコンチネンタルホテル

カフェトスカ

クイーンズモール

Le Ciel

日本丸

動く歩道

桜木町駅

赤レンガパーク

ワールドポーターズ

トポス

ブリーズベイ
ホテル

down beat

deja-vu

Moon Phase

丸井横浜関内店
馬車道館

MOGA MOBO

USAGI TO KAME

AQUA OLIVINE

海岸通

神奈川県庁
本庁舎

横浜信金
本店

都橋交番

KUSI-TEI

Bar Bar Bar

関内駅

関内仲通り

大岡川

丸井横浜関内店
イセザキ館

氷川丸

John John

横浜スタジアム

首都高速神奈川1号横羽線

大通り公園

山下公園

マリンタワー

小港町
二丁目

ALOHA CAFE

バーニーズ
ニューヨーク
横浜店

山手警察署

Bar NEPTUNE

本牧通

石川町駅

横浜中華街

港の見える丘公園前交番

谷戸坂

港の見える丘
公園

鶴屋町
三丁目

KAIKAGETSU YOKOHAMASONONI

環状1号線

首都高速神奈川3号狩場線

外国人墓地

YAMATE JU-BAN KAN

首都高速神奈川2号三ツ沢線

三越

横浜駅

横浜
高島屋

A map of the Yokohama area from a feature article on Yokohama in the magazine "Monthly M."

雑誌『マンスリー・エム』より。横浜特集内で使用した横浜地区のマップ。

Japan　2002

AD: Takeshi Hamada　I: Tokuma　DF: Dynamite Brothers Syndicate Co., Ltd.　CL: Bell System 24　S: Bowlgraphics

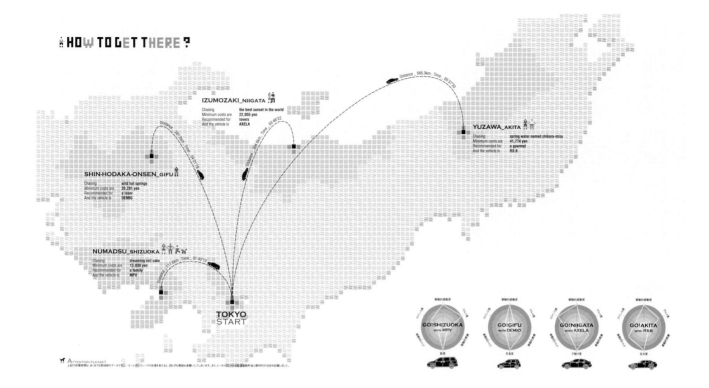

Information to aid in maximizing the pleasure of spur of the moment day trips by car from Tokyo from the magazine "Metro Minutes."

雑誌『メトロミニッツ』より。東京から衝動的に日帰りドライブを満喫するための情報。

Japan 2004
D, I: Tokuma CW: Junichi Kobayashi CL: Starts Publishing Co. S: Bowlgraphics

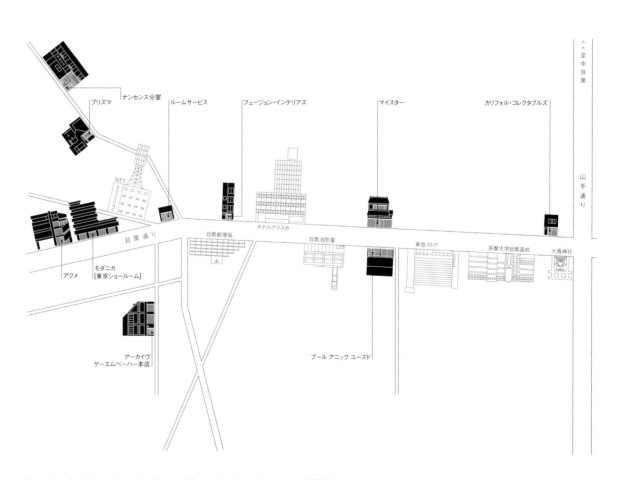

A map introducing interior design shops on Meguro-dori from the magazine "TITLe."

雑誌『TITLe』より。目黒通りのインテリアショップを紹介したマップ。

Japan 2004
AD: Tetsushi Kawamura I: Tokuma DF: Atomosphere, Ltd. CL: Bungeishunju Ltd. S: Bowlgraphics

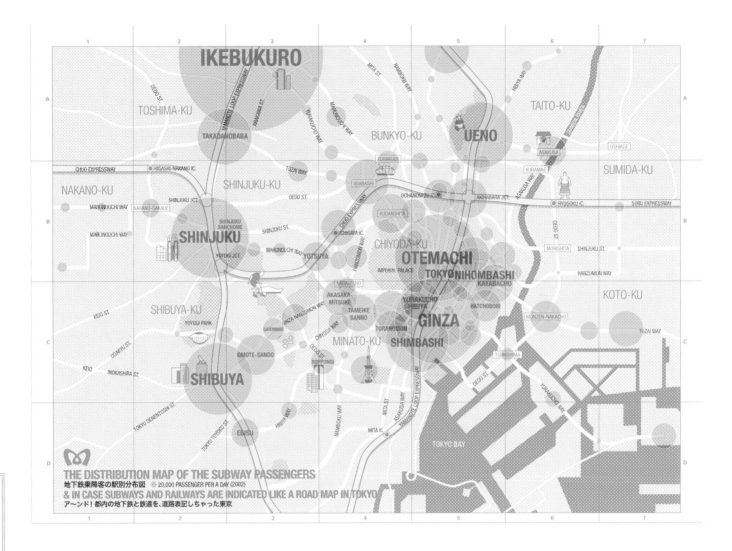

The Tokyo railroad network expressed as road ways also showing the distribution of passengers boarding and alighting at each station, from the magazine "Metro Minutes."

雑誌『メトロミニッツ』より。東京都内の鉄道網を道路に見立てて表現。さらに駅別乗降客の分布も表記。

Japan　2004
AD, D: Takashi Tokuma　I: Tokuma　DF: Dynamite Brothers Syndicate Co., Ltd.　CL: Starts Publishing Co.　S: Bowlgraphics

Visualization of the main rail lines and stations related to topics dealt with in the magazine "Metro Minutes."

雑誌『メトロミニッツ』より。
雑誌内で扱うトピックを中心に主要部の駅と路線をビジュアル化した。

Japan　2003
AD: Shinsuke Koshio　D: Miki Shimizu
CL: Starts Publishing Co.　S: Sunday-Vision

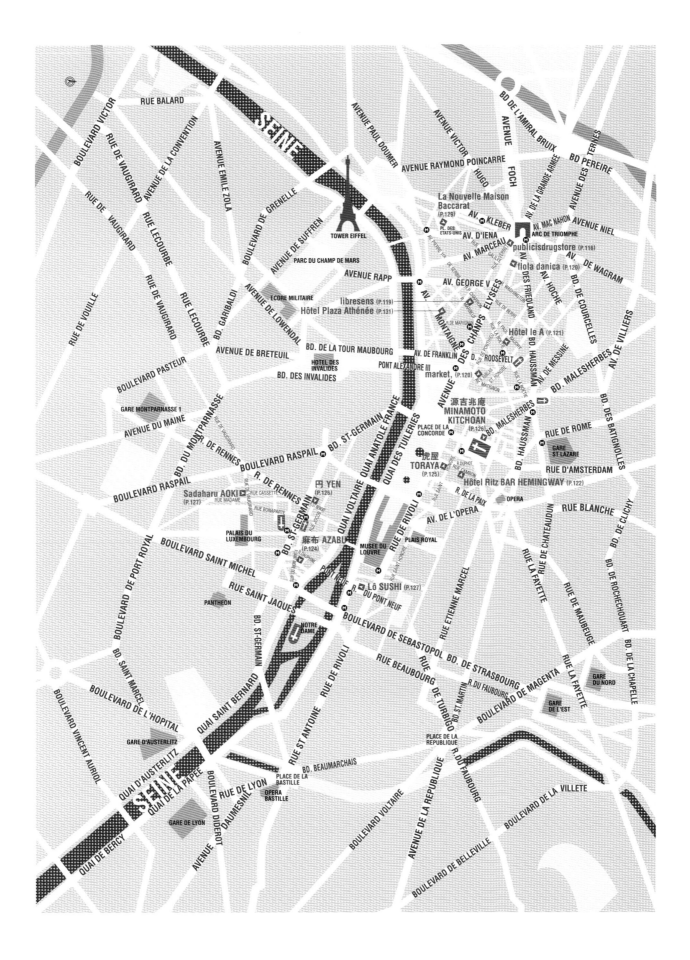

A map of Paris streets from a feature article on Paris in the magazine "Tokyo Calendar."

雑誌『東京カレンダー』より。パリの特集内で使用したパリ市街のマップ。

Japan 2004

AD: Mayuko Horikawa   I: Tokuma   DF: Dynamite Brothers Syndicate Co., Ltd.   CL: Access Publishing Co., Ltd.   S: Bowlgraphics

A map of Tokyo centered on the headquarters of a broadcasting company.

放送会社の本社を中心とした東京のマップ。

Japan 2004

AD: Kazunari Shimajiri   D: Mizuna Kojima   I, S: Teppei Watanabe   CW: Toru Ejima / Takaaki Kubota   DF: Sony Music Communications Inc.   CL: J-Wave, Inc.

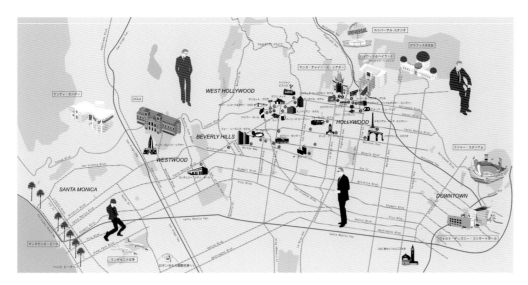

Los Angeles guide map centered around
Hollywood.

ハリウッドを中心としたロサンゼルスのガイドマップ。

Japan　2004
I, S: Teppei Watanabe
CL: Shochiku Co., Ltd.

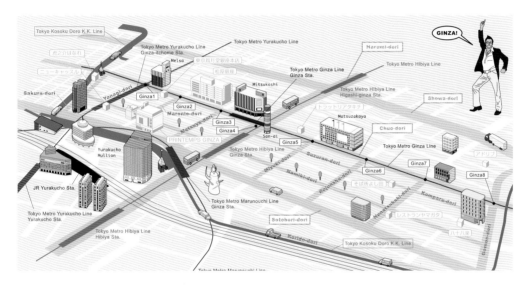

Ginza guide map.

銀座のガイドマップ。

Japan　2004
AD: Aoco (Pangaea)　D: Uru-uru
P: Naomichi Seo　I, S: Teppei Watanabe
CW: Ayako Otsuka
Compilation: Nobuyuki Hirai
CL: Starts Publishing Co.

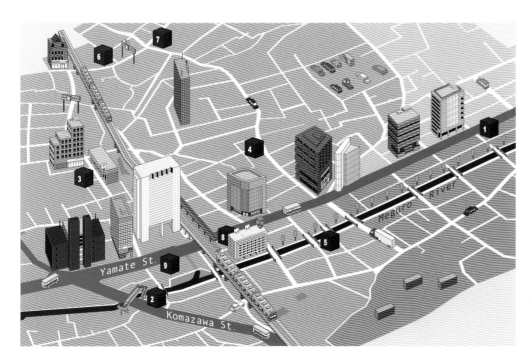

Naka-Meguro guide map.

中目黒のガイドマップ。

Japan　2003
AD: Aoco (Pangaea)　D: Uru-uru
P: Takashi Misawa / Takashi Nishizawa /
Katsumi Sato　I, S: Teppei Watanabe
CW, Compilation: Mihoko Nemoto
CL: Starts Publishing Co.

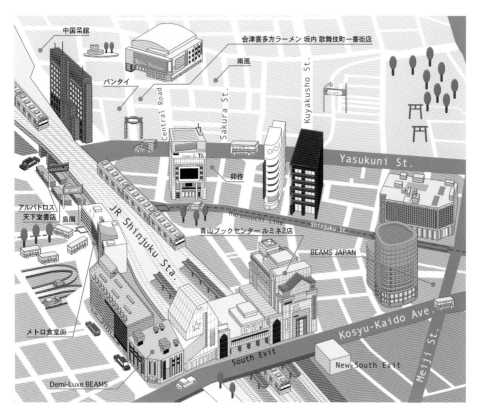

Shinjuku guide map.

新宿のガイドマップ。

Japan　2003
CL: Starts Publishing Corporation　AD: Aoco(Pangaea)
D: Uru-Uru　P: Takashi Nishizawa / Naomichi Seo
I, S: Teppei Watanabe　CW, Kousei: Mihoko Nemoto

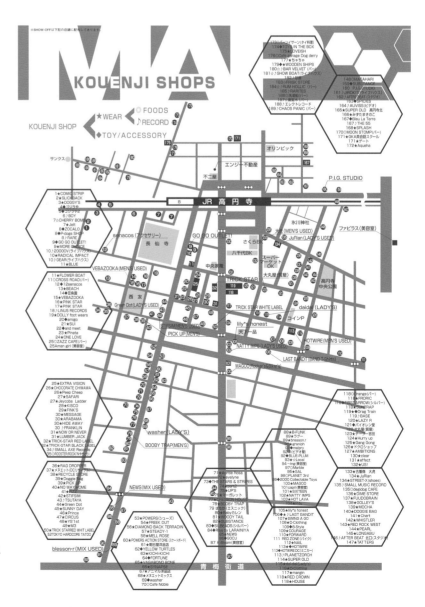

A map indicating stores in Koenji that distribute the free paper "SHOW-OFF."

フリーペーパー『SHOW-OFF』を配布している高円寺内の店舗を示すマップ。

Japan　2000
DF: Lovin' Graphic　CL, S: Show-Off

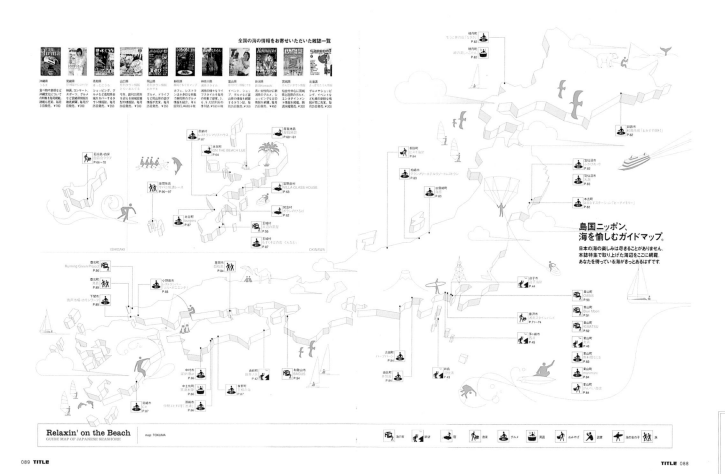

全国の海の情報をお寄せいただいた雑誌一覧

島国ニッポン、
海を愉しむガイドマップ。

日本の海の楽しみは尽きることがありません。
本誌特集で取り上げた海辺をここに網羅。
あなたを待っている海がきっとあるはずです。

Relaxin' on the Beach
GUIDE MAP OF JAPANESE SEASHORE　　map: TOKUMA

A map showing the distribution of beaches featured in Japan in a special article on beaches in the magazine "TITLe."

雑誌『TITLe』より。海辺の特集内で使用した日本国内の海辺の分布図。

Japan　2003

AD: Tetsushi Kawamura　I: Tokuma　DF: Atomosphere, Ltd.　CL: Bungeisyunju Ltd.　S: Bowlgraphics

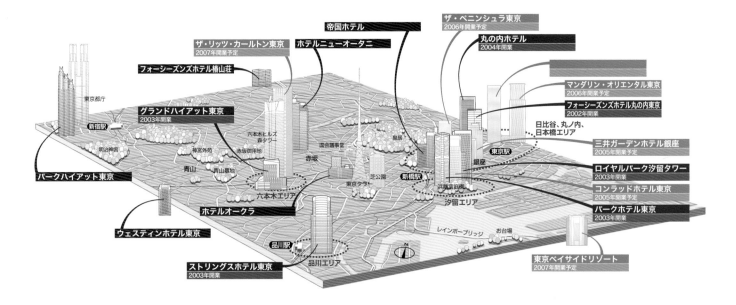

東京都庁

ザ・リッツ・カールトン東京
2007年開業予定

帝国ホテル

ザ・ペニンシュラ東京
2006年開業予定

丸の内ホテル
2004年開業

フォーシーズンズホテル椿山荘

ホテルニューオータニ

マンダリン・オリエンタル東京
2006年開業予定

グランドハイアット東京
2003年開業

フォーシーズンズホテル丸の内東京
2002年開業

新宿駅

明治神宮

六本木ヒルズ
森タワー

神宮外苑

赤坂御用地

青山

青山墓地

国会議事堂

皇居

日比谷、丸ノ内、
日本橋エリア

三井ガーデンホテル銀座
2005年開業予定

赤坂

銀座

東京駅

ロイヤルパーク汐留タワー
2003年開業

パークハイアット東京

六本木エリア

東京タワー

芝公園

新橋駅

浜離宮庭園

汐留エリア

コンラッドホテル東京
2005年開業予定

パークホテル東京
2003年開業

ホテルオークラ

ウェスティンホテル東京

品川駅

品川エリア

レインボーブリッジ

お台場

N

ストリングスホテル東京
2003年開業

東京ベイサイドリゾート
2007年開業予定

Illustrations of buildings arranged on a map describing the inroads of foreign-owned hotels from the magazine "Weekly Diamond."

雑誌『週刊ダイヤモンド』より。外資系ホテル進出ラッシュを、地図上に建物イラストを配置して説明。

Japan   2004
CD: Hiroyuki Kimura   D: Sachiko Hagiwara   DF, S: Tube Graphics   CL: Diamond Inc.

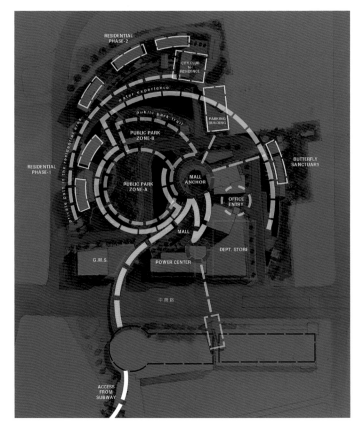

Node

Office Entry

Water Experience

Main Flow

Private Path in the Residential Area

Public Park Trail

A diagram showing the arrangement of spatial elements related to the various facilities planned within the development area.

開発地区内に計画される多種用途の施設を、空間の環境要素により関連付けた配置を表す分布図。

Japan   2001
CD, AD: Kiharu Tsuge   D: Hikaru Sasaki   DF, S: Tsuge Design Management   CL: Hamano Institute Inc.

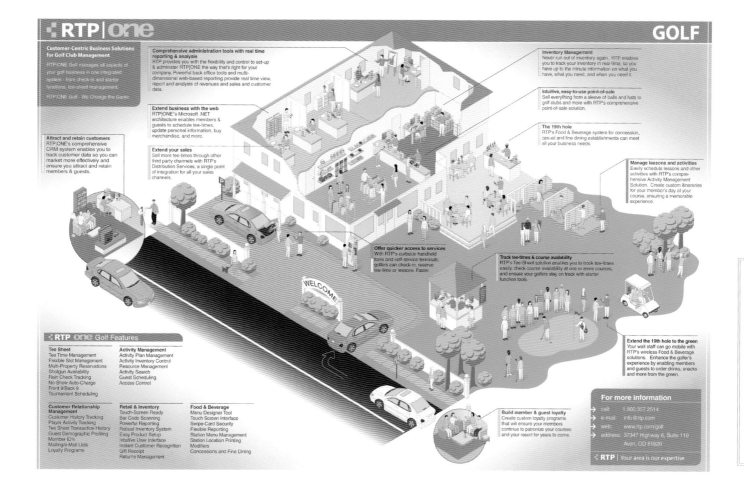

A diagram showing features of a golf resort point-of-sale software package.

ゴルフ・リゾートのセールス・ポイントを伝えるソフトウェア・パッケージの特徴を図解。

USA 2004
D, I, CW, S: William H. Bardel   CL: Resort Technology Partners

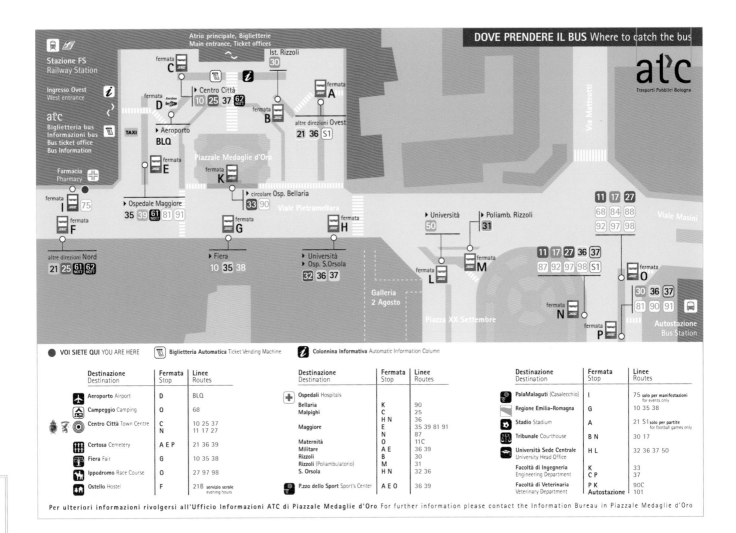

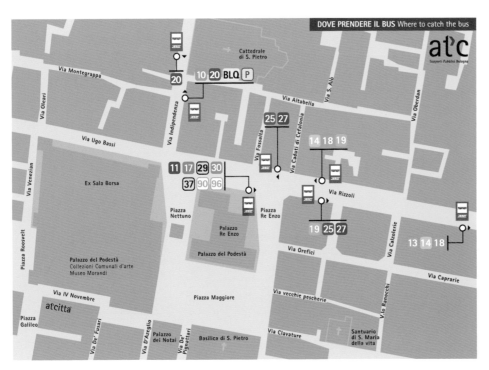

Various diagrams showing time tables, locations of bus stops, route maps of the public transportation.

公共の交通機関の路線図、バス停の場所、時刻表を示す様々な案内図。

Italy 2001
CD: Barbara Cuniberti   D: Elena Corradini / Martina Zucchini   DF, S: Kuni   CL: ATC-Azienda Trasporti Pubblici

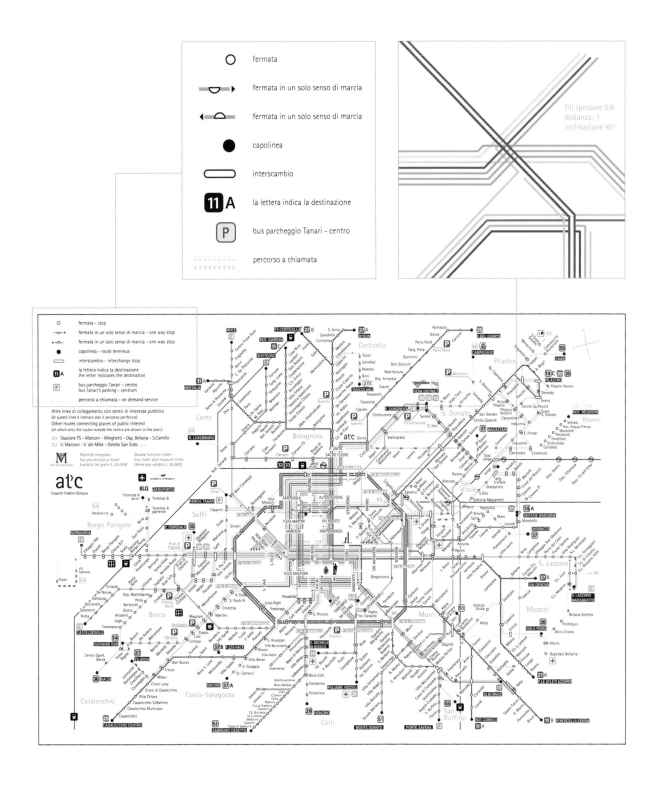

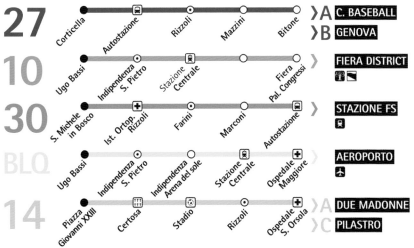

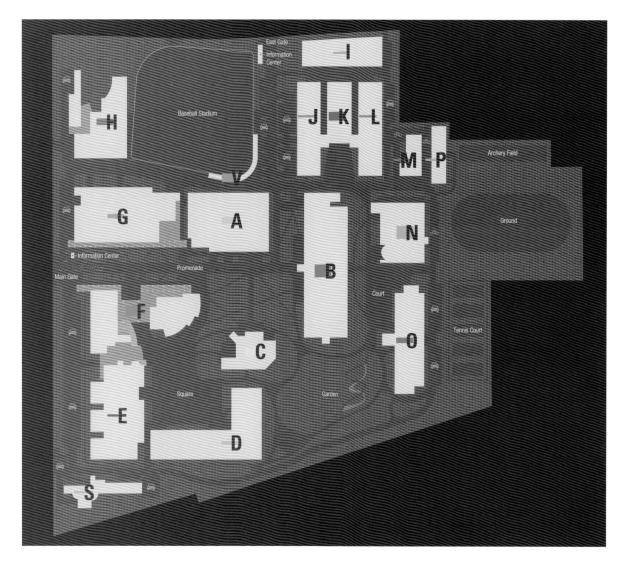

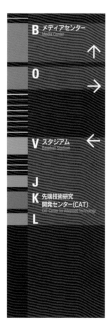
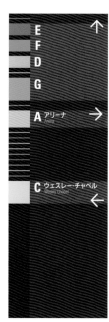
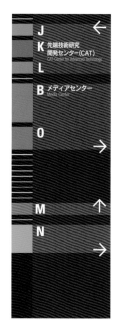

A map and guided diagram of the Aoyama Gakuin University Sagamihara Campus.
青山学院大学相模原キャンパス内のマップと案内表示。

Japan 2002
CD, AD, D, S: Kei Miyazaki   D: Natsuko Hosokawa   DF: KMD Inc.   CL: Aoyama Gakuin University

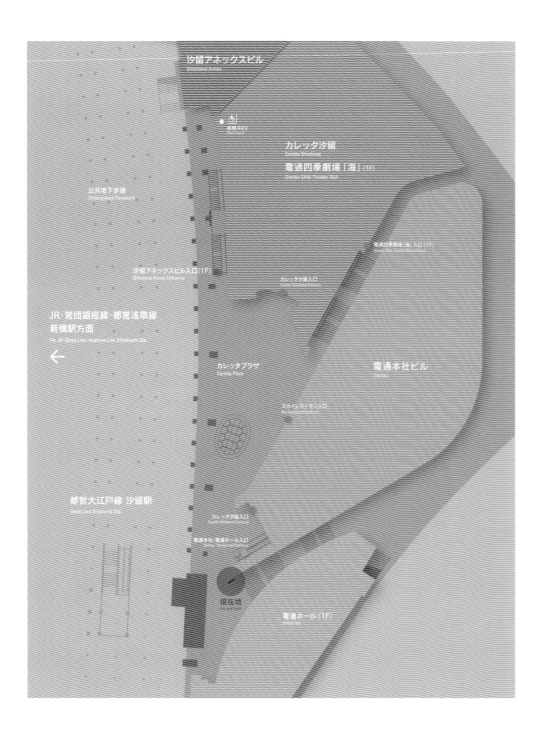

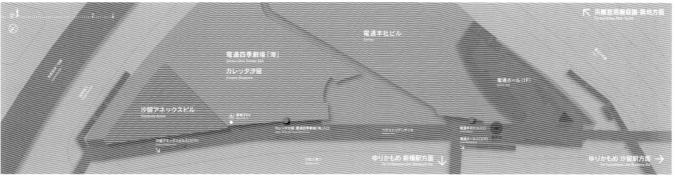

Guide to the area (Shiodome area A) surrounding Dentsu corporate headquarters.

電通本社周辺（汐留A街区）の案内図。

Japan 2002
CD, AD, D, S: Kei Miyazaki　D: Masako Nishikata　DF: KMD Inc.　CL: Dentsu Inc.

This application is less linear and more organic, with Resolve clusters along winding secondary paths. All routes and groups are defined by trusses, flags, or colored screens. Designed to support some collaboration and teamwork, this plan is primarily composed of individual spaces.

Think high.
Make use of overhead space with sliding trusses. A sliding truss connecting two constellations creates a threshold that can tie constellations together to identify teams and also assist in wayfinding.

Making room.
A 4' work surface on a 5' arm leaves room for attaching storage on either side: a ladder shelf or cabinet on one side, a tool rail or monitor pod on the other.

Making more room.
Work surfaces oriented in an "outbound" position create a peninsula off the pole, making the work space feel larger and freeing up infrastructure to support additional storage elements.

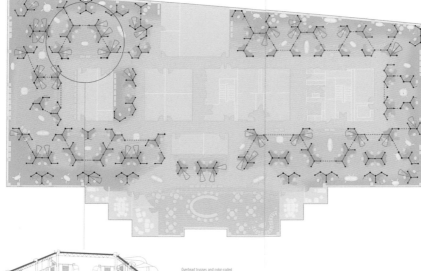

Primary circulation route.

Secondary traffic paths meander through constellations to provide opportunities for chance encounters and impromptu conversations.

Cul-de-sacs offer quiet places for casual meeting.

Trusses create a rhythm through the space that aids wayfinding and adds vertical dimension to the environment.

Overhead trusses and color-coded boundary screens and flags along the aisles highlight traffic paths and identify groups.

38 · DESIGNING RESOLVE ENVIRONMENTS   PLANNING · 39

Diagrams indicate floorplan examples to help interior designers and architects in designing office spaces.
インテリア・デザイナーや建築家がオフィス・スペースをデザインする際に役立つフロアプラン。

USA 2000
CD, AD, S: Yang Kim   AD, D: Brian Hauch   P: Herman Miller archives   I: Amy Franceschini   CW: Deb Wierenga   DF: BBK Studio   CL: Herman Miller

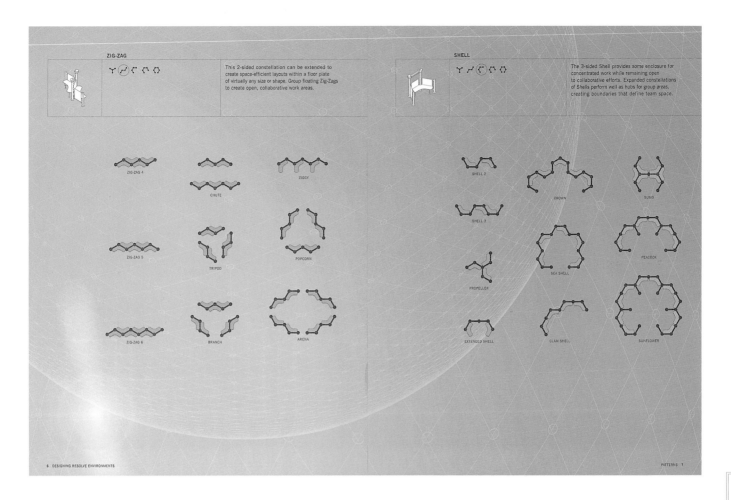

ZIG-ZAG

This 2-sided constellation can be extended to create space-efficient layouts within a floor plate of virtually any size or shape. Group floating Zig-Zags to create open, collaborative work areas.

ZIG-ZAG 4

CHUTE

ZIGGY

ZIG-ZAG 5

TRIPOD

POPCORN

ZIG-ZAG 6

BRANCH

ARENA

SHELL

The 3-sided Shell provides some enclosure for concentrated work while remaining open to collaborative efforts. Expanded constellations of Shells perform well as hubs for group areas, creating boundaries that define team space.

SHELL 2

SHELL 3

PROPELLER

CROWN

SEA SHELL

EXTENDED SHELL

SUMO

PEACOCK

CLAM SHELL

SUNFLOWER

Extended Honey

Clustered in groups of four along an expansive window wall, Extended Honey constellations support the computing, meeting, and paper-based work of their multitasking occupants.

EXTENDED HONEY

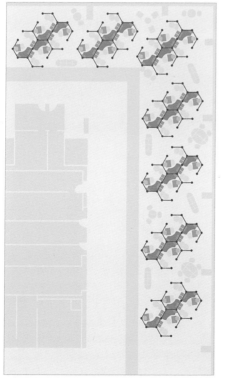

Dogbone, Extended Honey

Closely placed architectural columns in this long, narrow space are easily accommodated by Dogbone constellations placed at angles and linked with sliding trusses that carry power and telecommunications cables over the entrances to team areas.

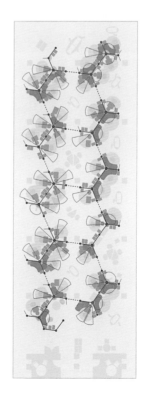

DOGBONE

EXTENDED HONEY

  1/16 SCALE

  1/16 SCALE

183

340 Madison
Space Plan Studies

Legal – 39,000rsf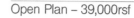

Open Plan – 39,000rsf

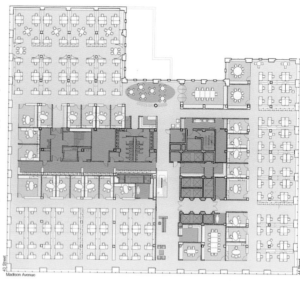

340 Madison
Stacking Plan

Floor		rsf
	22	23,000rsf
	21	24,000rsf
	20	24,000rsf
	19	27,000rsf
	18	27,000rsf
	17	30,000rsf
	16	38,000rsf
	15	39,000rsf
	14	39,000rsf
Crossover Floor	**12**	39,000rsf
	11	39,000rsf
	10	39,000rsf
	9	39,000rsf
	8	39,000rsf
	7	39,000rsf
	6	39,000rsf
	5	29,000rsf
	4	29,000rsf
	3	29,000rsf
	2	29,000rsf
	1	Lobby/Retail
	LL	Lower Level

Freight　Hi-Rise　Lo-Rise

Floor guide and plan from an overview book for a major new office buildings in the midtown Manhattan.
マンハッタンのミッドタウンに建つ新しいオフィスビルの案内書から抜粋したフロアガイドとフロアプラン。

USA 2003
CD, D: Graham Hanson   P: Wayne Sorce   CW: Sheldon Werdiger   DF, S: Graham Hanson Design   CL: Macklowe Properties

O ESCRITÓRIO DO FUTURO

Projeto do que pode ser o escritório do século 21, desenvolvido por Piratininga Arquitetos Associados a pedido da Folha; a principal inovação está em alterar o layout do ambiente de trabalho ao longo de um único dia conforme as necessidades específicas da empresa

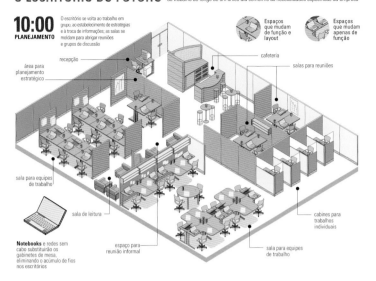

10:00 PLANEJAMENTO

O escritório se volta ao trabalho em grupo, ao estabelecimento de estratégias e à troca de informações; as salas se moldam para abrigar reuniões e grupos de discussão

Espaços que mudam de função e layout

Espaços que mudam apenas de função

recepção
área para planejamento estratégico
cafeteria
salas para reuniões
sala para equipes de trabalho
sala de leitura
cabines para trabalhos individuais
Notebooks e redes sem cabo substituirão os gabinetes de mesa, eliminando o acúmulo de fios nos escritórios
espaço para reunião informal
sala para equipes de trabalho

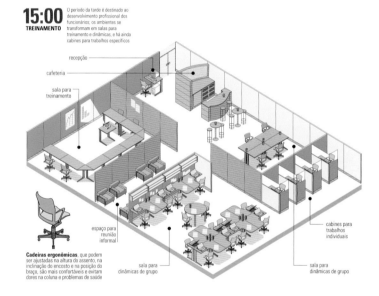

15:00 TREINAMENTO

O período da tarde é destinado ao desenvolvimento profissional dos funcionários; os ambientes se transformam em salas para treinamento e dinâmicas, e há ainda cabines para trabalhos específicos

recepção
cafeteria
sala para treinamento
espaço para reunião informal
Cadeiras ergonômicas, que podem ser ajustadas na altura do assento, na inclinação do encosto e na posição do braço, são mais confortáveis e evitam dores na coluna e problemas de saúde
sala para dinâmicas de grupo
cabines para trabalhos individuais
sala para dinâmicas de grupo

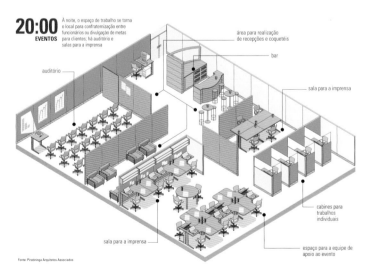

20:00 EVENTOS

À noite, o espaço de trabalho se torna o local para confraternização entre funcionários ou divulgação de metas para clientes; há auditório e salas para a imprensa

auditório
área para realização de recepções e coquetéis
bar
sala para a imprensa
cabines para trabalhos individuais
sala para a imprensa
espaço para a equipe de apoio ao evento

Fonte: Piratininga Arquitetos Associados

Illustration showing the different layouts of office space and explaining that offices will be more dynamic in the future.

オフィス・スペースの様々なレイアウトを紹介。オフィスは将来的にもっとダイナミックになるだろうと予測している。

Brazil 2000

CD, S: Eduardo Asta   CW: Mauricio Puls / Thales de Menezes / Leonardo Cruz   CL: Folha de São Paulo

Access

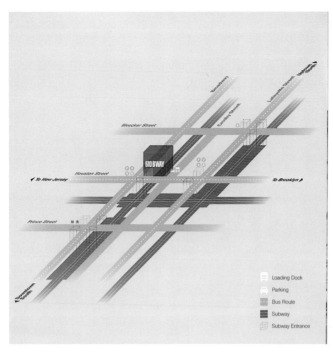

610 B'WAY

Loading Dock
Parking
Bus Route
Subway
Subway Entrance

Subway

Ⓙ Service between Jamaica–179 Street, Queens and Coney Island–Stilwell Avenue, Brooklyn

Ⓕ Service between Forest Hills–71 Avenue, Queens and Lower East Side–2nd Avenue, Manhattan

Ⓢ Shuttle service between Grand Street and West 4th Street, Manhattan

Ⓝ Service between Astoria–Ditmars Boulevard, Queens and 86 Street, Brooklyn

Ⓡ Service between Forest Hills–71 Avenue, Queens and 95 Street–Fort Hamilton, Brooklyn

Ⓖ Service between Pelham Bay Park–Bronx and Brooklyn Bridge–City Hall, Manhattan

Bus

M1 Service between Harlem and the East Village or South Ferry

M5 Service between Washington Heights and Greenwich Village

M6 Service between South Ferry and Midtown Manhattan

M21 Local crosstown service between Bellevue Hospital and West Village

Pedestrian

There are three major subway lines and six trains servicing 610 Broadway, including the N, R, 6, F, V and S trains. The MTA records indicate the daily pedestrian turnstile count at the local stations to be approximately 75,000 persons.

Vehicular

610 Broadway is located at the intersection of Houston Street and Broadway with direct access from the North, South and river to river. Traffic counts at this intersection have shown the vehicular hourly volume to be 2,000 cars on Houston Street and 1,200 cars on Broadway.

The building has an interior loading dock and on-site public parking off Crosby Street.

Stacking Plan

Floor	Ceiling	RSF
6	13' – 6"	10,050 plus 3,360sf outdoor terrace
5	15' – 0"	15,350
4	15' – 0"	15,350
3	15' – 0"	15,350
2	15' – 0"	15,350
Ground	19' – 0"	12,000
Cellar	10' – 0"	9,000
Parking 1	9' – 0"	14,750
Parking 2	9' – 0"	15,000

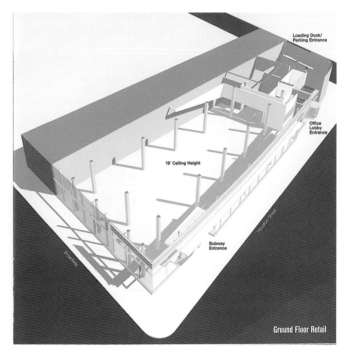

Loading Dock/Parking Entrance

Office Lobby Entrance

19' Ceiling Height

Houston Street

Broadway

Subway Entrance

Ground Floor Retail

Map from an overview book for a major new showroom building in the SOHO area of New York City.

ニューヨーク市のソーホー地区にある新しいショールームビルの案内書から抜粋したマップとフロアプラン。

USA　2003

CD, D: Graham Hanson　D: Jiranuch Sanguaree　CW: Sheldon Werdiger　DF, S: Graham Hanson Design　CL: Macklowe Properties

With 11 stories above ground and 3 below, Tokyo's first convention & art center is a magnificent venue embracing a glass atrium and four buildings each housing a unique hall.

Four buildings, each housing a unique hall, plus the distinctive atrium of the Glass Building. This is the Tokyo International Forum. 7 Multisized halls, the Exhibition Hall, and conference rooms cater to a wide range of needs and requests. Each of these refined spaces boasts the finest equipment and facilities.

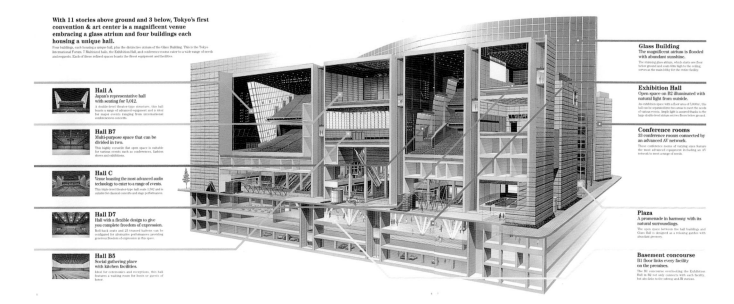

Hall A
Japan's representative hall with seating for 5,012.
A double-level theater-type structure, this hall boasts a range of advanced equipment and is ideal for major events ranging from international conferences to concerts.

Hall B7
Multi-purpose space that can be divided in two.
This highly versatile flat open space is suitable for various events such as conferences, fashion shows and exhibitions.

Hall C
Venue boasting the most advanced audio technology to cater to a range of events.
This triple-level theater-type hall seats 1,502 and is suitable for classical concerts and stage performances.

Hall D7
Hall with a flexible design to give you complete freedom of expression.
Roll-back seats and 25 trussed battens can be configured for alternative performances providing generous freedom of expression in this space.

Hall B5
Social gathering place with kitchen facilities.
Ideal for ceremonies and receptions, this hall features a waiting room for hosts or guests of honor.

Glass Building
The magnificent atrium is flooded with abundant sunshine.
The stunning glass atrium, which starts one floor below ground and soars 60m high to the ceiling, serves as the main lobby for the entire facility.

Exhibition Hall
Open space on B2 illuminated with natural light from outside.
An exhibition space with a floor area of 5,000m², this hall can be separated into two areas to meet the needs of various events. Ample light is assured thanks to the large double-level atrium set two floors below ground.

Conference rooms
33 conference rooms connected by an advanced AV network.
These conference rooms of varying sizes feature the most advanced equipment including an AV network to meet a range of needs.

Plaza
A promenade in harmony with its natural surroundings.
The open space between the hall buildings and Glass Hall is designed as a relaxing garden with abundant greenery.

Basement concourse
B1 floor links every facility on the premises.
The B1 concourse overlooking the Exhibition Hall in B2 not only connects with each facility, but also links to the subway and JR stations.

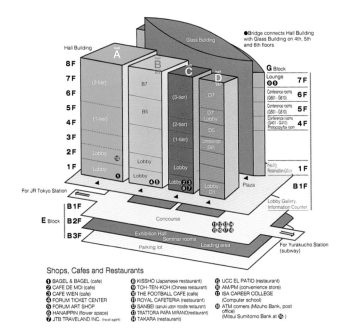

Shops, Cafes and Restaurants

❶ BAGEL & BAGEL (cafe)
❷ CAFE DE MOI (cafe)
❸ CAFE WIEN (cafe)
❹ FORUM TICKET CENTER
❺ FORUM ART SHOP
❻ HANAIPPIN (flower space)
❼ JTB TRAVELAND INC. (travel agent)
❽ KISSHO (Japanese restaurant)
❾ TOH-TEN-KOH (Chinese restaurant)
❿ THE FOOTBALL CAFE (cafe)
⓫ ROYAL CAFETERIA (restaurant)
⓬ SANBEI (sanuki udon noodle restaurant)
⓭ TRATTORIA PAPA MIRANO (restaurant)
⓮ TAKARA (restaurant)
⓯ UCC EL PATIO (restaurant)
⓰ AM/PM (convenience store)
⓱ ISA CAREER COLLEGE (Computer school)
⓲ ATM corners (Mizuho Bank, post office) (Mitsui Sumitomo Bank at ⓰)

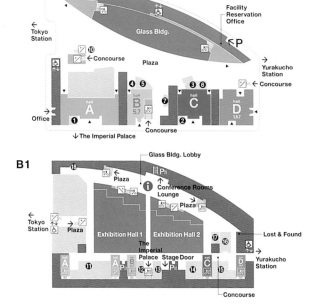

Guide to conference rooms, halls and facilities in a building.

大規模公共施設「東京国際フォーラム」内のホール、会議室等の案内図。

Japan 2003
DF: McCann-Erickson Inc.   S: Tokyo International Forum Co., Ltd.

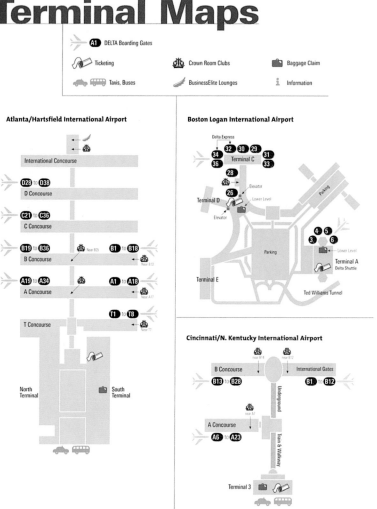

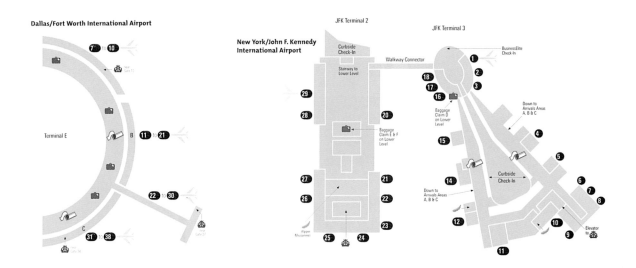

SKY April 2000 **141**

Maps of 6 airport terminals from the in-flight magazine.

機内誌から抜粋した6つの空港ターミナルのマップ。

USA 2000

AD: Ann Harvey   D, I, S: Nigel Holmes   DF: Explanation Graphics   CL: Delta Airlines Sky Magazine

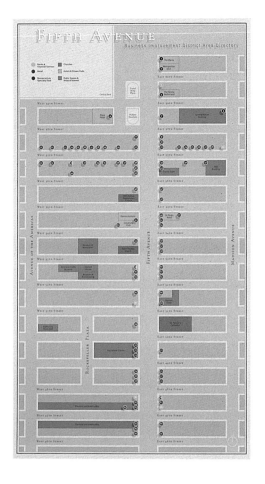

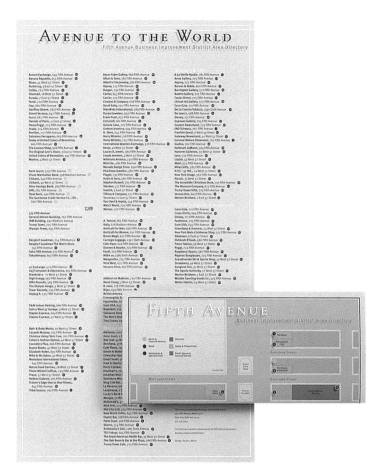

A visitor information map/guide.

来場者のためのインフォメーション・マップ兼ガイド。

USA 2003

D: L. Richard Poulin / Douglas Morris   DF, S: Poulin + Morris Inc.   CL: Fifth Avenue Business Development

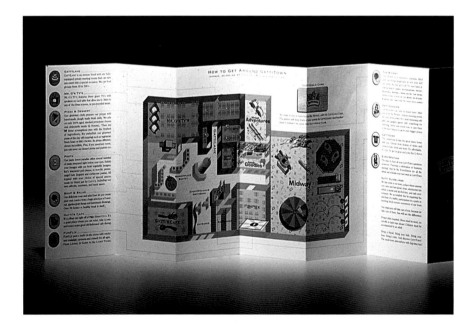

Maps to and around Gattitown, a Mr. Gatti's restaurant that includes buffets, an arcade, and a gift shop.

ビュッフェ、アーケード、ギフトショップを含むレストラン、Gattitownのフロアガイド。

USA 2002

AD, D, CW: Rex Peteet   D: Carrie Echo   DF, S: Sibley Peteet   CL: Mr. Gatti's

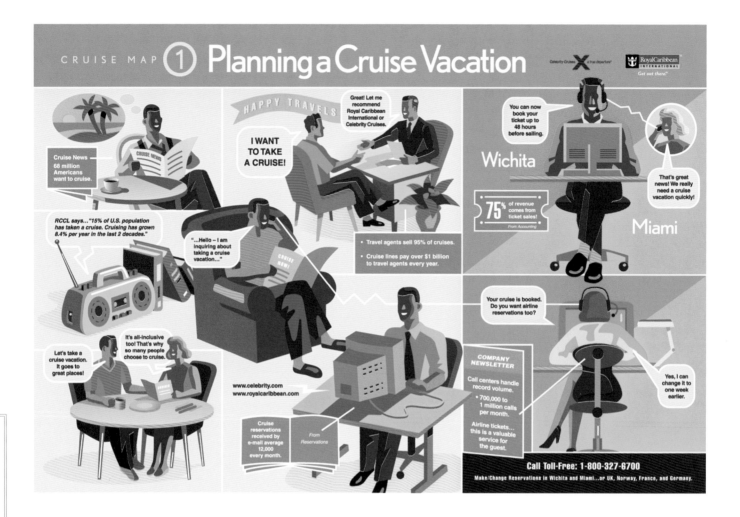

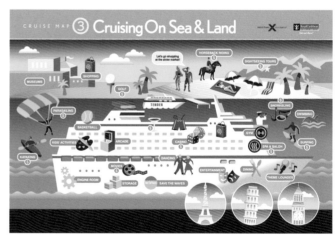

Employee training maps designed to show call-center employees how a cruise "works" from a customer's perspective.

顧客の立場から見たクルーズの流れをコールセンターの従業員に説明するためにデザインされた、研修用のイラストレーション。

USA 2004

CD, S: Sonia Greteman   AD, D: James Strange   DF: Greteman Group   CL: Royal Caribbean Cruises Ltd.

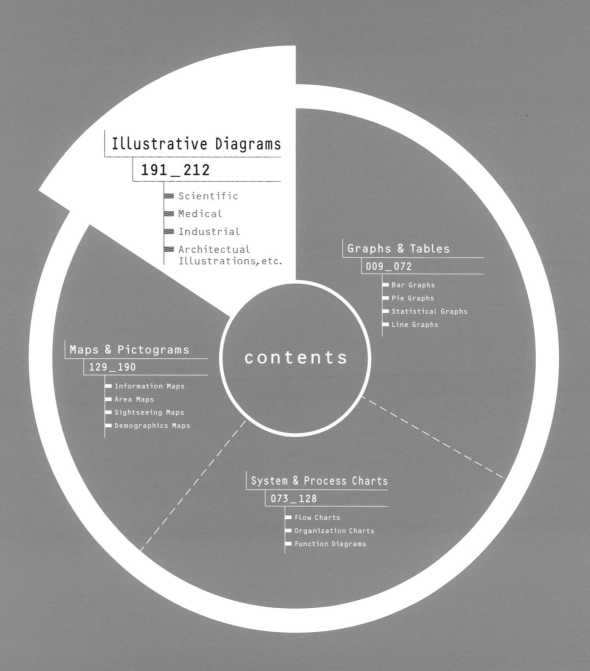

contents

Advanced PEG Molecule

In an aqueous medium, the long chain-like PEG molecule is heavily hydrated and in rapid motion. This rapid motion causes the PEG to sweep out a large volume and prevents the approach and interference of other molecules.

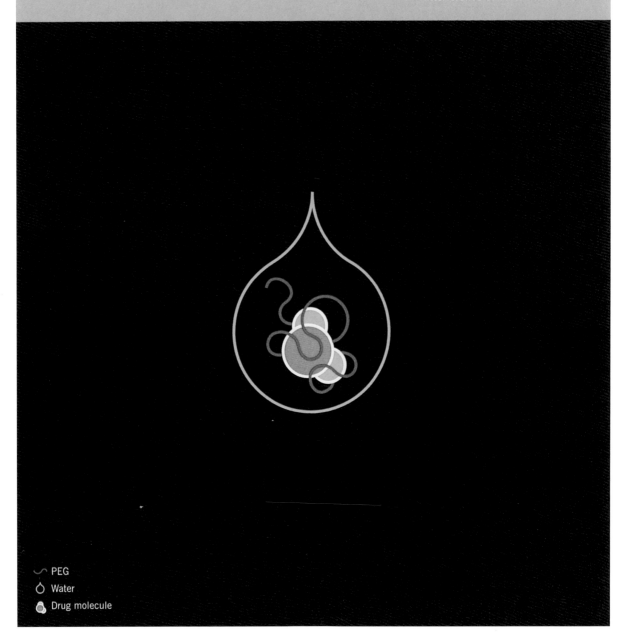

⌒ PEG
⬭ Water
🫧 Drug molecule

From the corporate brochure for Nektar Therapeutics, a pharmaceutical company. Charts explain their technologies and drug formulations.
製薬会社のNektar Therapeutics社の会社案内より。同社のテクノロジーや製剤設計を説明するチャート。

USA 2003
CD, AD: Bill Cahan   AD, D: Sharrie Brooks   I: Doug Struthers   CW: Nicole Litchfield   DF, S: Cahan & Associates   CL: Nektar Therapeutics

Advanced **PEGylation**

The mPEG-SPA Advanced PEGylation reagent is an example of Nektar's clinically proven stable attachment chemistry, which enables improved therapeutic safety and efficacy and decreased dosing frequency.

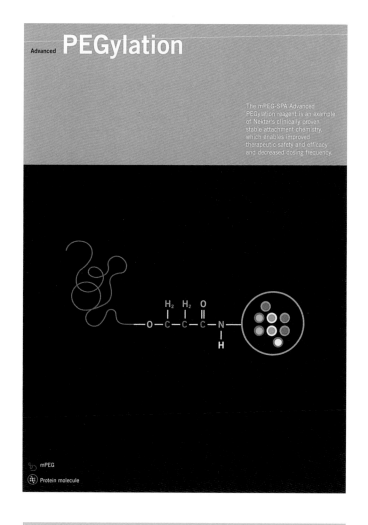

- mPEG
- Protein molecule

Hydrogel PEG Matrix

Composed of chemically cross-linked or physically associated PEGs that create three-dimensional structures, Nektar Hydrogels degrade slowly over time and can dramatically decrease dosing frequency by prolonging drug absorption and release.

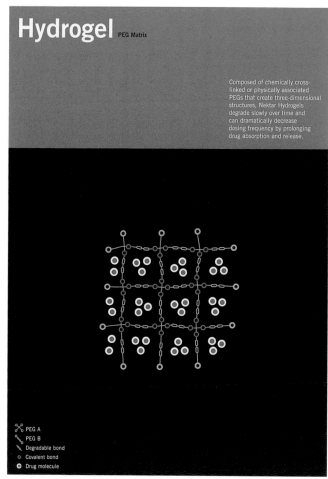

- PEG A
- PEG B
- Degradable bond
- Covalent bond
- Drug molecule

Particle Engineering

In order to effectively administer therapeutics to the deep lung, research indicates that drug particles must have a small, controlled size of under five microns and be highly dispersible. Nektar optimizes particles for efficient and reproducible pulmonary delivery.

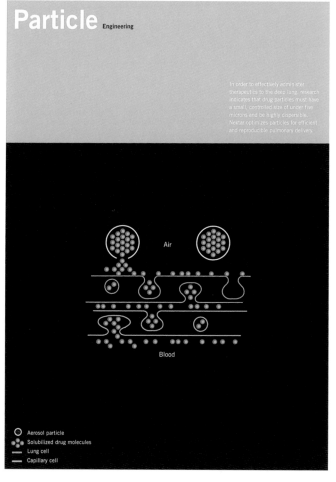

Air

Blood

- Aerosol particle
- Solubilized drug molecules
- Lung cell
- Capillary cell

Amorphous Formulations

Nektar applies innovative screening and modeling methods to determine long-term stability of amorphous formulations, including the formulation's ability to withstand the range of environmental conditions experienced during storage and patient use.

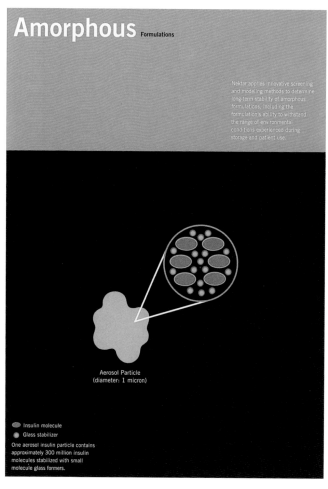

Aerosol Particle
(diameter: 1 micron)

- Insulin molecule
- Glass stabilizer

One aerosol insulin particle contains approximately 300 million insulin molecules stabilized with small molecule glass formers.

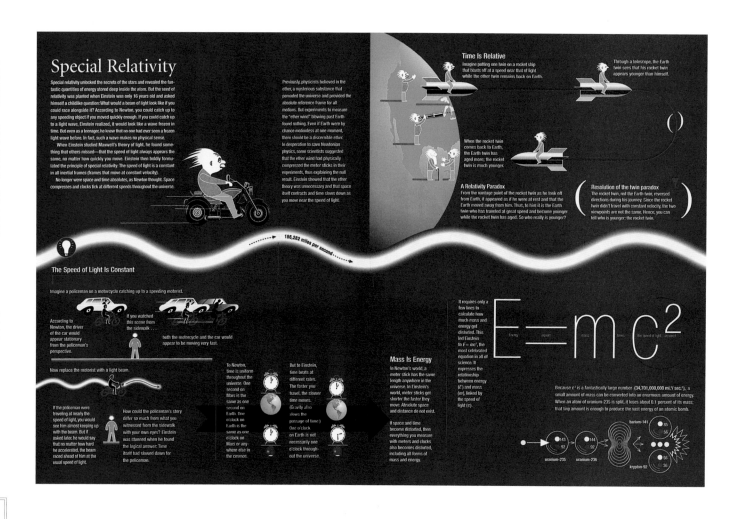

A series of diagrams from a magazine article. Explaining Einstein's theories.

雑誌の記事から抜粋。アインシュタインの理論を説明する図。

USA   2004

CD: Michael Mrak   AD: John Gilman   D, I, S: Nigel Holmes   CW: Michio Kaku   DF: Explanation Graphics   CL: Discover

General Relativity

Special relativity was incomplete because it made no mention of acceleration or gravity. Einstein then made the next key observation: Motion under gravity and motion in an accelerated frame are indistinguishable. Since a light beam will bend in a rocket that is accelerating, a light beam must also bend under gravity.

To show this, Einstein introduced the concept of curved space. In this interpretation, planets move around the sun not because of a gravitational pull but because the sun has warped the space around it, and space itself pushes the planets. Gravity does not pull you into a chair; space pushes on you, creating the feeling of weight. Space-time has been replaced by a fabric that can stretch and bend.

General relativity can describe the extreme warping of space caused by the gravity of a massive dead star—a black hole. When we apply general relativity to the universe as a whole, one solution naturally describes an expanding cosmos that originated in a fiery big bang.

If the sun were to disappear suddenly, what would happen? Newton would say that the entire universe would instantly feel the loss of the sun's gravity. Einstein recognized that nothing—not even gravity—can travel faster than light. Since sunlight takes eight minutes to travel from the sun to Earth, Einstein believed that it would likewise take eight minutes for Earth to respond to the sun's disappearance.

Curved Space-Time

One key to Einstein's thinking is to analyze a spinning disk. Since the rim of the disk travels faster than the center of the disk, the theory of relativity states that the rim is compressed more than the center. If so, the disk must be distorted (its circumference is no longer pi times its diameter). The surface of the disk is, in fact, curved.

Einstein showed that space itself could be similarly curved and that curved space could explain gravity.

Put a bowling ball on a bedsheet and shoot a marble past it. The marble will move in a curved line. A Newtonian physicist would say that the bowling ball exerts a "force" that "pulls" on the marble, making it move in a curved line. A relativist would say that the ball curves the bedsheet and that the bedsheet "pushes" against the marble.

Now replace the bowling ball with the sun and the marble with Earth. By analogy, gravity does not pull Earth around the sun. Rather, the sun bends space around it, and curved space pushes Earth so that it moves around the sun.

(If we remove the bowling ball, the fabric springs back to its normal shape and releases a wave that spreads out. If the sun disappeared, it would take eight minutes for the analogous gravity waves to reach Earth.)

This effect will also bend starlight.

In 1919, during an eclipse of the sun, two expeditions actually measured the bending of starlight as it passed by the sun, shifting the apparent position of the stars. This sealed Einstein's fame.

As it passes by the sun, starlight is bent by the sun's distortion of space. As a result, the stars appear to move.

Black Holes

If a star grows enormously dense, either through collapse or by accumulating matter, its gravity creates a rip in space-time. The result: a black hole, an object from which even light cannot escape. Hundreds of black holes have been detected, many lurking in the centers of galaxies.

Wormholes

Einstein and Nathan Rosen introduced the concept of a "bridge" that might link to a location on the other side of a black hole. Einstein did not believe a person could pass through this bridge, since the gravitational forces would be lethal. (Since then, solutions have been found in which travel through a wormhole might be possible, although this is still controversial.)

The Big Bang

The entire universe can be regarded as a by-product of curved space and time. Curved space-time is analogous to the surface of a balloon. If you blew up a balloon covered with dots, each dot would appear to be speeding away from the other dots. We seem to live on the surface of a four-dimensional balloon that is expanding in a similar manner. Our telescopes show galaxies speeding away from us in all directions.

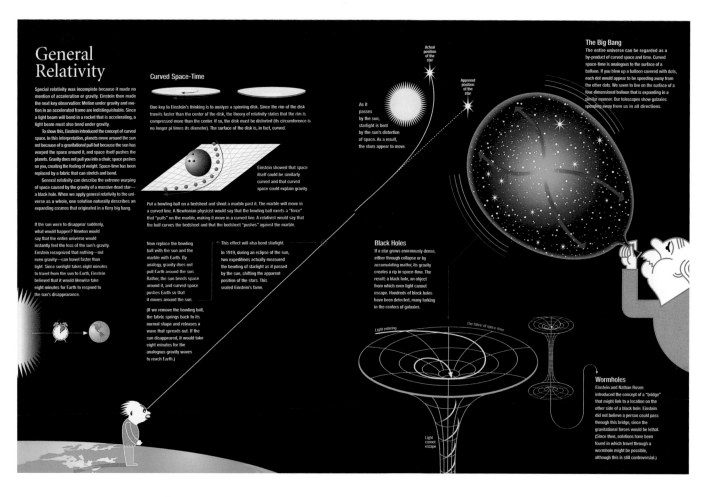

Actual position of the star

Apparent position of the star

Light entering

The fabric of space-time

Light cannot escape

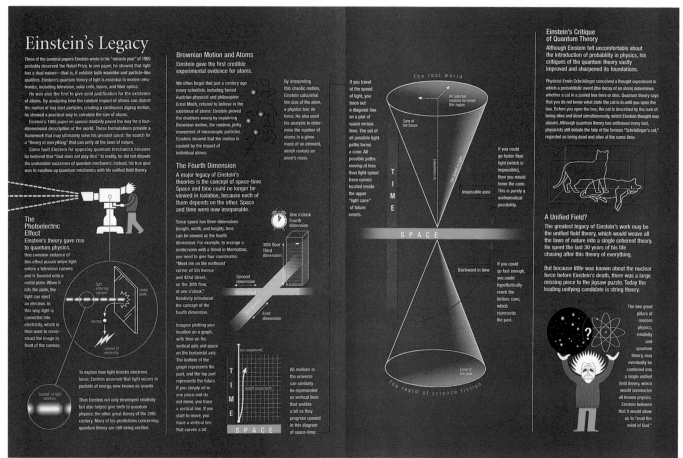

Einstein's Legacy

Three of the seminal papers Einstein wrote in his "miracle year" of 1905 probably deserved the Nobel Prize. In one paper, he showed that light has a dual nature—that is, it exhibits both wavelike and particle-like qualities. Einstein's quantum theory of light is essential to modern electronics, including television, solar cells, lasers, and fiber optics.

He was also the first to give solid justification for the existence of atoms. By analyzing how the random impact of atoms can distort the motion of tiny dust particles, creating a continuous zigzag motion, he showed a practical way to calculate the size of atoms.

Einstein's 1905 paper on special relativity paved the way for a four-dimensional description of the world. These formulations provide a framework that may ultimately solve his greatest quest: the search for a "theory of everything" that can unify all the laws of nature.

Some fault Einstein for opposing quantum mechanics because he believed that "God does not play dice." In reality, he did not dispute the undeniable successes of quantum mechanics. Instead, his true goal was to swallow up quantum mechanics with his unified field theory.

The Photoelectric Effect

Einstein's theory gave rise to quantum physics.

One common instance of this effect occurs when light enters a television camera and is focused onto a metal plate. When it hits the plate, the light can eject an electron. In this way, light is converted into electricity, which is then used to reconstruct the image in front of the camera.

light entering camera

metal plate

electron

current of electricity

"packet" of light (photon)

To explain how light knocks electrons loose, Einstein assumed that light occurs in packets of energy, now known as quanta.

Thus Einstein not only developed relativity but also helped give birth to quantum physics, the other great theory of the 20th century. Many of his predictions concerning quantum theory are still being verified.

Brownian Motion and Atoms

Einstein gave the first credible experimental evidence for atoms.

We often forget that just a century ago many scientists, including famed Austrian physicist and philosopher Ernst Mach, refused to believe in the existence of atoms. Einstein proved the doubters wrong by explaining Brownian motion, the random, jerky movement of microscopic particles. Einstein showed that the motion is caused by the impact of individual atoms.

By interpreting this chaotic motion, Einstein calculated the size of the atom, a physics tour de force. He also used his analysis to determine the number of atoms in a given mass of an element, which reveals an atom's mass.

The Fourth Dimension

A major legacy of Einstein's theories is the concept of space-time. Space and time could no longer be viewed in isolation, because each of them depends on the other. Space and time were now inseparable.

Since space has three dimensions (length, width, and height), time can be viewed as the fourth dimension. For example, to arrange a rendezvous with a friend in Manhattan, you need to give four coordinates: "Meet me on the northeast corner of 5th Avenue and 42nd Street, on the 30th floor, at one o'clock." Relativity introduced the concept of the fourth dimension.

Imagine plotting your location on a graph, with time on the vertical axis and space on the horizontal axis. The bottom of the graph represents the past, and the top part represents the future. If you simply sit in one place and do not move, you trace a vertical line. If you start to move, you trace a vertical line that curves a bit.

One o'clock Fourth dimension

30th floor Third dimension

Second dimension

First dimension

TIME

SPACE

(no movement)

(slight movement)

All motions in the universe can similarly be represented as vertical lines that wobble a bit as they progress upward in this diagram of space-time.

The real world

Cone of the future

All possible motions lie inside this region

TIME

SPACE

Impossible area

Cone of the past

The realm of science fiction

If you travel at the speed of light, you trace out a diagonal line on a plot of space versus time. The set of all possible light paths forms a cone. All possible paths moving at less than light speed trace curves located inside the upper "light cone" of future events.

If you could go faster than light (which is impossible), then you would leave the cone. This is purely a mathematical possibility.

If you could go fast enough, you could hypothetically reach the bottom cone, which represents the past.

Backward in time

Einstein's Critique of Quantum Theory

Although Einstein felt uncomfortable about the introduction of probability in physics, his critiques of the quantum theory vastly improved and sharpened its foundations.

Physicist Erwin Schrödinger conceived a thought experiment in which a probabilistic event (the decay of an atom) determines whether a cat in a sealed box lives or dies. Quantum theory says that you do not know what state the cat is in until you open the box. Before you open the box, the cat is described by the sum of being alive and dead simultaneously, which Einstein thought was absurd. Although quantum theory has withstood every test, physicists still debate the fate of the famous "Schrödinger's cat," regarded as being dead and alive at the same time.

A Unified Field?

The greatest legacy of Einstein's work may be the unified field theory, which would weave all the laws of nature into a single coherent theory. He spent the last 30 years of his life chasing after this theory of everything.

But because little was known about the nuclear force before Einstein's death, there was a large missing piece to the jigsaw puzzle. Today the leading unifying candidate is string theory.

The two great pillars of modern physics, relativity and quantum theory, may eventually be combined into a single unified field theory, which would summarize all known physics. Einstein believed that it would allow us to "read the mind of God."

The Java That Really Did Change the World

On average, everyone in the **U.S.** drinks a cup and a half of coffee daily:
(That's far less than folks in the **Netherlands;** they down four cups a day:)
Here's why we humans like caffeine so much (and why spiders don't).

BY NIGEL HOLMES

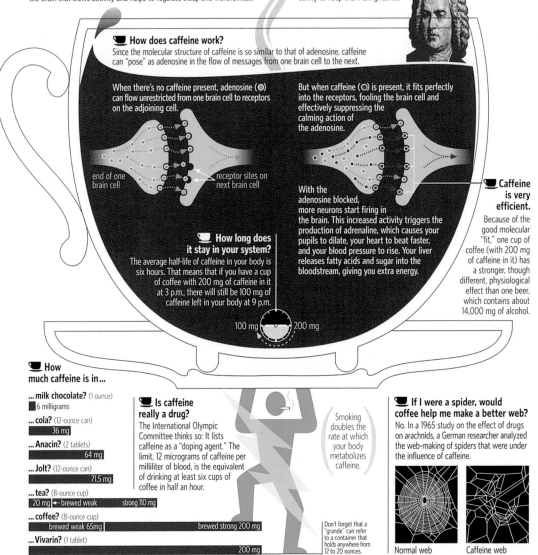

What is caffeine?

Caffeine is a stimulant found in more than 60 plants, including coffee beans and tea leaves, but also guarana seeds and some holly. In its pure form, it is a white, bitter-tasting crystalline powder. The chemical structure, first identified in 1819, is nearly identical to that of **adenosine,** a chemical in the brain that slows activity and helps to regulate sleep and wakefulness.

A very short history.

The Chinese discovered the effects of caffeine, in the form of medicinal tea, some 5,000 years ago, and legend has it that 15th-century Sufis in Yemen drank coffee to stay awake during night prayers. Coffee was introduced to Europe at the beginning of the 1600s. By the early 1700s, **Bach** had written his "Coffee Cantata" operetta while intellectuals such as Voltaire and Rousseau, frequenters of Paris's many coffeehouses, praised the drink's ability to keep them Enlightened.

How does caffeine work?

Since the molecular structure of caffeine is so similar to that of adenosine, caffeine can "pose" as adenosine in the flow of messages from one brain cell to the next.

When there's no caffeine present, adenosine (◉) can flow unrestricted from one brain cell to receptors on the adjoining cell.

end of one brain cell

receptor sites on next brain cell

But when caffeine (○) is present, it fits perfectly into the receptors, fooling the brain cell and effectively suppressing the calming action of the adenosine.

With the adenosine blocked, more neurons start firing in the brain. This increased activity triggers the production of adrenaline, which causes your pupils to dilate, your heart to beat faster, and your blood pressure to rise. Your liver releases fatty acids and sugar into the bloodstream, giving you extra energy.

How long does it stay in your system?

The average half-life of caffeine in your body is six hours. That means that if you have a cup of coffee with 200 mg of caffeine in it at 3 p.m., there will still be 100 mg of caffeine left in your body at 9 p.m.

100 mg　200 mg

Caffeine is very efficient.

Because of the good molecular "fit," one cup of coffee (with 200 mg of caffeine in it) has a stronger, though different, physiological effect than one beer, which contains about 14,000 mg of alcohol.

How much caffeine is in...

...milk chocolate? (1 ounce)
6 milligrams

...cola? (12-ounce can)
36 mg

...Anacin? (2 tablets)
64 mg

...Jolt? (12-ounce can)
71.5 mg

...tea? (8-ounce cup)
20 mg ◄ brewed weak　　strong 110 mg

...coffee? (8-ounce cup)
brewed weak 65mg　　brewed strong 200 mg

...Vivarin? (1 tablet)
200 mg

Is caffeine really a drug?

The International Olympic Committee thinks so: It lists caffeine as a "doping agent." The limit, 12 micrograms of caffeine per milliliter of blood, is the equivalent of drinking at least six cups of coffee in half an hour.

Smoking doubles the rate at which your body metabolizes caffeine.

Don't forget that a "grande" can refer to a container that holds anywhere from 12 to 20 ounces.

If I were a spider, would coffee help me make a better web?

No. In a 1965 study on the effect of drugs on arachnids, a German researcher analyzed the web-making of spiders that were under the influence of caffeine.

Normal web　　Caffeine web

SOURCES: National Coffee Assn.: *The World of Caffeine,* Bennett Alan Weinberg and Bonnie K. Bealer; Duke University Medical Center; International Food Information Council; International Olympic Committee; *A Spider's Web,* Peter N. Witt et al.

JANUARY 2002 **BUSINESS 2.0 29**

Diagrams explaining how caffeine affects the brain.

カフェインがどのように脳に影響を与えるかを図解したもの。

USA　2002

CD: Susan Casey　AD: Susan Scandrett　D, I, CW, S: Nigel Holmes　DF: Explanation Graphics　CL: E-Company

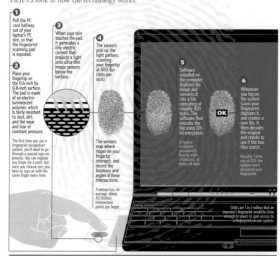

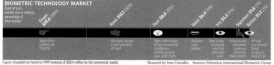

a

b

c

An explanation of the fingerprint recognition system. (a)
Diagram showing the process of champagne making. (b)
Illustration accompanying an article about the French TGV train. How is french TGV to go so fast? (c)

指紋識別システムに関する説明図。 (a)
シャンパンができるまでの過程図。 (b)
TGV（フランス新幹線）がなぜ速く走れるのかを図解。 (c)

USA 2001 (a, c) / 2003 (b)
CD: Susan Casey (a)   AD: Susan Scandrett (a) / Holly Holliday (b, c)   D, I, S: Nigel Holmes   CW: Nigel Holmes (a)   DF: Explanation Graphics
CL: E-Company (a) / Attaché Magazine (b, c)

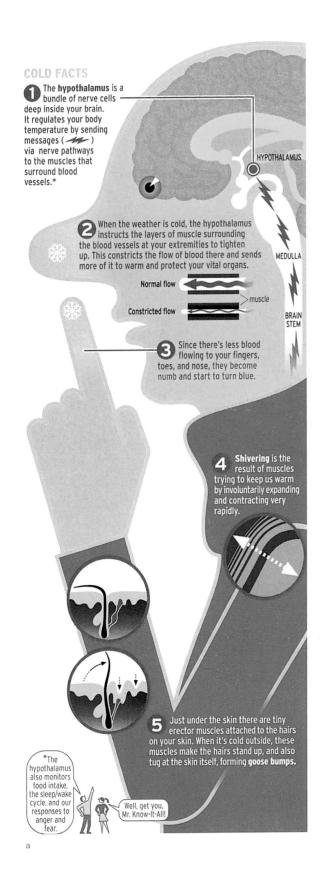

COLD FACTS

① The **hypothalamus** is a bundle of nerve cells deep inside your brain. It regulates your body temperature by sending messages (⚡) via nerve pathways to the muscles that surround blood vessels.*

HYPOTHALAMUS

② When the weather is cold, the hypothalamus instructs the layers of muscle surrounding the blood vessels at your extremities to tighten up. This constricts the flow of blood there and sends more of it to warm and protect your vital organs.

MEDULLA

Normal flow
Constricted flow
← muscle

BRAIN STEM

③ Since there's less blood flowing to your fingers, toes, and nose, they become numb and start to turn blue.

④ **Shivering** is the result of muscles trying to keep us warm by involuntarily expanding and contracting very rapidly.

⑤ Just under the skin there are tiny erector muscles attached to the hairs on your skin. When it's cold outside, these muscles make the hairs stand up, and also tug at the skin itself, forming **goose bumps.**

*The hypothalamus also monitors food intake, the sleep/wake cycle, and our responses to anger and fear.

Well, get you, Mr. Know-It-All!

a

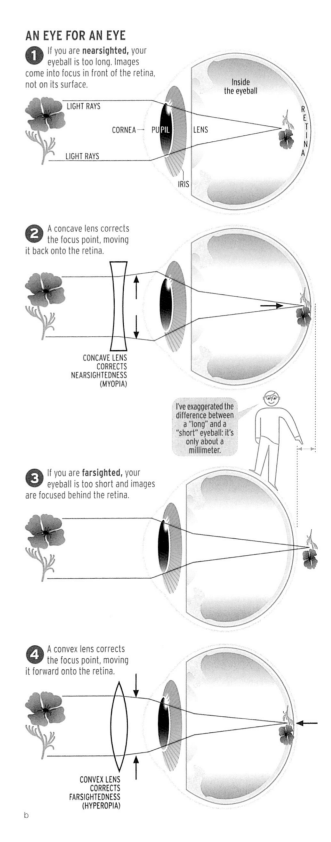

AN EYE FOR AN EYE

① If you are **nearsighted,** your eyeball is too long. Images come into focus in front of the retina, not on its surface.

Inside the eyeball

LIGHT RAYS
CORNEA → PUPIL   LENS   RETINA
LIGHT RAYS
IRIS

② A concave lens corrects the focus point, moving it back onto the retina.

CONCAVE LENS CORRECTS NEARSIGHTEDNESS (MYOPIA)

I've exaggerated the difference between a "long" and a "short" eyeball: it's only about a millimeter.

③ If you are **farsighted,** your eyeball is too short and images are focused behind the retina.

④ A convex lens corrects the focus point, moving it forward onto the retina.

CONVEX LENS CORRECTS FARSIGHTEDNESS (HYPEROPIA)

b

Illustration explains the facts on common cold symptom. (a)
How an eye focuses. (b)

風邪の症状に関する事実を説明するイラストレーション。 (a)
眼球が焦点を合わせるしくみを説明するイラストレーション。 (b)

USA　2001 (a) / 2003 (b) / 2004 (c, d)
AD: Holly Holliday　D, I, S: Nigel Holmes　DF: Explanation Graphics　CL: Attaché Magazine

A SWEET STREAM

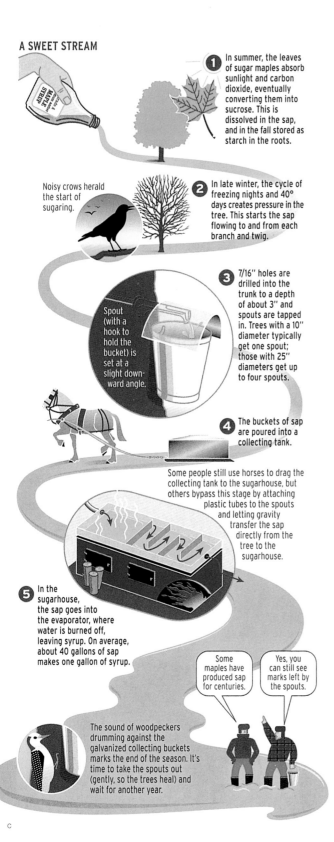

1 In summer, the leaves of sugar maples absorb sunlight and carbon dioxide, eventually converting them into sucrose. This is dissolved in the sap, and in the fall stored as starch in the roots.

Noisy crows herald the start of sugaring.

2 In late winter, the cycle of freezing nights and 40° days creates pressure in the tree. This starts the sap flowing to and from each branch and twig.

3 7/16″ holes are drilled into the trunk to a depth of about 3″ and spouts are tapped in. Trees with a 10″ diameter typically get one spout; those with 25″ diameters get up to four spouts.

Spout (with a hook to hold the bucket) is set at a slight downward angle.

4 The buckets of sap are poured into a collecting tank.

Some people still use horses to drag the collecting tank to the sugarhouse, but others bypass this stage by attaching plastic tubes to the spouts and letting gravity transfer the sap directly from the tree to the sugarhouse.

5 In the sugarhouse, the sap goes into the evaporator, where water is burned off, leaving syrup. On average, about 40 gallons of sap makes one gallon of syrup.

Some maples have produced sap for centuries.

Yes, you can still see marks left by the spouts.

The sound of woodpeckers drumming against the galvanized collecting buckets marks the end of the season. It's time to take the spouts out (gently, so the trees heal) and wait for another year.

c

PROJECTING A GOOD IMAGE

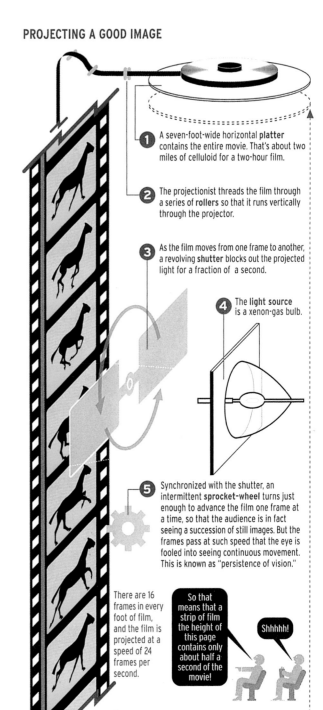

1 A seven-foot-wide horizontal **platter** contains the entire movie. That's about two miles of celluloid for a two-hour film.

2 The projectionist threads the film through a series of **rollers** so that it runs vertically through the projector.

3 As the film moves from one frame to another, a revolving **shutter** blocks out the projected light for a fraction of a second.

4 The **light source** is a xenon-gas bulb.

5 Synchronized with the shutter, an intermittent **sprocket-wheel** turns just enough to advance the film one frame at a time, so that the audience is in fact seeing a succession of still images. But the frames pass at such speed that the eye is fooled into seeing continuous movement. This is known as "persistence of vision."

There are 16 frames in every foot of film, and the film is projected at a speed of 24 frames per second.

So that means that a strip of film the height of this page contains only about half a second of the movie!

Shhhhh!

6 After passing through the projector, the film is wound onto a **second platter**, which is positioned directly under the first.

d

Informational graphics describing how movies are projected. (c)
Illustration explaining the process of maple syrup production. (d)

メイプル・シロップの製造過程を説明するイラストレーション。(c)
映画がどのように映し出されるかを説明するグラフィック。(d)

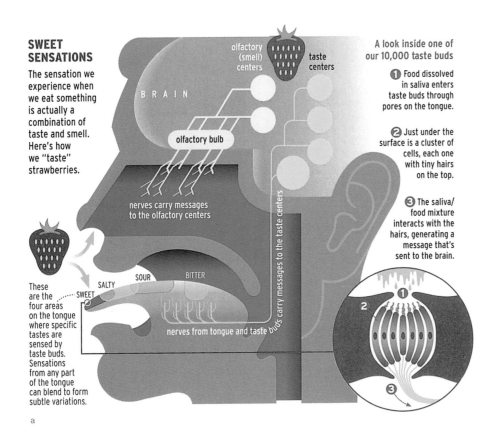

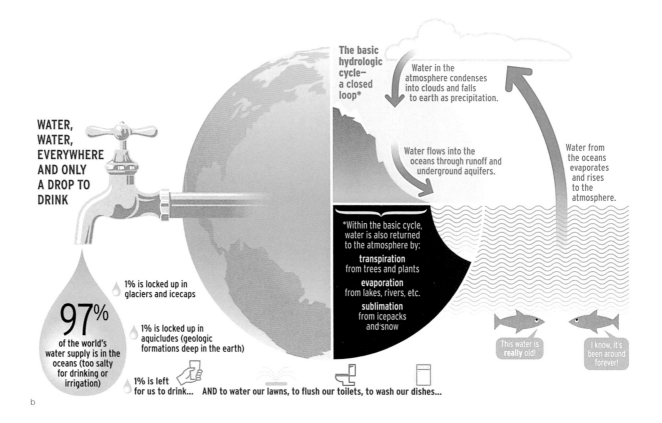

Illustration explaining the mechanism for gustatory and olfactory sensation. How we "taste" strawberries. (a)
An explanation of the basic hydrologic cycle. (b)

味覚と嗅覚の仕組みを説明する図。どうやってイチゴを味わうか。 (a)
基本的な水の循環の説明図。 (b)

USA   2002 (a) / 2003 (b)
AD: Holly Holliday   D, I, S: Nigel Holmes   DF: Explanation Graphics   CL: Attaché Magazine

2

MONKS, VEGETABLES & GENES

It all began when a quiet monk named Mendel decided to study his vegetables instead of just eating them.

Living in a quiet monastery in Moravia, a country that no longer exists, Mendel puttered around the garden experimenting with various types of peas.

He found that **when** 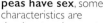 **peas have sex**, some characteristics are dominant and some tend to disappear for a generation. From this he deduced that you can statistically predict what the next generations will look like.

Mendel published, joined management, retired, and perished. It took decades until researchers discovered his work and began to build a pyramid of knowledge based on "Mendelian Genetics."

(So we can begin to understand why someone has blonde or red hair; why only one brother is tall and thin; why your sister is good looking while you…)

The Monk in the Garden
Robin Marantz Henig

a

3

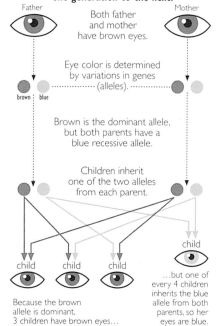

How some traits are passed from one generation to the next.

Father · Mother

Both father and mother have brown eyes.

Eye color is determined by variations in genes (alleles).

brown · blue

Brown is the dominant allele, but both parents have a blue recessive allele.

Children inherit one of the two alleles from each parent.

child

child · child · child

Because the brown allele is dominant, 3 children have brown eyes…

…but one of every 4 children inherits the blue allele from both parents, so her eyes are blue.

The smallest ever
GUIDE TO LIFE SCIENCES
(for busy people)

JUAN ENRIQUEZ • RODRIGO MARTINEZ
Life Sciences Project, Harvard Business School

NIGEL HOLMES
Designer

Produced by
THE VAN HEYST GROUP

6

SIZE MATTERS: quarks to the universe

	quark	atom	molecule	base pairs	DNA	chromosome pair	cell	human
how big?	we don't know	0.2 nm	0.2– 20 nm	see next page	6 ft per human cell		2μm– 0.2 mm	6 ft high –you wish– (1.8 trillion nm)
how many?				3.2 billion base pairs in human genome	30,000+ genes in humans	23 pairs in every human cell	100 trillion in the human body	6.2 billion on earth
and…		1 million atoms side-by-side equal the thickness of one of your hairs	life is a series of long molecules strung together	base pairs: **A**denine + **T**hiamine **C**ytosine + **G**uanine	**genes** are sections of DNA that carry specific instructions (**genome:** whole of an organism's gene code)	hold different sections of your gene code	hardware that executes the gene code	

nm	nanometer	one billionth of a meter	10^{-9}
μm	micrometer	one millionth of a meter	10^{-6}
mm	millimeter	one thousandth of a meter	10^{-3}
m	meter	one meter	10^{0}

www.powersof10.com

7

earth 12,760 kms diameter (0.0000000013 light years)

Caution: figures are illustrative. Many are estimates or averages.

milky way 100,000 l.y. across

known universe 40 billion l.y. across

b

A series of diagrams from the little book explaining the human genome. How some traits are passed from one generation to the next. (a) Size matters : quarks to the universe. (b)

ヒトゲノムを説明する小冊子から抜粋した一連のダイアグラム。ある体質が次の世代に受け継がれる仕組み。(a)
クォークから宇宙までの大きさを表すダイアグラム。(b)

USA 2003

CD, AD, D, I, S: Nigel Holmes   CW: Juan Enriquez / Rodrigo Martinez   DF: Explanation Graphics   CL: Van Heyst Group

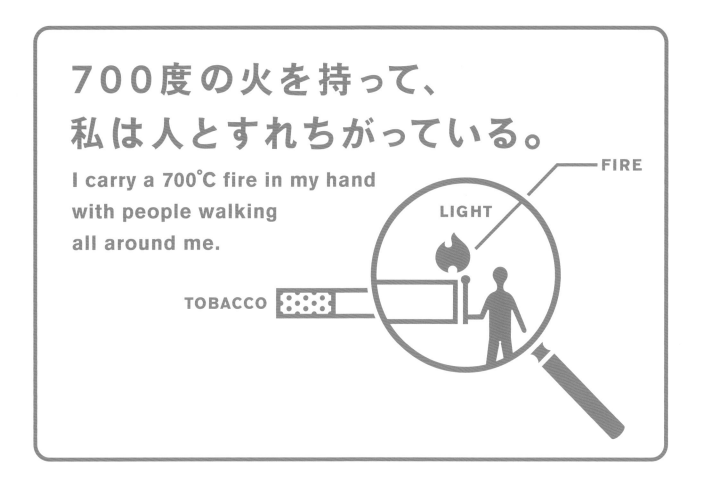

７００度の火を持って、
私は人とすれちがっている。

**I carry a 700°C fire in my hand
with people walking
all around me.**

FIRE

LIGHT

TOBACCO

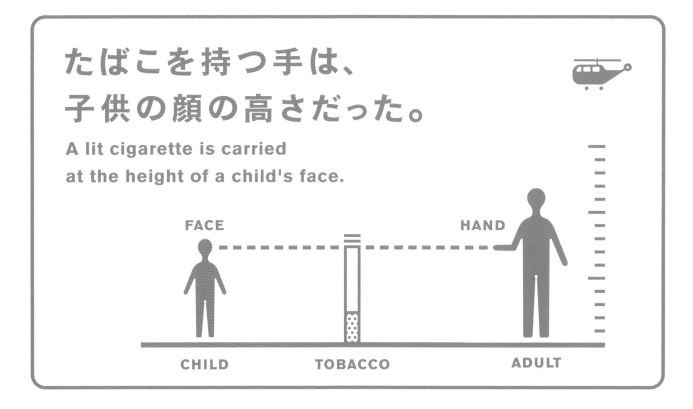

たばこを持つ手は、
子供の顔の高さだった。

**A lit cigarette is carried
at the height of a child's face.**

FACE

HAND

CHILD

TOBACCO

ADULT

A diagram designed to stimulate awareness, thought and action by presenting various scenes of thoughtless smoking manners.

何気なく行ってしまう喫煙マナー行動について多くのシーンを紹介し、気づき、考え、行動することを促すためのイラストレーション。

Japan 2004
CD: Hiroshi Aizawa AD, I: Bunpei Yorifuji D: Takuya Shibata CW: Kinya Okamoto DF: Bunpei Ginza CL, S: Japan Tobacco Inc.

私に手を振る人がいた。
煙を払う仕草だった。

A person was waving at me.
He was waving away
my smoke.

HAND WAVING　　　　PROTECTION

スタンド灰皿。火を消さないで
入れるのは、煙をふやす行為だ。

Stand ashtrays.
Disposing of a lit cigarette
in one just creates
more smoke.

TOBACCO

STAND ASHTRAY　　　　INCINERATOR

煙の行方。本人だけが、
他人事だった。

Where does the smoke go?
Only the person producing
it is unconcerned.

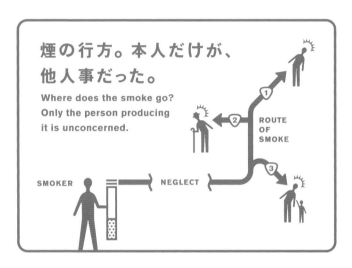

ROUTE
OF
SMOKE

SMOKER　　　NEGLECT

吸いがらを
排水溝に捨てた。
というか隠した。

I threw my cigarette butt
into the drain. That is to say,
I hid it in the drain.

DROP

TOBACCO

SEWER

体はよけた。
それでも煙は
ぶつかった。

I moved to avoid him.
But my smoke didn't.

SMOKE

SIDE STEP

TOBACCO

日本一、
目につくゴミは、
吸いがらかも。

Probably the kind of litter
I see most often in Japan
is cigarette butts.

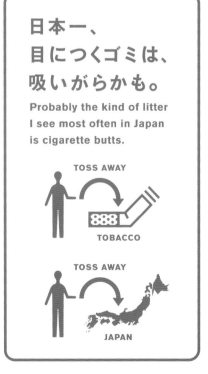

TOSS AWAY

TOBACCO

TOSS AWAY

JAPAN

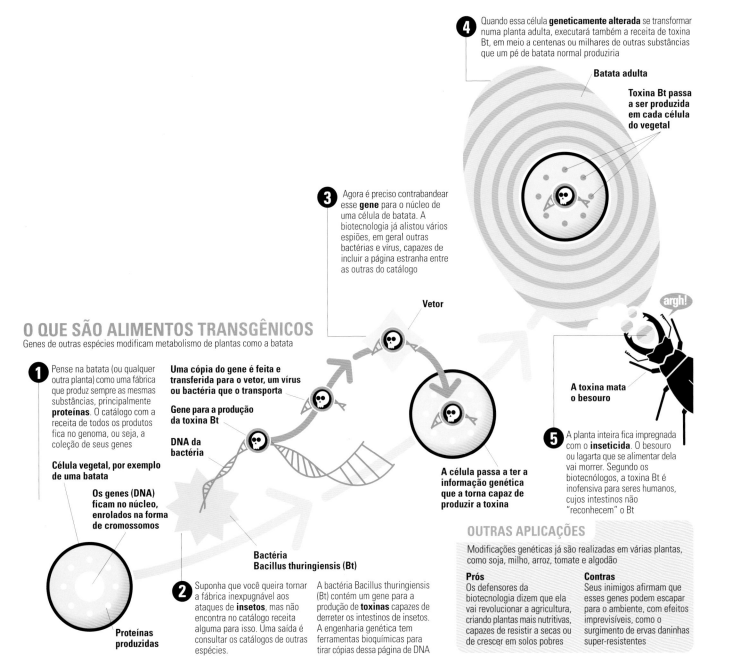

4 Quando essa célula **geneticamente alterada** se transformar numa planta adulta, executará também a receita de toxina Bt, em meio a centenas ou milhares de outras substâncias que um pé de batata normal produziria

Batata adulta

Toxina Bt passa a ser produzida em cada célula do vegetal

3 Agora é preciso contrabandear esse **gene** para o núcleo de uma célula de batata. A biotecnologia já alistou vários espiões, em geral outras bactérias e vírus, capazes de incluir a página estranha entre as outras do catálogo

Vetor

O QUE SÃO ALIMENTOS TRANSGÊNICOS

Genes de outras espécies modificam metabolismo de plantas como a batata

1 Pense na batata (ou qualquer outra planta) como uma fábrica que produz sempre as mesmas substâncias, principalmente **proteínas**. O catálogo com a receita de todos os produtos fica no genoma, ou seja, a coleção de seus genes

Célula vegetal, por exemplo de uma batata

Os genes (DNA) ficam no núcleo, enrolados na forma de cromossomos

Uma cópia do gene é feita e transferida para o vetor, um vírus ou bactéria que o transporta

Gene para a produção da toxina Bt

DNA da bactéria

Proteínas produzidas

Bactéria Bacillus thuringiensis (Bt)

2 Suponha que você queira tornar a fábrica inexpugnável aos ataques de **insetos**, mas não encontra no catálogo receita alguma para isso. Uma saída é consultar os catálogos de outras espécies.

A bactéria Bacillus thuringiensis (Bt) contém um gene para a produção de **toxinas** capazes de derreter os intestinos de insetos. A engenharia genética tem ferramentas bioquímicas para tirar cópias dessa página de DNA

A célula passa a ter a informação genética que a torna capaz de produzir a toxina

argh!

A toxina mata o besouro

5 A planta inteira fica impregnada com o **inseticida**. O besouro ou lagarta que se alimentar dela vai morrer. Segundo os biotecnólogos, a toxina Bt é inofensiva para seres humanos, cujos intestinos não "reconhecem" o Bt

OUTRAS APLICAÇÕES

Modificações genéticas já são realizadas em várias plantas, como soja, milho, arroz, tomate e algodão

Prós
Os defensores da biotecnologia dizem que ela vai revolucionar a agricultura, criando plantas mais nutritivas, capazes de resistir a secas ou de crescer em solos pobres

Contras
Seus inimigos afirmam que esses genes podem escapar para o ambiente, com efeitos imprevisíveis, como o surgimento de ervas daninhas super-resistentes

Will transgenic foods be the final solution to hunger? Diagrams explaining what is transgenic foods, and creating a starting point for readers to think about this question.

遺伝子組み換え食品は飢餓の最終的な解決策になるのだろうか？ 遺伝子組み換え食品とは何かを説明し、読者がこの問題について考えるための出発点となる図。

Brazil   2000

CD, S: Eduardo Asta   CW: Mauricio Puls / Thales de Menezes / Leonardo Cruz   CL: Folha de São Paulo

O PRESENTE E O FUTURO NA CONSTRUÇÃO CIVIL

ARTESANAL — INDUSTRIAL

Tecnologia predominante hoje, assemelha-se ao processo utilizado na feitura de uma bolo. Na construção, a estrutura é composta por uma massa equacionada de concreto e barras de aço, depositada no interior de fôrmas de madeira. Quando essa mistura seca, as fôrmas são retiradas, deixando prontas as vigas de concreto e aço. Esse processo artesanal de construção é demorado, com elevado desperdício de materiais e utiliza mão-de-obra pouco qualidade e mal remunerada

Já utilizada hoje em menor escala, a tecnologia dos pré-fabricados é a principal tendência na construção para o futuro. Seu sistema assemelha-se mais a um jogo infantil com pequenas peças de plástico de montar. Todos os componentes vêm finalizados da fábrica e nas dimensões exatas, prontos para serem montados, no canteiro de obras. Há redução do tempo de duração da obra, do desperdício de materiais e da mão-de-obra, que deverá ter melhor qualificação

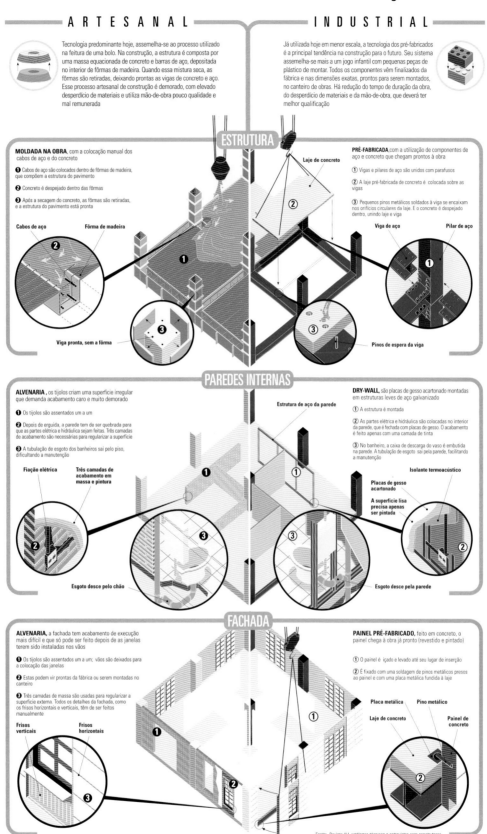

ESTRUTURA

MOLDADA NA OBRA, com a colocação manual dos cabos de aço e do concreto

❶ Cabos de aço são colocados dentro de fôrmas de madeira, que compõem a estrutura do pavimento

❷ Concreto é despejado dentro das fôrmas

❸ Após a secagem do concreto, as fôrmas são retiradas, e a estrutura do pavimento está pronta

Cabos de aço — Fôrma de madeira

Viga pronta, sem a fôrma

PRÉ-FABRICADA, com a utilização de componentes de aço e concreto que chegam prontos à obra

① Vigas e pilares de aço são unidos com parafusos

② A laje pré-fabricada de concreto é colocada sobre as vigas

③ Pequenos pinos metálicos soldados à viga se encaixam nos orifícios circulares da laje. E o concreto é despejado dentro, unindo laje e viga

Laje de concreto

Viga de aço — Pilar de aço

Pinos de espera da viga

PAREDES INTERNAS

ALVENARIA, os tijolos criam uma superfície irregular que demanda acabamento caro e muito demorado

❶ Os tijolos são assentados um a um

❷ Depois de erguida, a parede tem de ser quebrada para que as partes elétrica e hidráulica sejam feitas. Três camadas de acabamento são necessárias para regularizar a superfície

❸ A tubulação de esgoto dos banheiros sai pelo piso, dificultando a manutenção

Fiação elétrica — Três camadas de acabamento em massa e pintura

Esgoto desce pelo chão

DRY-WALL, são placas de gesso acartonado montadas em estruturas leves de aço galvanizado

① A estrutura é montada

② As partes elétrica e hidráulica são colocadas no interior da parede, que é fechada com placas de gesso. O acabamento é feito apenas com uma camada de tinta

③ No banheiro, a caixa de descarga do vaso é embutida na parede. A tubulação de esgoto sai pela parede, facilitando a manutenção

Estrutura de aço da parede

Isolante termoacústico

Placas de gesso acartonado

A superfície lisa precisa apenas ser pintada

Esgoto desce pela parede

FACHADA

ALVENARIA, a fachada tem acabamento de execução mais difícil e que só pode ser feito depois de as janelas terem sido instaladas nos vãos

❶ Os tijolos são assentados um a um; vãos são deixados para a colocação das janelas

❷ Estas podem vir prontas da fábrica ou serem montadas no canteiro

❸ Três camadas de massa são usadas para regularizar a superfície externa. Todos os detalhes da fachada, como os frisos horizontais e verticais, têm de ser feitos manualmente

Frisos verticais — Frisos horizontais

PAINEL PRÉ-FABRICADO, feito em concreto, o painel chega a obra já pronto (revestido e pintado)

① O painel é içado e levado até seu lugar de inserção

② É fixado com uma soldagem de pinos metálicos presos ao painel e com uma placa metálica fundida à laje

Placa metálica — Pino metálico

Laje de concreto — Painel de concreto

Fonte: Revista AU, catálogos técnicos e entrevistas com construtoras

From a newspaper article that says a house will be built as a car in the future.
Illustration explaining the difference between the present and future construction process step by step.

将来、住宅が車の様に組み立てられるようになるという新聞記事のイラスト。現在と将来の建築プロセスの違いを順を追って説明している。

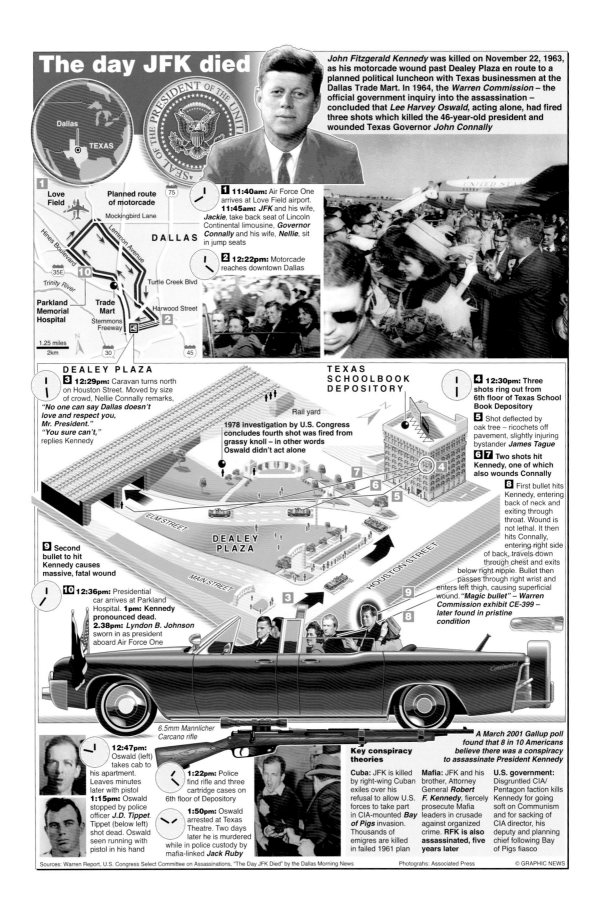

The day JFK died

John Fitzgerald Kennedy was killed on November 22, 1963, as his motorcade wound past Dealey Plaza en route to a planned political luncheon with Texas businessmen at the Dallas Trade Mart. In 1964, the *Warren Commission* – the official government inquiry into the assassination – concluded that *Lee Harvey Oswald*, acting alone, had fired three shots which killed the 46-year-old president and wounded Texas Governor *John Connally*

Dallas
TEXAS

1 Love Field

Planned route of motorcade

Mockingbird Lane

Hines Boulevard
Lemmon Avenue

DALLAS

Trinity River

10

Turtle Creek Blvd

Parkland Memorial Hospital

Trade Mart

Stemmons Freeway

Harwood Street

2

1.25 miles
2km

1 **11:40am:** Air Force One arrives at Love Field airport.
11:45am: *JFK* and his wife, *Jackie*, take back seat of Lincoln Continental limousine, *Governor Connally* and his wife, *Nellie*, sit in jump seats

2 **12:22pm:** Motorcade reaches downtown Dallas

DEALEY PLAZA

3 **12:29pm:** Caravan turns north on Houston Street. Moved by size of crowd, Nellie Connally remarks,
"No one can say Dallas doesn't love and respect you, Mr. President."
"You sure can't," replies Kennedy

Rail yard

1978 investigation by U.S. Congress concludes fourth shot was fired from grassy knoll – in other words Oswald didn't act alone

TEXAS SCHOOLBOOK DEPOSITORY

4 **12:30pm:** Three shots ring out from 6th floor of Texas School Book Depository

5 Shot deflected by oak tree – ricochets off pavement, slightly injuring bystander *James Tague*

6 7 Two shots hit Kennedy, one of which also wounds Connally

8 First bullet hits Kennedy, entering back of neck and exiting through throat. Wound is not lethal. It then hits Connally, entering right side of back, travels down through chest and exits below right nipple. Bullet then passes through right wrist and enters left thigh, causing superficial wound. *"Magic bullet"* – *Warren Commission* exhibit CE-399 – later found in pristine condition

9 Second bullet to hit Kennedy causes massive, fatal wound

DEALEY PLAZA

ELM STREET
MAIN STREET
HOUSTON STREET

10 **12:36pm:** Presidential car arrives at Parkland Hospital. **1pm:** Kennedy pronounced dead.
2.38pm: *Lyndon B. Johnson* sworn in as president aboard Air Force One

6.5mm Mannlicher Carcano rifle

12:47pm: Oswald (left) takes cab to his apartment. Leaves minutes later with pistol
1:15pm: Oswald stopped by police officer *J.D. Tippet*. Tippet (below left) shot dead. Oswald seen running with pistol in his hand

1:22pm: Police find rifle and three cartridge cases on 6th floor of Depository

1:50pm: Oswald arrested at Texas Theatre. Two days later he is murdered while in police custody by mafia-linked *Jack Ruby*

Key conspiracy theories

A March 2001 Gallup poll found that 8 in 10 Americans believe there was a conspiracy to assassinate President Kennedy

Cuba: JFK is killed by right-wing Cuban exiles over his refusal to allow U.S. forces to take part in CIA-mounted *Bay of Pigs* invasion. Thousands of emigres are killed in failed 1961 plan

Mafia: JFK and his brother, Attorney General *Robert F. Kennedy*, fiercely prosecute Mafia leaders in crusade against organized crime. **RFK is also assassinated, five years later**

U.S. government: Disgruntled CIA/ Pentagon faction kills Kennedy for going soft on Communism and for sacking of CIA director, his deputy and planning chief following Bay of Pigs fiasco

Sources: Warren Report, U.S. Congress Select Committee on Assassinations, "The Day JFK Died" by the Dallas Morning News   Photograhs: Associated Press   © GRAPHIC NEWS

40th anniversary of President John F. Kennedy's assassination. Graphic shows chronology of events in Dallas and details main conspiracy theories. 8 in 10 Americans believe there was a conspiracy to kill JFK.

ジョン・F・ケネディ元大統領暗殺の40周年。ダラスでの出来事を順を追って紹介し、主な陰謀説を解説する図。
アメリカ人の10人のうち8人がJFKを殺害する陰謀があったと信じている。

UK 2003
Creative Team: Duncan Mil / Phi Bainbridge / Jordi Bou / Mark McLellan   Copywriter & Research: Julie Mullins
DF, S: Graphic News Ltd.   CL: Various Newspapers & Magazines

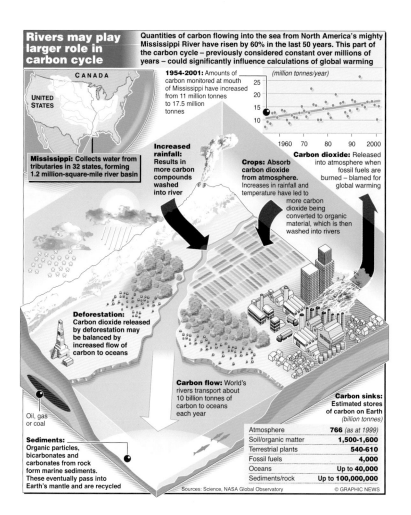

Rivers may play larger role in carbon cycle

Quantities of carbon flowing into the sea from North America's mighty Mississippi River have risen by 60% in the last 50 years. This part of the carbon cycle – previously considered constant over millions of years – could significantly influence calculations of global warming

1954-2001: Amounts of carbon monitored at mouth of Mississippi have increased from 11 million tonnes to 17.5 million tonnes

(million tonnes/year)

25
20
15
10

1960 70 80 90 2000

CANADA

UNITED STATES

Mississippi: Collects water from tributaries in 32 states, forming 1.2 million-square-mile river basin

Increased rainfall: Results in more carbon compounds washed into river

Crops: Absorb carbon dioxide from atmosphere. Increases in rainfall and temperature have led to more carbon dioxide being converted to organic material, which is then washed into rivers

Carbon dioxide: Released into atmosphere when fossil fuels are burned – blamed for global warming

Deforestation: Carbon dioxide released by deforestation may be balanced by increased flow of carbon to oceans

Oil, gas or coal

Sediments: Organic particles, bicarbonates and carbonates from rock form marine sediments. These eventually pass into Earth's mantle and are recycled

Carbon flow: World's rivers transport about 10 billion tonnes of carbon to oceans each year

Carbon sinks: Estimated stores of carbon on Earth
(billion tonnes)

Atmosphere	766 (as at 1999)
Soil/organic matter	1,500-1,600
Terrestrial plants	540-610
Fossil fuels	4,000
Oceans	Up to 40,000
Sediments/rock	Up to 100,000,000

Sources: Science, NASA Global Observatory   © GRAPHIC NEWS

ミシシッピ川から海へと流れ込んだ炭酸ガスの量は、過去半世紀で60%上昇した。図表は、以前は何百万年以上も継続していたと考えられていた炭酸ガスの循環が、地球温暖化の問題にどのような影響を与えているかを示している。

Quantities of carbon flowing into the sea from Mississippi River have risen by 60% in the last half century.
Graphic shows how this part of the carbon cycle previously considered constant over millions of years could significantly influence calculations of global warming.

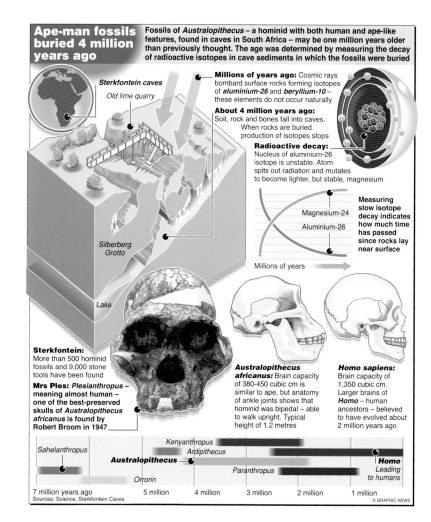

Ape-man fossils buried 4 million years ago

Fossils of *Australopithecus* – a hominid with both human and ape-like features, found in caves in South Africa – may be one million years older than previously thought. The age was determined by measuring the decay of radioactive isotopes in cave sediments in which the fossils were buried

Sterkfontein caves

Old lime quarry

Millions of years ago: Cosmic rays bombard surface rocks forming isotopes of *aluminium-26* and *beryllium-10* – these elements do not occur naturally

About 4 million years ago: Soil, rock and bones fall into caves. When rocks are buried production of isotopes stops

Radioactive decay: Nucleus of aluminium-26 isotope is unstable. Atom spits out radiation and mutates to become lighter, but stable, magnesium

Magnesium-24

Aluminium-26

Measuring slow isotope decay indicates how much time has passed since rocks lay near surface

Millions of years

Silberberg Grotto

Lake

Sterkfontein: More than 500 hominid fossils and 9,000 stone tools have been found

Mrs Ples: *Plesianthropus* – meaning almost human – one of the best-preserved skulls of *Australopithecus africanus* is found by Robert Broom in 1947

Australopithecus africanus: Brain capacity of 380-450 cubic cm is similar to ape, but anatomy of ankle joints shows that hominid was bipedal – able to walk upright. Typical height of 1.2 metres

Homo sapiens: Brain capacity of 1,350 cubic cm. Larger brains of *Homo* – human ancestors – believed to have evolved about 2 million years ago

Sahelanthropus	Kenyanthropus				Homo
	Ardipithecus				Leading to humans
Australopithecus					
Orrorin		Paranthropus			

7 million years ago   5 million   4 million   3 million   2 million   1 million

Sources: Science, Sterkfontein Caves   © GRAPHIC NEWS

New Australopithecus fossils from caves in South-Africa— along with a nearly complete skeleton discovered there in 1997— may have been buried about 4 million years ago, as much as 1 million years earlier than previously thought.

南アフリカの洞くつで1997年に発見されたほぼ完全な骨格に加えて、新たに発見されたアウストラロピテクスの化石は、以前考えられていたよりも100万年近くさかのぼる、400万年前に埋葬されていた可能性があることを示す図。

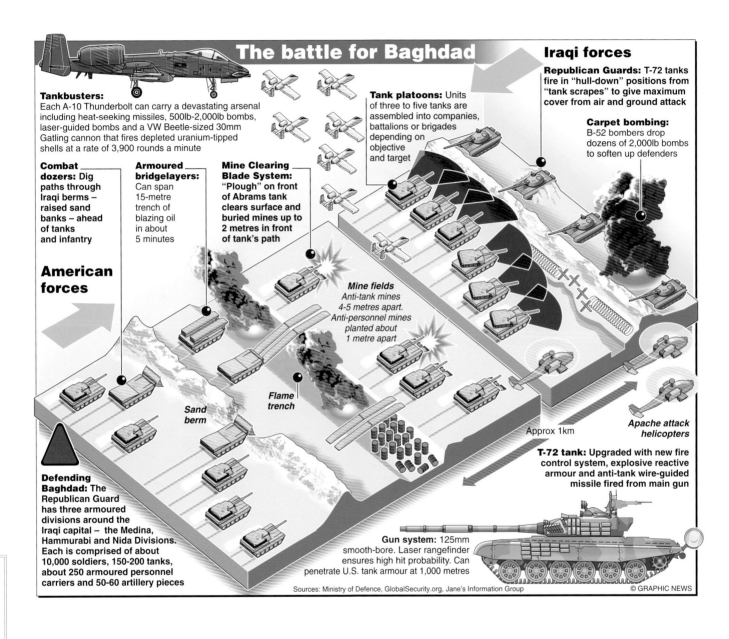

The battle for Baghdad

Iraqi forces

Republican Guards: T-72 tanks fire in "hull-down" positions from "tank scrapes" to give maximum cover from air and ground attack

Carpet bombing: B-52 bombers drop dozens of 2,000lb bombs to soften up defenders

Tankbusters: Each A-10 Thunderbolt can carry a devastating arsenal including heat-seeking missiles, 500lb-2,000lb bombs, laser-guided bombs and a VW Beetle-sized 30mm Gatling cannon that fires depleted uranium-tipped shells at a rate of 3,900 rounds a minute

Tank platoons: Units of three to five tanks are assembled into companies, battalions or brigades depending on objective and target

Combat dozers: Dig paths through Iraqi berms – raised sand banks – ahead of tanks and infantry

Armoured bridgelayers: Can span 15-metre trench of blazing oil in about 5 minutes

Mine Clearing Blade System: "Plough" on front of Abrams tank clears surface and buried mines up to 2 metres in front of tank's path

American forces

Mine fields Anti-tank mines 4-5 metres apart. Anti-personnel mines planted about 1 metre apart

Sand berm

Flame trench

Approx 1km

Apache attack helicopters

T-72 tank: Upgraded with new fire control system, explosive reactive armour and anti-tank wire-guided missile fired from main gun

Defending Baghdad: The Republican Guard has three armoured divisions around the Iraqi capital – the Medina, Hammurabi and Nida Divisions. Each is comprised of about 10,000 soldiers, 150-200 tanks, about 250 armoured personnel carriers and 50-60 artillery pieces

Gun system: 125mm smooth-bore. Laser rangefinder ensures high hit probability. Can penetrate U.S. tank armour at 1,000 metres

Sources: Ministry of Defence, GlobalSecurity.org, Jane's Information Group　© GRAPHIC NEWS

Graphic shows likely tactics to be adopted by U.S. forces attempting to dislodge Republican Guards defending Bughdad.

バグダッドを守るイラク共和国防衛軍の撤退をもくろむ、米軍が採択したと思われる計画を説明する図。

UK　2003
Creative Team: Duncan Mil / Phi Bainbridge / Jordi Bou / Mark McLellan　Copywriter & Research: Julie Mullins　DF, S: Graphic News Ltd.　CL: Various Newspapers & Magazines

Wal-Mart's annual sales of **$244.5 billion** are almost as great as **Switzerland's GDP.**

Wal-Mart sold enough Ol' Roy multiflavored **dog biscuits** in one year to circle the earth twice.

If Wal-Mart were a country, it would be China's eighth-largest trading partner, with **$12 billion** in imports.*

Wal-Mart is the largest corporate employer in the U.S., with **1.2 million workers.**

Wal-Mart accounts for 25 percent of Clorox's sales, 18 percent of Procter & Gamble's and **3 percent of all sales** in the world.

*2002. Sources: Bloomberg; Clorox and Procter & Gamble SEC filings; Wal-Mart

Low prices, high numbers Wal-Mart makes its fortune on volume. These numbers show just how big the biggest company is.

Diagram illustrating key facts about Wal-Mart, the world's largest company.
世界有数の企業であるWal-Mart社の重要な事実を示すイラストレーション。

No refills These top-selling drugs will lose patent protection in the next three years.

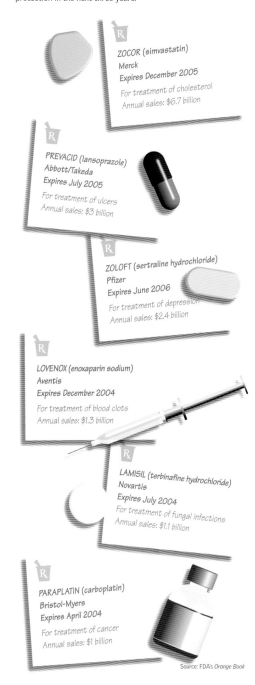

ZOCOR (simvastatin)
Merck
Expires December 2005
For treatment of cholesterol
Annual sales: $6.7 billion

PREVACID (lansoprazole)
Abbott/Takeda
Expires July 2005
For treatment of ulcers
Annual sales: $3 billion

ZOLOFT (sertraline hydrochloride)
Pfizer
Expires June 2006
For treatment of depression
Annual sales: $2.4 billion

LOVENOX (enoxaparin sodium)
Aventis
Expires December 2004
For treatment of blood clots
Annual sales: $1.3 billion

LAMISIL (terbinafine hydrochloride)
Novartis
Expires July 2004
For treatment of fungal infections
Annual sales: $1.1 billion

PARAPLATIN (carboplatin)
Bristol-Myers
Expires April 2004
For treatment of cancer
Annual sales: $1 billion

Source: FDA's *Orange Book*

Diagram illustrating drug patents expiration dates.
医薬品の特許期限を表したイラストレーション。

USA   2004
AD: Carol Macrini   D, I, S: Eliot Bergman   CL: Bloomberg Markets Magazine

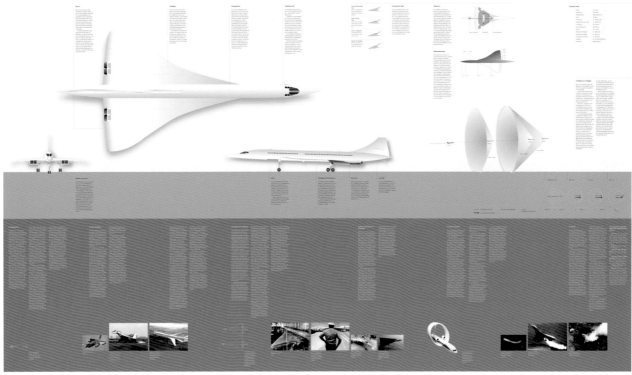

a

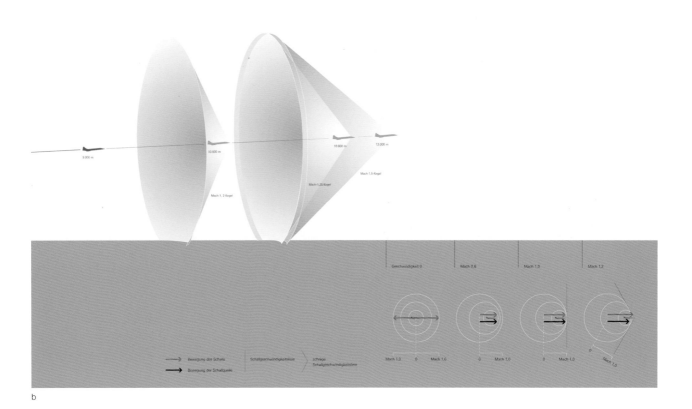

b

A poster deals with the plane's technology and explains supersonic flight in almost three-dimensional representation.
The bottom segment presents the history of the Concorde. (a)
Graphic explanation of supersonic flight in almost three-dimensional representation. (b)

航空技術に関するポスター。コンコルドを立体的な表現を用いて説明している。下の部分では歴史を紹介。 (a)
超音速飛行を立体的な表現を用いて説明したグラフィック。 (b)

Germany   2001
D, I: Lars Wentrup   DF, S: Nieschlag + Wentrup

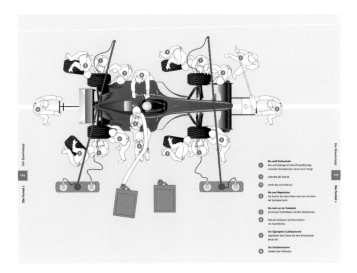

The logistics of a pit stop during a Formula 1 car racing.

F1レース中のピット・ストップの後方支援を表す図。

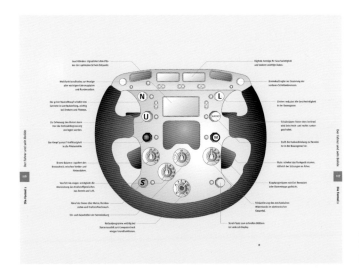

A steering wheel of a Formula 1 racing car and its functions.

F1のレーシング・カーのハンドルと、その性能を説明する図。

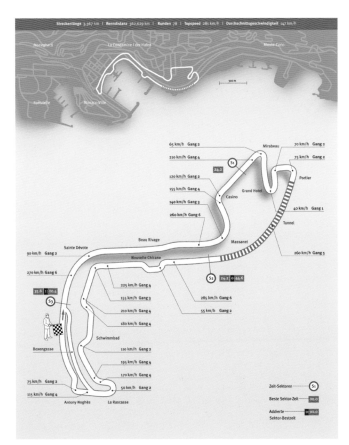

Illustration showing the location of the course in the city of Monaco and the course in detail with additional information.

モナコのレーシング・コースの位置や、
コース中の詳しい情報を示すイラストレーション。

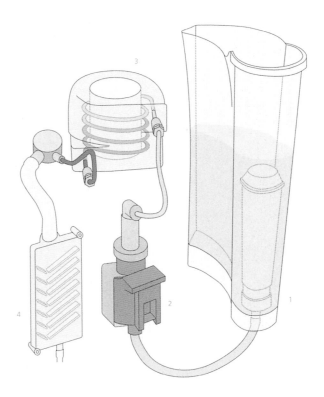

1> The removable water tank lasts a long time between fillings (at a recommended 40 ml per cup) and you can check water level at a glance. Always use cool water that is filtered or bottled, never distilled or softened.

2> The pump delivers 15 bars of pressure (good for two cups) instantaneously and ensures an ideal 25 to 30 seconds for extraction (i.e., when water is in contact with the grounds). If extraction time is too fast, espresso will taste bitter and have little or no crema; too slow, and it will taste burnt.

3> With Thermobloc technology, water is forced through an ultra-compact labyrinth of stainless steel (not aluminum) heating pipes to immediately reach an optimum 92°C. If the water is too cool, the espresso will be weak; too hot, and the grounds will be scalded.

4> Excess water is directed into the drip tray; it doesn't sit in the machine, so each new cup always uses fresh water.

Diagrams indicate how to position the Krups line of espresso makers thoughtfully designed for coffee enthusiasts.
コーヒー好きのために工夫してデザインされたエスプレッソ・メーカー、Krupsシリーズの設置方法を図解。

Canada   2004
CD, AD: Frank Viva   D, I: Todd Temporale   P: Ron Baxter Smith / Hill Peppard   CW: Doug Dolan   DF, S: Viva Dolan Communications & Design Inc.   CL: Groupe Seb

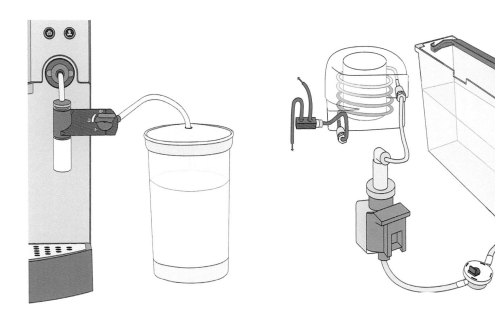

Diagrams are used in a brochure about Krups espresso machines to reinforce the high level of engineering.
ブローシャーに使用したKrupsエスプレッソ・マシンの高度な技術を強調するための図。

Canada   2004
CD, AD: Frank Viva   D, I: Todd Temporale   DF, S: Viva Dolan Communications & Design Inc.   CL: Groupe Seb

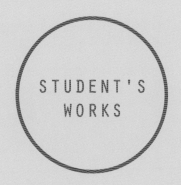

STUDENT'S WORKS

Students' works from the Diagram Design course
in the Department of Visual Communication Design at Musashino Art University

武蔵野美術大学視覚伝達デザイン学科ダイアグラムデザインコース学生作品

Several years ago I initiated a Diagram Design course at the Department of Visual Communication Design at Musashino Art University. In today's society, we live our everyday lives surrounded by a variety of media and information. In my class I classify diagrams into six categories—tables, graphs, schematics, pictograms, illustrations, and maps—and challenge students to express divers information diagrammatically.

In the first semester students study the fundamentals of diagrammatic expression; in the second they hone in on specific themes, applying and developing them as graphic works. The inspirational work is analog; the finish work is generated on computer. Students also monitor each other's work in progress. By scrutinizing other people's ideas, their own design becomes more logical. They also collect their own data, the analysis and organization of which leads to original ideas and concepts. At the end, we critique the works in terms of expressing a visual language, function, and aesthetic sensibilities.

As part of basic graphic training, the diagrams course expands the way students think and aides in refining their design abilities.

*The works shown here represent students' solutions to assignments given in my Diagram Design course.

武蔵野美術大学視覚伝達デザイン学科コースでは数年前から「ダイアグラムデザインコース」を新設しました。私たちは今、日常の社会で多種多様のメディアと情報に囲まれて生きています。授業ではダイアグラムを6つ（①表組 ②図表 ③図式 ④図譜 ⑤図解 ⑥地図）のカテゴリーに分類し、さまざまなデータを図的に表現することを課題としています。

前半では基本を学び、後半ではテーマを絞り込み、応用と展開で作品化しています。インスピレーションはアナログで、フィニッシュはコンピュータで仕上げます。また、これらの作業はお互いにその場でチェックし合います。他の人の考えを黙過せず凝視することによって論理的なデザインに到達します。データの収集は学生の個人作業で分類・整理させ、発想と結び付けていきます。

最後に、デザインされた作品が視覚言語や機能性や美しさを表現できたかを決定します。

このダイアグラムの授業はグラフィックデザインの基礎トレーニングとして学生たちの発想を広げ、同時に高度なデザイン能力を引き出すために役立ちます。

*ここに掲載された作品は「ダイアグラムデザインコース」授業課題です。

Tetsuya Ohta : graphic designer

Graduated from Kuwasawa Design Laboratory in 1963. After working at Ikko Tanaka Design Office, established the present Ohta Tetsuya Design Office in 1975. His Diagram exhibitions were held at Ginza Graphic Gallery (ggg) in 1991, and Morisawa Typography Space (MOTS) in 2000. Among the awards he has received are: the Ministry of International Trade and Industry Award of the Japan Book Design Concours, and the Tokyo TDC Award in 1991; the ADC Award and Hiroshi Hara Award in 1992; and the Ministry of Education, Culture, Sports, Science and Technology Award of the Japan Book Design Concours in 2002. In 1989 he published "Changes in Logos and Trademarks in Japan" and "Iro no mihoncho (Color Swatchbook)." He teaches the Diagram Design course in the Department of Visual Communication Design at Musashino Art University.

太田徹也（グラフィックデザイナー）

1963年桑沢デザイン研究所卒。田中一光デザイン室を経て1975年太田徹也デザイン室設立、現在に至る。1991年「ダイアグラム展」ギンザグラフィックギャラリー（ggg）、2000年「ダイアグラム展」モリサワ・タイポグラフィ・スペース（MOTS）。1991年全国装幀コンクール、カタログポスター展「通産大臣賞」、東京タイポディレクターズクラブ「会員・銅賞」、1992年東京アートディレクターズクラブ「ADC賞」「原弘賞」、2002年全国装幀コンクール「文部科学大臣賞」などを受賞。1989年『CI＝マーク・ロゴの変遷』六耀社、『色の見本帖』ごま書房（共著）を出版。武蔵野美術大学視覚伝達デザイン学科ダイアグラムデザインコース講師。

A correlation graph of characters in the TV anime series "Kyojin no Hoshi."
テレビアニメ『巨人の星』における人物相関図。

D: Takuya Nagami

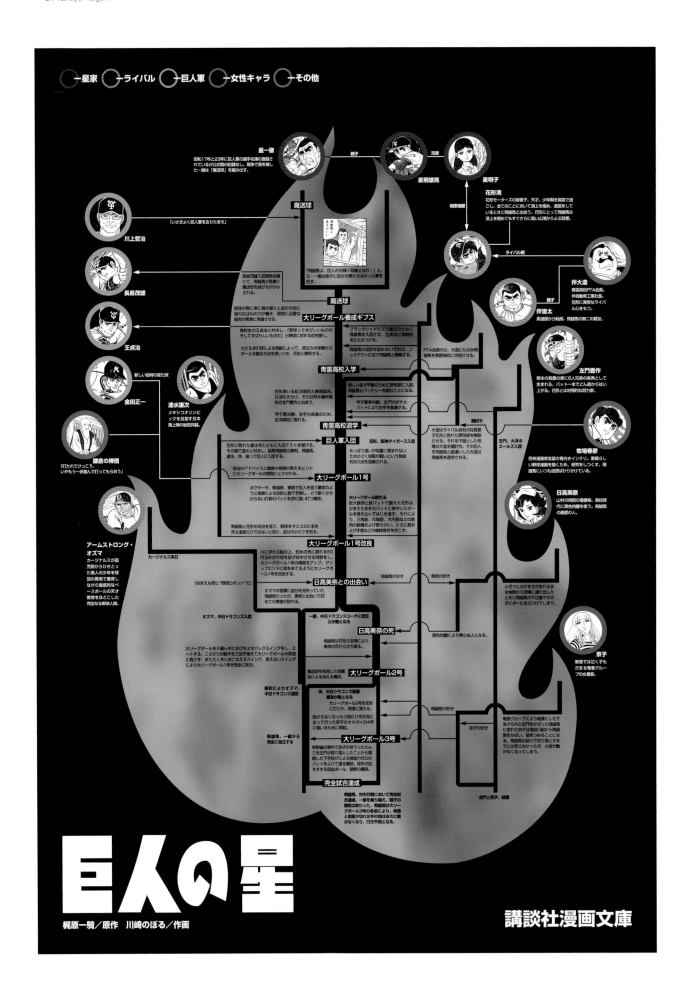

A map expressing the sounds heard en route from home to school.
自宅から学校までの通学途中に耳にする音を表現したサウンドマップ。

D: Misato Yasui

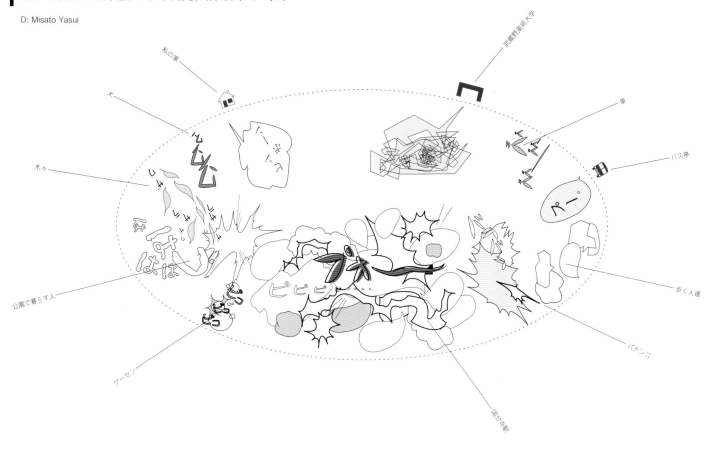

A diagram expressing the surrounds encountered when walking from home to school.
自宅から学校まで歩いたときの周囲の環境を表現したダイアグラム。

D: Arata Yabuuchi

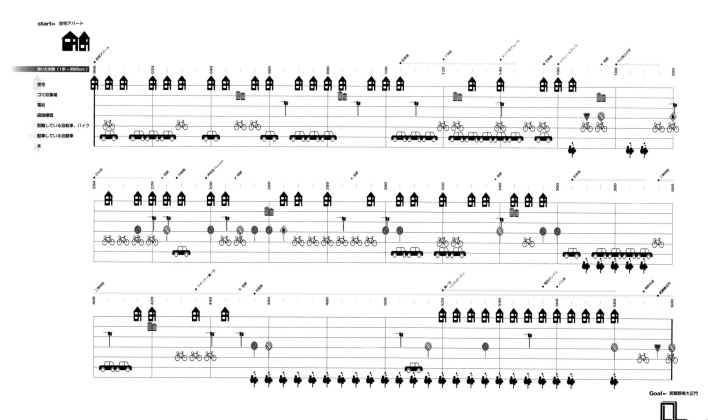

A map expressing the sounds heard en route from home to school.
自宅から学校までの通学途中に耳にする音を表現したサウンドマップ。

D: Inka Shinbo

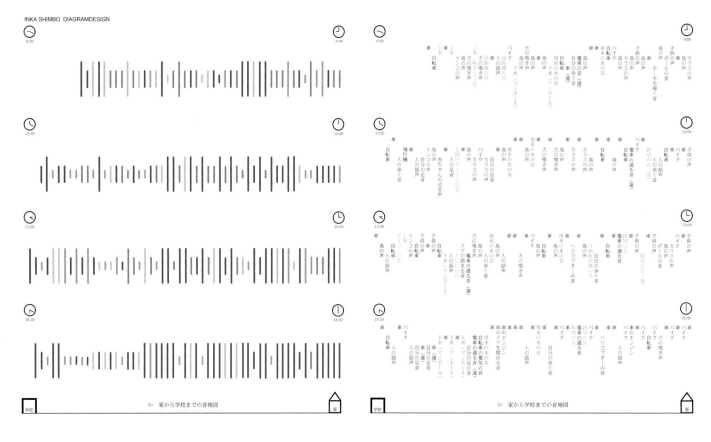

A map expressing the changes in elevation en route to school.
通学路の高低差を表現したマップ。

D: Sachiyo Ojima

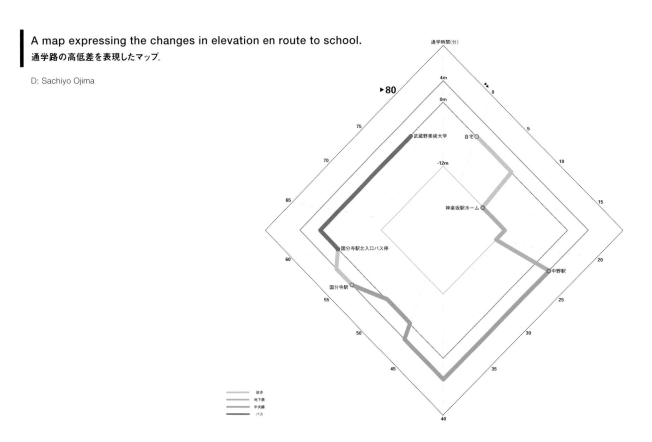

A map expressing the number of steps between home and school.
自宅から学校までの歩数を表現したマップ。

D: Natsuko Otaka

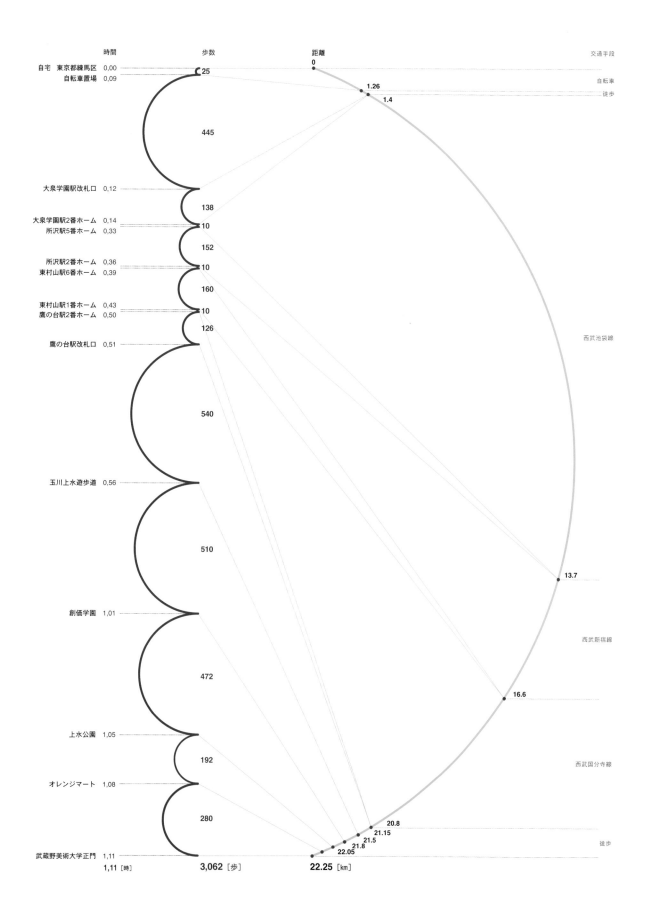

時間　　　　　　　歩数　　　　　距離　　　　　　　　　　　交通手段
0

自宅　東京都練馬区　0,00　　　　25　　　　　　　　　　　　　　　　　自転車
自転車置場　0,09　　　　　　　　　　　　　　1.26
　　　　　　　　　　　　　　　　　　　　　　　　1.4　　　　　　　　　徒歩
　　　　　　　　　　445

大泉学園駅改札口　0,12
　　　　　　　　　　138
大泉学園駅2番ホーム　0,14　　　10
所沢駅5番ホーム　0,33
　　　　　　　　　　152
所沢駅2番ホーム　0,36　　　　10
東村山駅6番ホーム　0,39
　　　　　　　　　　160
東村山駅1番ホーム　0,43　　　10　　　　　　　　　　　　　　　　　西武池袋線
鷹の台駅2番ホーム　0,50
　　　　　　　　　　126
鷹の台駅改札口　0,51

　　　　　　　　　　540

玉川上水遊歩道　0,56
　　　　　　　　　　　　　　　　　　　　　　13.7

　　　　　　　　　　510

創価学園　1,01
　　　　　　　　　　　　　　　　　　　　　　　　　西武新宿線
　　　　　　　　　　472
　　　　　　　　　　　　　　　　　　　16.6
上水公園　1,05
　　　　　　　　　　192
　　　　　　　　　　　　　　　　　　　　　　　西武国分寺線
オレンジマート　1,08
　　　　　　　　　　280　　　　　　　20.8
　　　　　　　　　　　　　　　　　21.15
　　　　　　　　　　　　　　　21.5
　　　　　　　　　　　　　　21.8　　　　　　　　　　徒歩
武蔵野美術大学正門　1,11　　　　22.05
　　　1,11 [時]　　3,062 [歩]　　22.25 [km]

A map showing nationwide time differences for the first sunrise of 2004 using Tokyo as the standard.
2004年元旦の初日の出、東京を基準とした日本各地の時間差を表したマップ。

D: Kei Minemura

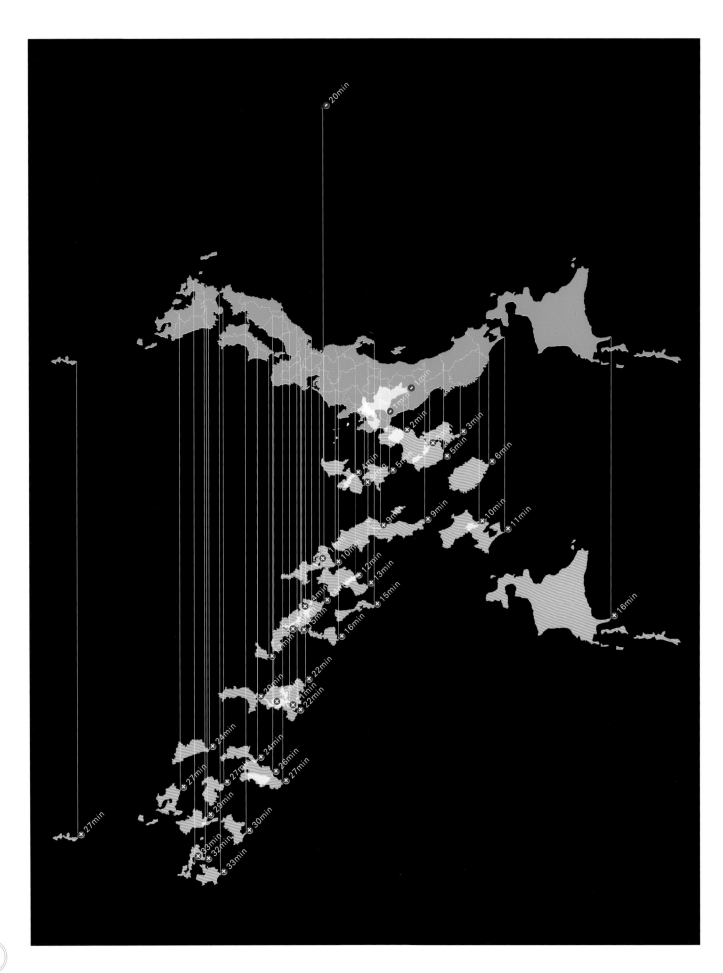

A map showing population density and rate of increase by prefecture.
都道府県別の人口密度と人口増加率を表すマップ。

D: Yayoi Yamamoto

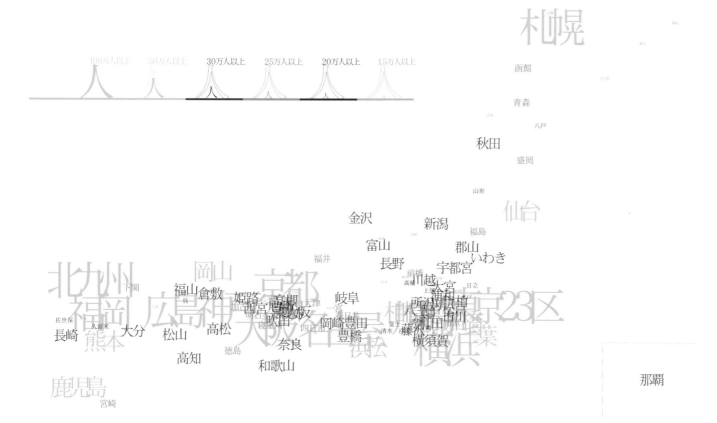

A map showing the surface area of major lakes in Japan.
日本国内の主要な湖の面積を表すマップ。

D: Ricaco Nagashima

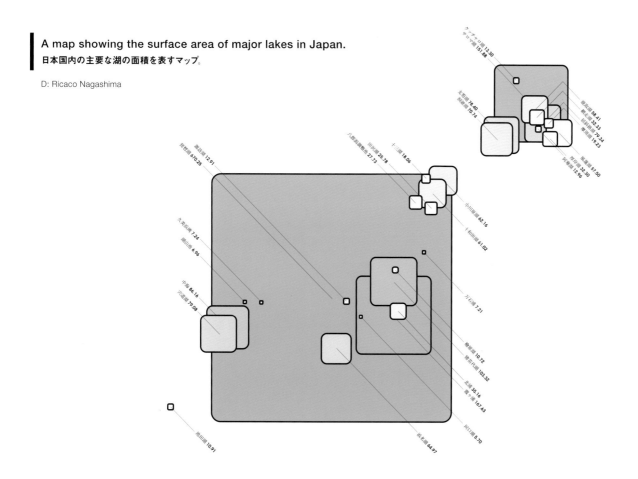

A map showing scale of earthquakes occurring in Japan.
日本で起きた地震の規模を表したマップ。

D: Hideki Sugimoto

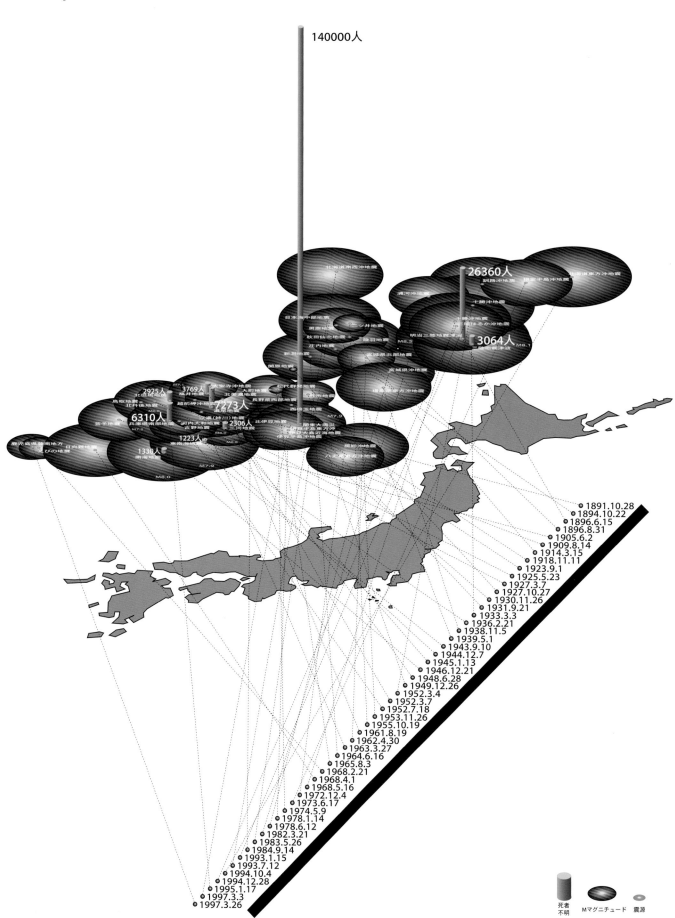

A map showing the severity of acid rain worldwide.
世界の酸性雨の状況を表すマップ。

D: Nakazo Katayama

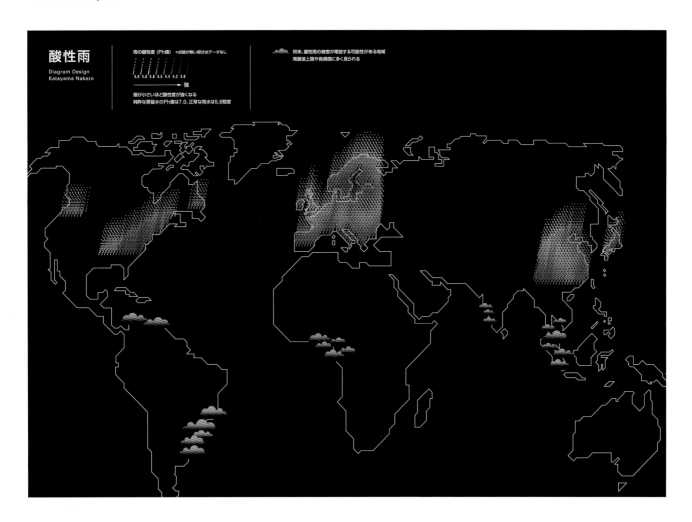

A map showing the severity of pollution of Japanese rivers.
日本国内の河川の水質汚濁状況を表すマップ。

D: Satoko Shoda

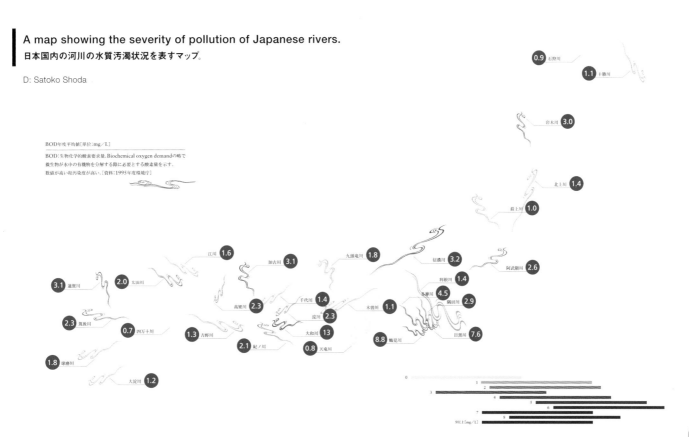

A map showing the rate of criminal arrests in Japan.
日本の犯罪検挙率を表すマップ。

D: Yu Osaki

順位	都道府県	(%)	順位	都道府県	(%)
1	高知県	58.4	24	愛媛県	28.7
2	鳥取県	54.5	25	石川県	28.5
3	島根県	44.8	26	兵庫県	27.4
4	長崎県	43.8	27	大分県	27.0
5	徳島県	43.5	28	東京都	26.3
6	秋田県	41.7	29	青森県	26.1
7	新潟県	41.1	30	岩手県	25.6
8	福井県	39.6	31	京都府	25.5
9	奈良県	39.4	32	和歌山県	25.5
10	鹿児島県	37.9	33	栃木県	24.6
11	山形県	36.8	34	神奈川県	24.5
12	山口県	36.5	35	長野県	23.7
13	熊本県	36.1	36	茨城県	21.7
14	香川県	35.8	37	山梨県	21.4
15	群馬県	35.6	38	滋賀県	21.1
16	広島県	34.0	39	静岡県	21.0
17	福島県	33.8	40	宮城県	19.2
18	岡山県	32.7	41	福岡県	17.7
19	宮崎県	29.8	42	愛知県	17.6
20	富山県	29.8	43	岐阜県	16.9
21	三重県	29.8	44	埼玉県	16.7
22	佐賀県	29.0	45	大阪府	16.3
23	沖縄県	29.0	46	北海道	16.0
			47	千葉県	16.0

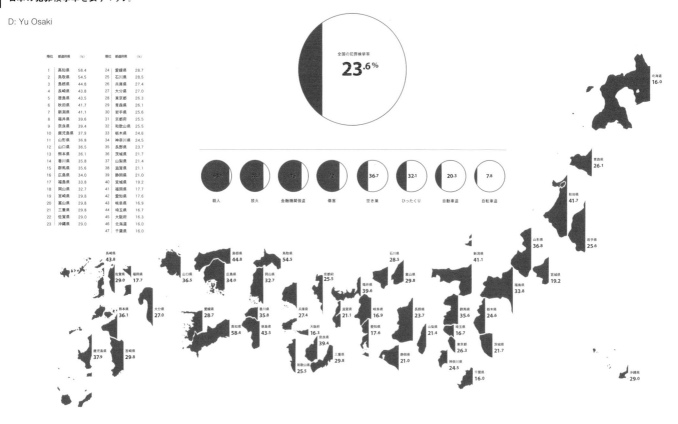

全国の犯罪検挙率
23.6%

殺人 95.9　放火 76.7　金融機関強盗 75.0　傷害 72.0　空き巣 36.7　ひったくり 32.1　自動車盗 20.3　自転車盗 7.8

A distribution map showing the use of the words "baka" and "aho" (both meaning "fool" or "idiot") throughout Japan.
日本全国の「バカ」と「アホ」ということばの使用分布を示すマップ。

D: Miwa Akabane

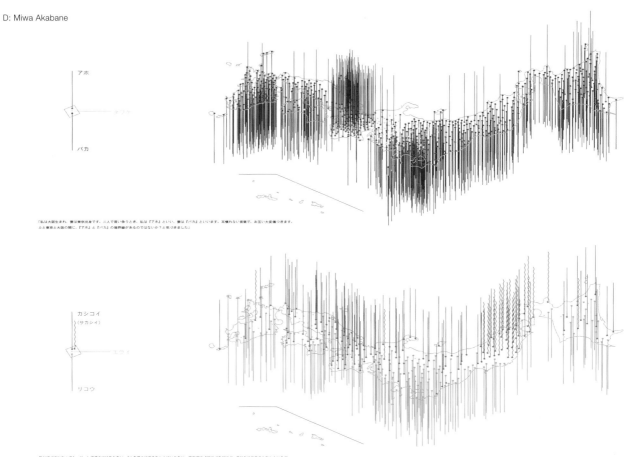

「私は大阪生まれ、妻は東京出身です。二人で言い争うとき、私は『アホ』といい、妻は『バカ』といいます。耳慣れない言葉で、お互い大変傷つきます。
ふと東京と大阪の間に、『アホ』と『バカ』の境界線があるのではないか？と気づきました」

ねしはバカになっても、けっしてアホにはならない。「人をアホにするな」とはいわない。東京では「兄はバカだけど、弟はおりコウさんね」というが、
大阪では「兄はアホやけど、弟はカシコイね」という。

INDEX

CLIENT

世界のダイアグラムコレクション 2
Informational Diagram Collection

2009年 10月 5日　初版第1刷発行

Jacket Design
Noriyuki Shirasu
シラスノリユキ

Designer
Akiko Shiba
柴 亜季子

Editor
Yu Fukushi
福士 祐

Coordinator
Maya Kishida
岸田麻矢

Photographer
Kuniharu Fujimoto
藤本邦治

Translators
Maya Kishida, Pamela Miki
岸田麻矢／パメラ三木

Typesetter
Ayuko Ishibashi
石橋亞由子

Publisher
Shingo Miyoshi
三芳伸吾

発行元：ピエ・ブックス

〒170-0005　東京都豊島区南大塚2-32-4
編集　Tel: 03-5395-4820　Fax: 03-5395-4821
editor@piebooks.com
営業　Tel: 03-5395-4811　Fax: 03-5395-4812
sales@piebooks.com

印刷・製本　株式会社サンニチ印刷

ISBN978-4-89444-810-0 C3070
Printed in Japan